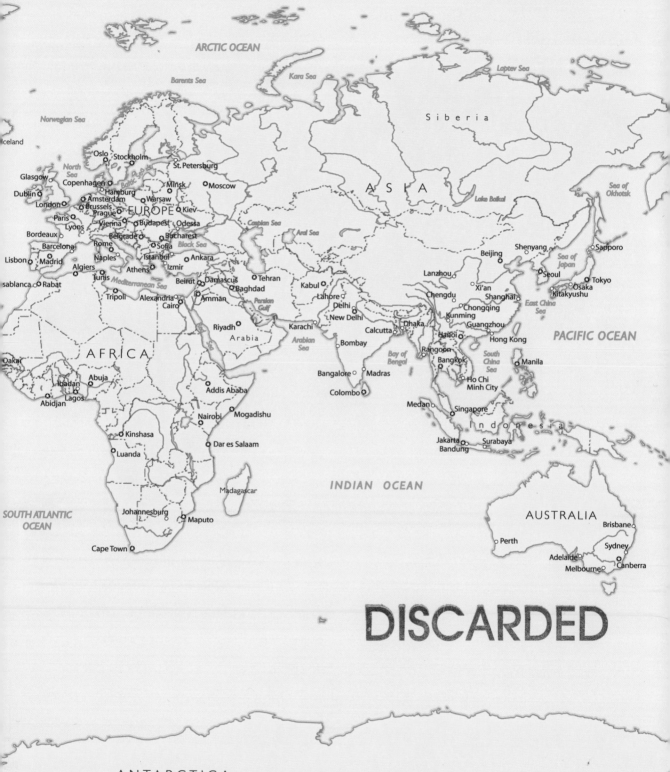

ARCTIC OCEAN

Barents Sea

Kara Sea

Laptev Sea

Norwegian Sea

Siberia

Iceland

North Sea

Oslo   Stockholm
St. Petersburg

Glasgow   Copenhagen   Minsk   Moscow
Dublin   Hamburg   Warsaw
London   Amsterdam
Brussels   Kiev
Paris   Prague   EUROPE   Budapest   Odessa
Lyons   Vienna
Bordeaux   Belgrade   Bucharest
Barcelona   Rome   Sofia
Lisbon   Madrid   Naples   Istanbul   Ankara
Algiers   Athens   Izmir
sablanca   Rabat   Tunis   Mediterranean Sea   Beirut   Damascus   Tehran
Tripoli   Alexandria   Amman   Baghdad
Cairo

Caspian Sea
Aral Sea
Black Sea

A   S   I   A

Lake Baikal

Sea of Okhotsk

Sea of Japan

Shenyang   Sapporo
Beijing
Lanzhou   Seoul   Tokyo
Xi'an   Osaka
Chengdu   Shanghai   Kitakyushu
Chongqing   East China Sea
Kunming   Guangzhou
Hong Kong

Kabul
Delhi
New Delhi
Karachi
Riyadh   Arabia

Persian Gulf
Arabian Sea

Lahore
Dhaka
Calcutta   Hanoi
Rangoon
Bangkok
Ho Chi Minh City

PACIFIC OCEAN

AFRICA

Dakar
Abuja
Ibadan
Lagos
Abidjan

Bombay
Bangalore   Madras
Colombo

Bay of Bengal

Manila

South China Sea

DAFRICA
Nairobi   Mogadishu
Addis Ababa

Medan
Singapore

Indonesia

Kinshasa
Luanda
Dar es Salaam

Jakarta   Surabaya
Bandung

INDIAN   OCEAN

Madagascar

AUSTRALIA

SOUTH ATLANTIC OCEAN

Johannesburg
Maputo

Brisbane
Perth
Sydney
Adelaide   Canberra
Melbourne

Cape Town

ANTARCTICA

EXPLORERS & DISCOVERERS

**PALM BEACH COUNTY
LIBRARY SYSTEM**
3650 Summit Boulevard
West Palm Beach, FL 33406-4198

EXPLORERS & DISCOVERERS

From Alexander the Great to Sally Ride

Volume
5

Nancy Pear
•
Daniel B. Baker

U·X·L®

AN IMPRINT OF GALE

DETROIT · NEW YORK · TORONTO · LONDON

Explorers and Discoverers

From Alexander the Great to Sally Ride

Nancy Pear and Daniel B. Baker

Volume 5

Staff

Jane Hoehner, *U•X•L Senior Editor*
Carol DeKane Nagel, *U•X•L Managing Editor*
Thomas L. Romig, *U•X•L Publisher*

Mary Beth Trimper, *Production Director*
Evi Seoud, *Production Manager*
Shanna Heilveil, *Production Associate*

Cynthia Baldwin, *Product Design Manager*
Pamela A. E. Galbreath, *Page and Cover Designer*

Jessica L. Ulrich, *Permissions Assistant*

Marco Di Vita, The Graphix Group, *Typesetter*

Library of Congress Cataloging-in-Publication Data
Explorers & Discoverers : from Alexander the Great to Sally Ride
    Volume 5/by Nancy Pear and Daniel B. Baker.
        p   cm.
    Includes biographical references and index.
    ISBN 0-7876-1990-6
1. Explorers—Biography—Encyclopedias, Juvenile. 2. Discoverers in
    Geography—Encyclopedias, Juvenile. 3. Travelers—Biography—
    Encyclopedias, Juvenile. I. Pear, Nancy. II. Baker, Daniel B.
    G200.S22 1995
    920.02—dc20   95-166826
                                                                         CIP

Printed in the United States of America

10 9 8 7 6 5 4 3 2

Contents of Volume 5

Biographical Listings

Preface

Explorers and Discoverers: From Alexander the Great to Sally Ride, Volume 5, features 30 biographies of 22 men, 7 women, 2 machines, and 1 institution that have expanded the horizons of our world and universe. Beginning with a fourth-century Chinese monk and extending to modern aeronauts and astronauts, *Explorers and Discoverers, Volume 5* tells of the lives and times of well-known explorers as well as many lesser-known women and non-Europeans who have also made significant discoveries. Who these travelers were, when and how they lived and traveled, why their journeys were significant, and what the consequences of their discoveries were are all answered within these biographies.

The 30 biographical entries of *Explorers and Discoverers, Volume 5* are arranged in alphabetical order. More than 60 illustrations and maps bring the subjects to life as well as provide geographic details of specific journeys. Additionally, 16 maps of major regions of the world lead off the volume, and a chronology of exploration by region, a list of explorers by place of birth, and an extensive cumulative index conclude the volume.

Comments and Suggestions

We welcome your comments on this work as well as your suggestions for individuals to be featured in future editions of *Explorers and Discoverers*. Please write: Editors, *Explorers and Discoverers,* U•X•L, 835 Penobscot Bldg., Detroit, Michigan 48226-4094; call toll-free: 1-800-877-4253; or fax: 313-961-6348.

Introduction

Explorers and Discoverers, Volume 5 takes the reader on an adventure with twenty-seven men and women who have made significant contributions to human knowledge about the earth, the universe, and ourselves. Journeying through the centuries, we will conquer frontiers and sail uncharted waters. We will trek across treacherous mountains, scorching deserts, steamy jungles, and icy glaciers. We will plumb the depths of the ocean, dwell in outer space, and share in intriguing rituals and customs of unfamiliar peoples. We will unearth prehistoric fossils that offer a glimpse into our distant past. Encountering isolation, disease, and even death, we will come to know the grave sacrifices that discovery sometimes exacts. But we will also experience the joys of achievement!

Before joining the explorers and discoverers, however, it is worthwhile to consider why they venture into the unknown. Certainly a primary motivation is curiosity: they want to find out what is on the other side of a mountain, or they are intrigued by rumors about a strange new land, or they simply enjoy wandering the world. Yet adventurers often—indeed, usually—embark on a journey of discovery under less spontaneous circumstances.

Many of the great explorers were commissioned to lead an expedition with a specific mission. **Pedro de Alvarado,** for example, was enlisted by the Spanish colonial government of the New World to conquer the Indians of Mexico and Central America in an effort to expand Spain's land holdings and increase its wealth. Similarly, **Vitus Bering** led two enormous expeditions sponsored by Czar Peter the Great and Czarina Anna to explore Siberia's Pacific coast, the Russian rulers looking to expand their empire across the ocean. French scientist **Jean-Baptiste Charcot,** too, had the backing of his government in his later explorations of the Antarctic coast, where he claimed unknown territories for France. And in an effort that still astounds historians, seventeenth-century military officer **Pedro de Teixeira** managed to claim much of South America for his native Portugal during a continent-spanning expedition up the Amazon River. This was despite the 1494 Treaty of Tordesillas, which clearly gave most of South America to Spain.

Explorers also received backing from private sponsors or were motivated by economic self-interest. When the Dutch government withdrew its support from **Willem Barents**'s expeditions to find the Northeast Passage—a northern water route from Europe to the Orient—the enterprising merchants of Amsterdam continued to fund his efforts, looking for new markets in which to sell and trade their goods. Rather than watch his herds of livestock die from a prolonged drought, Australian settler **Gregory Blaxland** figured out a way to cross the Blue Mountains—thought to be impassable—to search for pastureland in the continent's interior, opening the way for future explorers. In the same unexpected manner, businessman **William Henry Ashley** and the fur trappers and traders that worked for his Rocky Mountain Fur Company cleared the way for future settlers of the American West. They did this by opening up land routes through the central Rocky Mountain region, including the South Pass, which would become the eastern end of the heavily traveled Oregon Trail.

Religious dedication has long been a strong motivating force behind exploration and travel into unknown lands. During the fifth century, for instance, Buddhist monk **Fa-Hsien** made an epic fifteen-year journey from China to India in search of religious texts. In 921–22 Islamic scholar **Ahmad Ibn Fadlan** made one of the first recorded trips into medieval Russia. Sent by the Islamic ruler, or caliph, of Baghdad, he was to instruct the Volga Bulgars—a Turkish tribe that lived on the Volga River—about the laws of Islam, for they were recent converts. Also eager to recruit religious converts was **Jacques Marquette,** a French Jesuit who traveled to North American and founded Catholic missions in the Great Lakes area during the seventeenth century. Skilled in Native American languages, Marquette was asked to accompany French-Canadian explorer Louis Jolliet on his expedition to explore the Mississippi River; the Jesuit accepted, seeing the trip as a wonderful opportunity to introduce Christianity to Indian tribes along the way.

Explorers have been inspired, too, by the quest for scientific knowledge. French scientist **Charles-Marie de La Condamine** endured incredible hardships during his expedition to South America. His mission was to measure the curvature of Earth at the equator in order to determine the true shape of the planet. Entomologist **Evelyn Cheesman** also worked in primitive conditions on the remote South Sea Islands where she spent many years collecting insect specimens. And **Louis** and **Mary Leakey** showed incredible dedication in their search for information about our ancient past. For nearly half a century they excavated the sediment walls of the Olduvai Gorge in northern Tanzania, unearthing prehistoric tools, fossils of extinct animals, and the remains of many types of human ancestors. Their finds (along with those of their son, **Richard Leakey**) would reshape scientific thinking about the course of human evolution.

And sometimes it is the little known people of distant lands that attract explorers. Publisher **May French Sheldon,** for instance, was appalled by the brutal ways of European colonizers in East Africa. Convinced that native inhabitants there would accept white people who treated them with kindness and respect, she traveled to the region and visited nearly three dozen different tribes, most of whom received her warmly. She, in turn, was one of the first Westerners to report on their lives and culture in a sympathetic and understanding way. Anthropologist **Vilhjalmur Stefansson** went to great lengths to study the Inuit (Eskimos) of the Canadian Arctic, learning their language, customs, and survival skills. Convinced that their way of life had much to teach polar explorers, he successfully put his theory to the test by living off the frigid land for five consecutive years.

But perhaps the foremost motivation to explore is the desire to be the first to accomplish a particular feat. **Alexine Tinné** was an adventurer driven—in several expeditions up the Nile River—to push farther and see more than any Westerner before her. Her obsession cost her the lives of her mother and aunt, who traveled with her; in a later attempt to be the first European woman to cross the Sahara Desert, Tinné herself was killed by bandits. Scientist **Nils Adolf Erik Nordenskjöld,** on the other hand, took a more reasoned approach when attempting to become the first explorer to travel the Northeast Passage. He studied why three centuries of navigational efforts had failed, and made the trip without difficulty in 1878–79, his achievement still celebrated in his Swedish homeland today. Modern-day balloonist **Steve Fossett** is learning as he goes in his attempts to be the first aeronaut to circle the globe. In his initial try he flew only 1,800 miles, but in his second attempt—although well short of his goal—he broke the ballooning distance record, with 9,672 miles traveled. He plans to try again. Viewed as a role model for youths, U.S. astronaut **Mae Jemison** became the first black woman to travel in space in 1992, aboard the space shuttle *Endeavour.* Overcoming the discrimination that girls and blacks often face in America, she hopes that her historic trip will encourage other blacks to pursue careers in space exploration, science, and technology.

By concentrating on biographies of individual explorers in this book we seem to suggest that many of these adventurers were loners who set out on their own to singlehandedly confront the unknown. But as a rule, explorers rarely traveled alone and they had help in achieving their goals. Therefore, use of an individual name is often only shorthand for the achievements of an expedition as a whole. Explorers were often accompanied by large groups of servants and porters— and most importantly—by native guides. Sometimes it was on these indigenous inhabitants that survival depended. When members of **Charles Francis Hall**'s polar expedition became stranded on an ice floe, it was the Inuit among them who ensured the group's survival, building igloos for shelter and hunting seals for food. The castaways endured at sea for nearly seven months.

Explorers and Discoverers, Volume 5 tells the stories of these men and women as well as those of others motivated by a daring spirit and an intense curiosity.

A final note of clarification: When we say that an explorer "discovered" a place, we do not mean that she or he was the first human ever to have been there. Although the discoverer may have been the first from his or her own country to set foot in a new land, most areas of the world during the great periods of exploration were already occupied or their existence had been verified by other people.

Picture Credits

The photographs and illustrations appearing in *Explorers and Discoverers, Volume 5,* were received from the following sources:

On the cover: John Smith; **The Granger Collection, New York:** Beryl Markham and Matthew A. Henson.

Archive Photos. Reproduced by permission: pp. 1, 93, 135; **Library of Congress.** pp. 7, 104; **The Granger Collection, New York. Reproduced by permission:** pp. 14, 85, 120, 126, 140; **Corbis-Bettmann. Reproduced by permission:** pp. 19, 22, 28, 40, 47, 49, 145, 155; **Sketches by William Bourne. Gale Research. Reproduced by permission:** pp. 24, 58; **Literary Estate of Evelyn Cheesman:** p. 35; **Photograph by Yun Suk bong. Archive Photos/Reuters. Reproduced by permission:** p. 62; **Ballantine Books, 1991. Reproduced by permission of Ballantine, a division of Random House, Inc.:** p. 79; **AP/Wide World Photos. Reproduced by permission:** pp. 80, 91, 92, 98, 112, 165, 167;

UPI/Corbis-Bettmann. **Reproduced by permission:** p. 82; **National Aeronautics and Space Administration (NASA). Reproduced by permission:** p. 109; **Photograph by Dominic Wong. Archive Photos/Reuters. Reproduced by permission:** p. 110; **Cover photograph by Barry Bishop. © National Geographic Society. Reproduced by permission:** p. 115; **Archive Photos/Popperfoto. Reproduced by permission:** p. 161.

Maps

The World

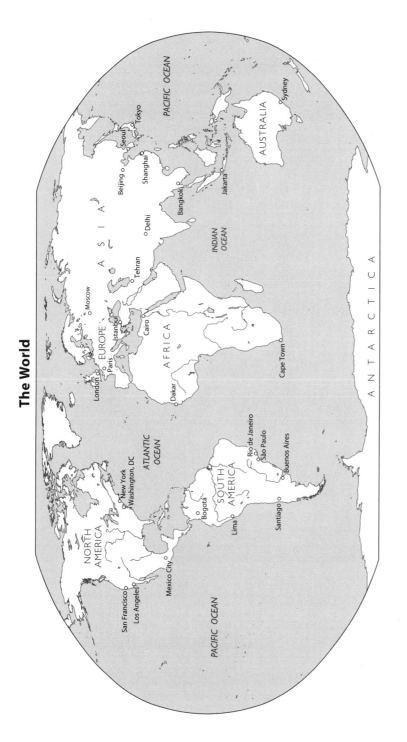

The World

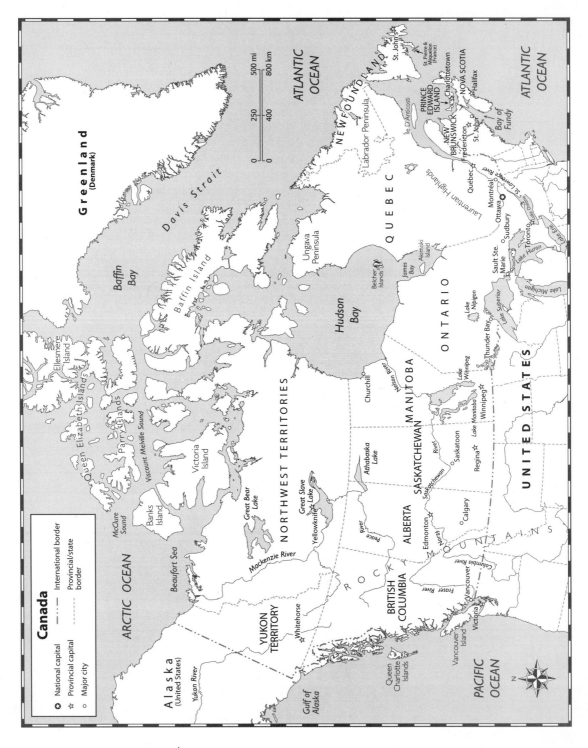

Canada

- ✪ National capital
- ☆ Provincial capital
- ○ Major city

- — International border
- --- Provincial/state border

Greenland
(Denmark)

ATLANTIC OCEAN

ATLANTIC OCEAN

500 mi
800 km

250
400

0
0

St. John's

St. Pierre & Miquelon (France)

Charlottetown

PRINCE EDWARD ISLAND

NOVA SCOTIA

Halifax

NEW BRUNSWICK

Fredericton

St. John

Bay of Fundy

Île D'Anticosti

Labrador Peninsula

NEWFOUNDLAND

Davis Strait

Baffin Bay

Baffin Island

QUEBEC

Laurentian Highlands

Québec

Montréal

Ottawa

St. Lawrence River

Sudbury

Lake Ontario

Lake Erie

Ungava Peninsula

Hudson Bay

James Bay

Akimiski Island

Belcher Islands

ONTARIO

Lake Huron

Sault Ste. Marie

Lake Michigan

Ellesmere Island

Queen Elizabeth Islands

Parry Islands

Viscount Melville Sound

Victoria Island

Lake Nipigon

Lake Superior

Thunder Bay

Churchill

Nelson River

Lake Winnipeg

MANITOBA

Winnipeg

UNITED STATES

McClure Sound

Banks Island

Great Bear Lake

NORTHWEST TERRITORIES

Great Slave Lake

Yellowknife

Athabaska Lake

Lake Manitoba

Saskatoon

SASKATCHEWAN

Saskatchewan River

Regina

Beaufort Sea

ARCTIC OCEAN

Mackenzie River

Peace River

ALBERTA

Edmonton

Calgary

North Saskatchewan River

R O C K Y   M O U N T A I N S

Columbia River

BRITISH COLUMBIA

Fraser River

YUKON TERRITORY

Whitehorse

Yukon River

Alaska
(United States)

Gulf of Alaska

Queen Charlotte Islands

Vancouver Island

Vancouver

Victoria

PACIFIC OCEAN

N

Americas–Canada.

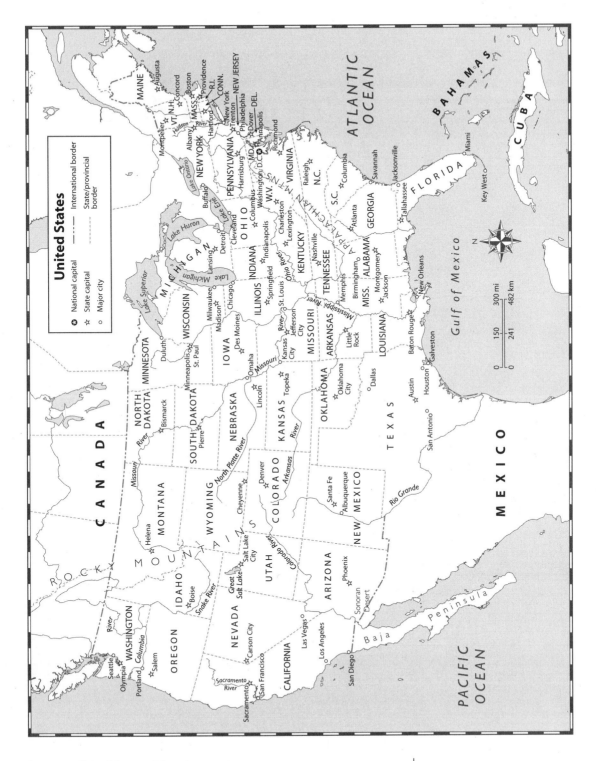

Americas—United States of America.

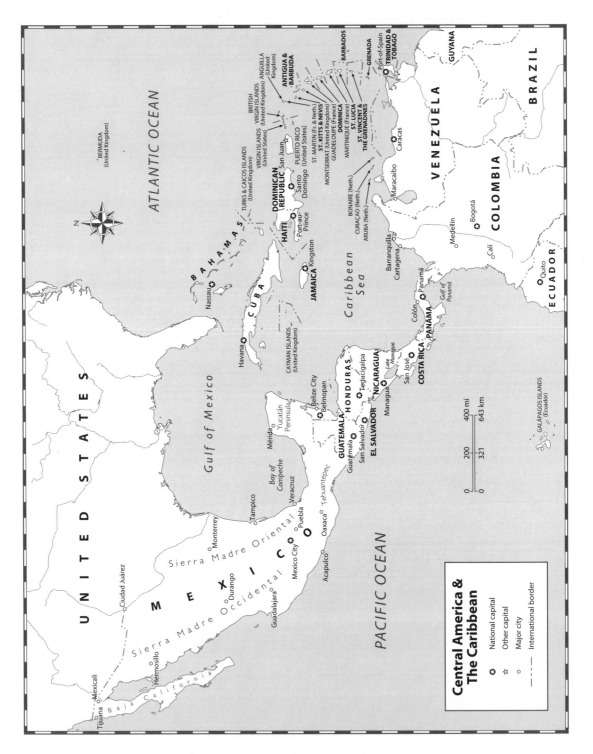

ATLANTIC OCEAN

BERMUDA
(United Kingdom)

N

ANGUILLA
(United Kingdom)

BRITISH
VIRGIN ISLANDS
(United Kingdom)

ANTIGUA &
BARBUDA

BARBADOS

GRENADA

TRINIDAD &
TOBAGO

GUYANA

Port-of-Spain

B R A Z I L

VENEZUELA

COLOMBIA

Caracas

ST. MARTIN (Fr. & Neth.)
ST. KITTS & NEVIS
GUADELOUPE (France)
MONTSERRAT (United Kingdom)
DOMINICA
MARTINIQUE (France)
ST. LUCIA
ST. VINCENT &
THE GRENADINES

VIRGIN ISLANDS
(United States)

PUERTO RICO
(United States)

San Juan

TURKS & CAICOS ISLANDS
(United Kingdom)

DOMINICAN
REPUBLIC

Santo
Domingo

HAITI

Port-au-
Prince

B A H A M A S

Nassau

Maracaibo

BONAIRE (Neth.)
CURAÇAO (Neth.)
ARUBA (Neth.)

Medellín

Bogotá

Cali

Caribbean
Sea

Barranquilla

Cartagena

Kingston

JAMAICA

C U B A

Havana

CAYMAN ISLANDS
(United Kingdom)

Panamá

Colón

Gulf of
Panamá

PANAMA

ECUADOR

Quito

COSTA RICA

San José

NICARAGUA

Lake
Managua

Managua

Tegucigalpa

HONDURAS

Belize City

Belmopan

Mérida

Yucatán
Peninsula

GUATEMALA

Guatemala

San Salvador

EL SALVADOR

U N I T E D   S T A T E S

Gulf of Mexico

Bay of
Campeche

Veracruz

Tampico

Monterrey

M E X I C O

Sierra Madre Oriental

Durango

Mexico City

Puebla

Oaxaca

Tehuantepec

Acapulco

Guadalajara

Sierra Madre Occidental

Ciudad Juárez

Hermosillo

B a j a   C a l i f o r n i a

Mexicali

Tijuana

PACIFIC OCEAN

GALÁPAGOS ISLANDS
(Ecuador)

400 mi   643 km

200   321

0   0

**Central America &
The Caribbean**

⊕ National capital

☆ Other capital

○ Major city

–·–·– International border

Americas—Mexico and Central America.

Maps │ xxii

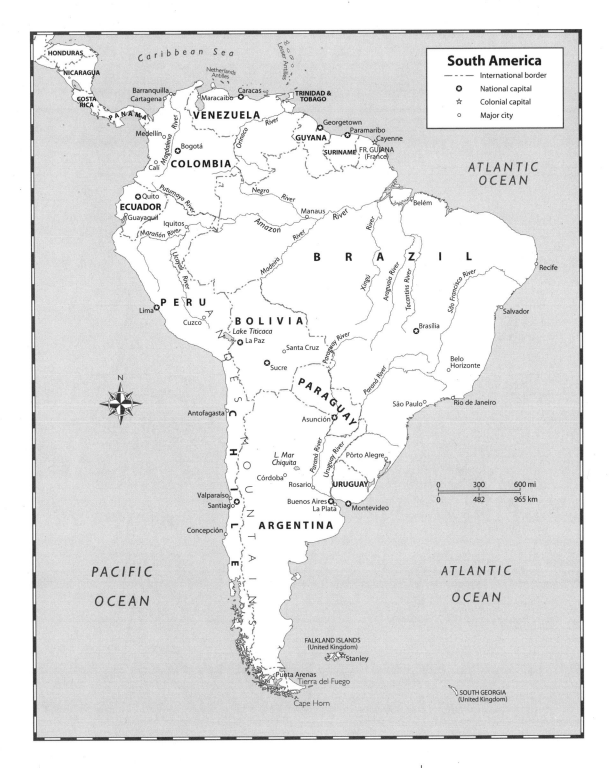

South America

- – – – International border
- ⊕ National capital
- ☆ Colonial capital
- ○ Major city

HONDURAS
NICARAGUA
COSTA RICA
PANAMA

Caribbean Sea
Netherlands Antilles
Lesser Antilles

Barranquilla
Cartagena
Maracaibo
Caracas
TRINIDAD & TOBAGO

VENEZUELA

Medellín
Bogotá
Orinoco River
Magdalena River

COLOMBIA
Cali

GUYANA
Georgetown
Paramaribo
Cayenne
SURINAME
FR. GUIANA (France)

Quito
ECUADOR
Guayaquil
Putumayo River

Iquitos
Marañón River

Negro River
Manaus
Amazon River
River

Belém

P E R U

Ucayali River
Madeira River

B R A Z I L

Xingú
Araguaia River
Tocantins River
São Francisco River

Recife

Lima
Cuzco

BOLIVIA
Lake Titicaca
La Paz
Santa Cruz
Sucre

Brasília
Salvador

Belo Horizonte

PARAGUAY
Paraguay River
Paraná River

São Paulo
Rio de Janeiro

Antofagasta

A N D E S   M O U N T A I N S

Asunción

L. Mar Chiquita
Córdoba
Rosario
Pôrto Alegre

Parana River
Uruguay River

URUGUAY

Valparaíso
Santiago

Buenos Aires
La Plata
Montevideo

Concepción

ARGENTINA

ATLANTIC OCEAN

PACIFIC OCEAN

ATLANTIC OCEAN

| 0 | 300 | 600 mi |
| 0 | 482 | 965 km |

FALKLAND ISLANDS (United Kingdom)
Stanley

Punta Arenas
Tierra del Fuego

SOUTH GEORGIA (United Kingdom)

Cape Horn

N

Americas–South America.

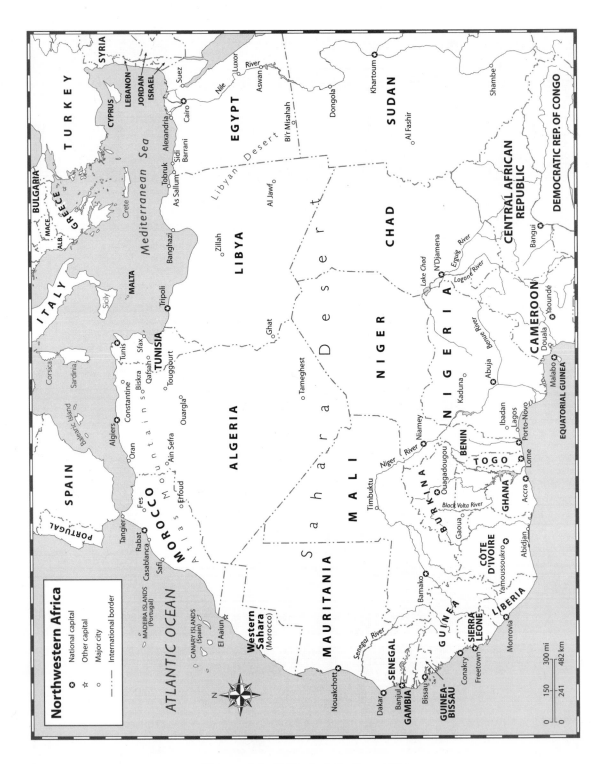

Northwestern Africa

- ✪ National capital
- ★ Other capital
- ○ Major city
- ‒‒‒ International border

TURKEY

SYRIA

BULGARIA

MACE.

ALB.

GREECE

CYPRUS

LEBANON

JORDAN

ISRAEL

Suez

Nile

Luxor

River

Aswan

Khartoum

Shambe

SUDAN

DEMOCRATIC REP. OF CONGO

Dongola

Al Fashir

Cairo

Alexandria

Sidi

Barrani

As Sallum

Tobruk

Bi'r Misahah

Al Jawf

Libyan Desert

EGYPT

Mediterranean Sea

Crete

Italy

Sicily

MALTA

Tripoli

Banghazi

Zillah

LIBYA

Ghat

CHAD

N'Djamena

Lake Chad

Erguig River

Logone River

Benue River

CENTRAL AFRICAN REPUBLIC

Bangui

CAMEROON

Yaoundé

Douala

Malabo

EQUATORIAL GUINEA

Corsica

Sardinia

Balearic Island

Sfax

Tunis

Qafsah

TUNISIA

Touggourt

Biskra

Constantine

Ouargla

Ain Sefra

Algiers

Oran

Sahara Desert

Tameghest

NIGER

Niamey

NIGERIA

Kaduna

Abuja

Ibadan

Lagos

Porto-Novo

BENIN

TOGO

Lome

GHANA

Accra

SPAIN

PORTUGAL

Fes

Tangier

Rabat

Casablanca

Safi

MOROCCO

Atlas Mountains

Effoud

MALI

Timbuktu

Niger River

Ouagadougou

BURKINA

Gaoua

Black Volta River

CÔTE D'IVOIRE

Abidjan

Yamoussoukro

LIBERIA

Monrovia

ATLANTIC OCEAN

MADEIRA ISLANDS (Portugal)

CANARY ISLANDS (Spain)

El Aaiun

Western Sahara (Morocco)

MAURITANIA

Nouakchott

Senegal River

SENEGAL

Dakar

Banjul

GAMBIA

Bissau

GUINEA-BISSAU

Conakry

GUINEA

Bamako

Freetown

SIERRA LEONE

150

300 mi

0

0

241

482 km

N

Africa and the Middle East—Northwest Africa.

Maps | xxiv

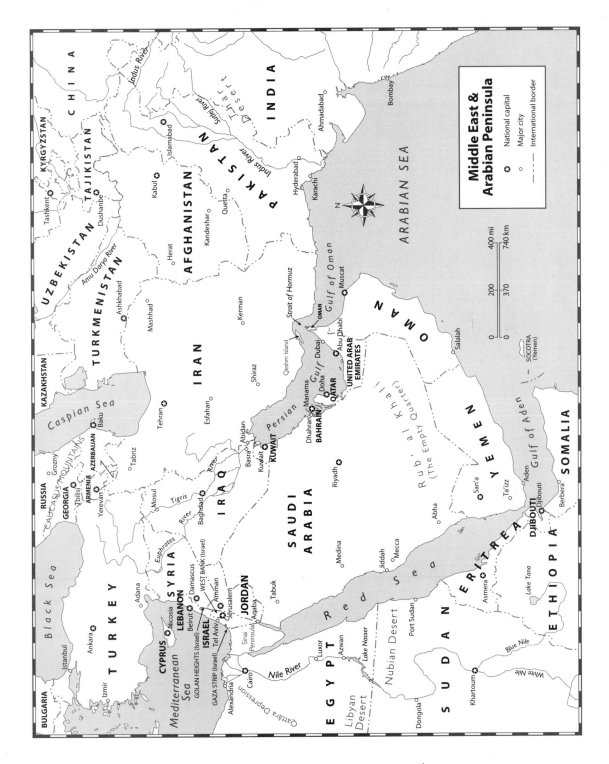

Africa and the Middle East—The Middle East and Arabia.

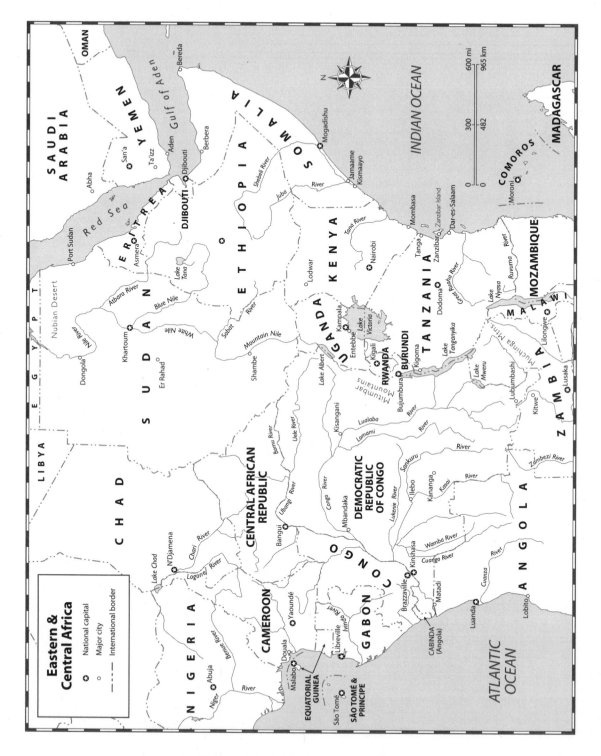

Africa and the Middle East–Eastern Africa.

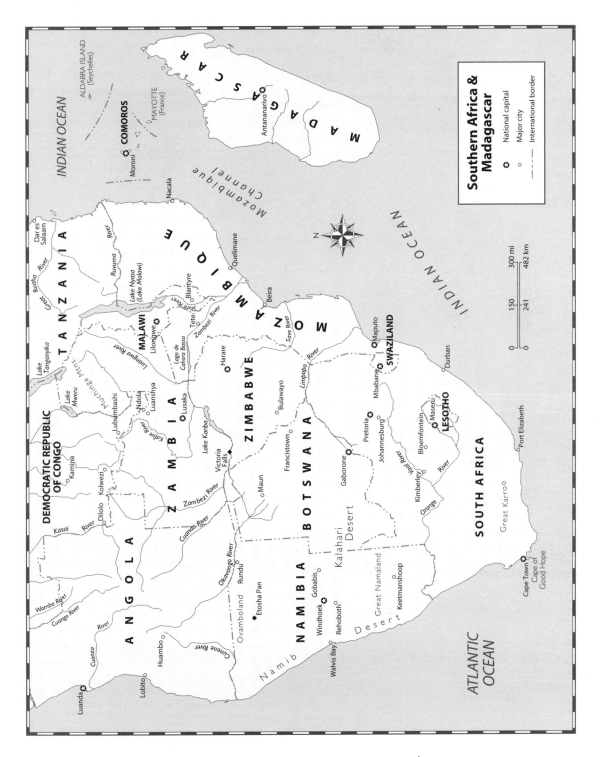

INDIAN OCEAN

ALDABRA ISLAND
(Seychelles)

MAYOTTE
(France)

COMOROS
Moroni

MADAGASCAR

Antananarivo

Mozambique Channel

Southern Africa &
Madagascar

National capital
Major city
International border

N

0   150   300 mi
0   241   482 km

Dar es
Salaam

Nacala

TANZANIA

Great Ruaha River

Ruvuma River

Lake Nyasa
(Lake Malawi)

Quelimane

Shire River

Blantyre

MALAWI

Tete

Lilongwe

Luangwa River

Lago de
Cahora Bassa

Zambezi River

MOZAMBIQUE

Lake
Tanganyika

Lake
Mweru

Muchinga Mtns.

Harare

Lubumbashi

Ndola

Luanshya

ZAMBIA

Lusaka

ZIMBABWE

Bulawayo

Save River

Beira

Limpopo River

Maputo

SWAZILAND

Mbabane

DEMOCRATIC REPUBLIC
OF CONGO

Kamjria

Kolwezi

Kafue River

Lake Kariba

Victoria
Falls

Francistown

Maun

Gaborone

BOTSWANA

Pretoria

Johannesburg

Durban

Maseru

LESOTHO

Bloemfontein

Kimberley

Vaal River

Dilolo

Kasai River

Zambezi River

Cuando River

Kalahari
Desert

Orange River

Port Elizabeth

SOUTH AFRICA

Great Karroo

Wamba River

ANGOLA

Cuango River

Cuanza River

Huambo

Okavango River

Rundu

Ovamboland

Etosha Pan

NAMIBIA

Gobabis

Windhoek

Rehoboth

Great Namaland

Keetmanshoop

Great
Namaland

Cape Town
Cape of
Good Hope

Cunene River

Namib Desert

Desert

Walvis Bay

Lobito

Luanda

ATLANTIC
OCEAN

INDIAN OCEAN

Africa and the Middle East–Southern Africa.

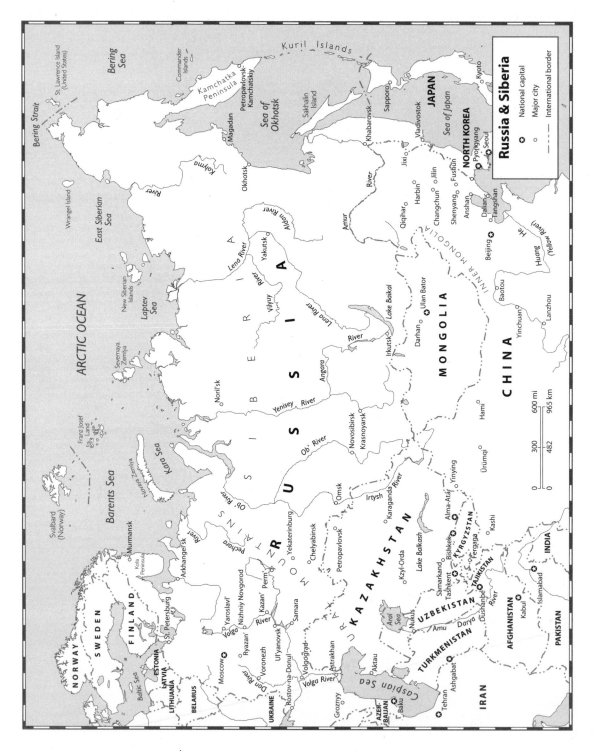

Asia–Siberia.

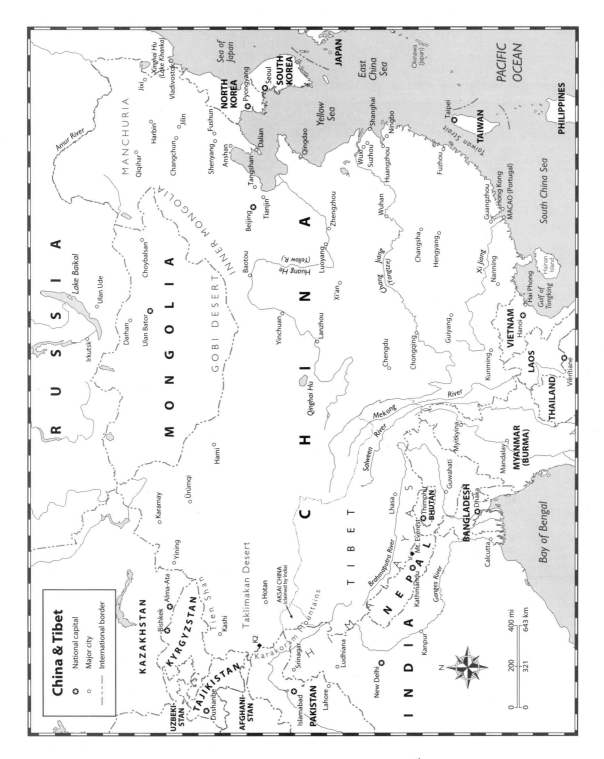

China & Tibet

- ✿ National capital
- ○ Major city
- –·–· International border

Asia—China and Tibet.

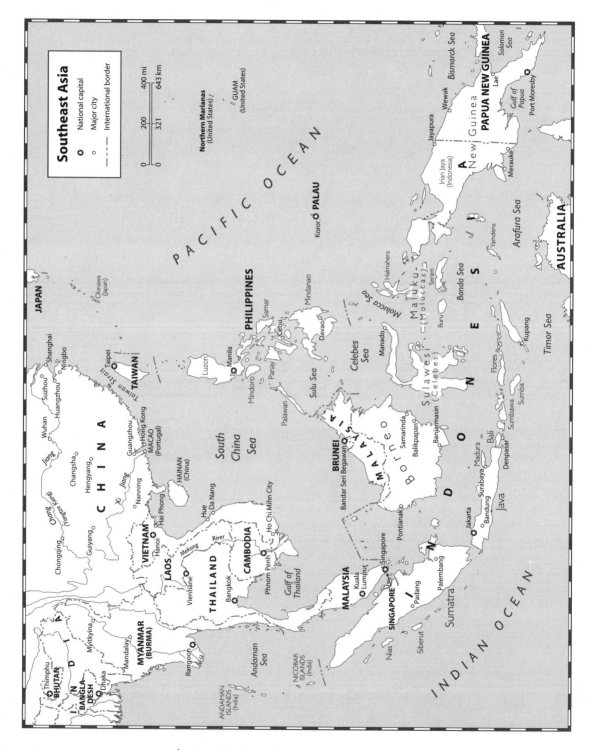

The map contains the following labels:

Legend:
Southeast Asia
⊕ National capital
○ Major city
– – – International border

0   200   400 mi
0   321   643 km

Oceans and Seas:
PACIFIC OCEAN
INDIAN OCEAN
South China Sea
Celebes Sea
Sulu Sea
Banda Sea
Arafura Sea
Timor Sea
Molucca Sea
Andaman Sea
Bismarck Sea
Solomon Sea
Gulf of Thailand
Gulf of Papua
Taiwan Strait

Countries and regions:
CHINA
JAPAN
TAIWAN
PHILIPPINES
VIETNAM
LAOS
THAILAND
CAMBODIA
MYANMAR (BURMA)
BANGLADESH
BHUTAN
INDIA
MALAYSIA
BRUNEI
SINGAPORE
INDONESIA
PAPUA NEW GUINEA
AUSTRALIA
PALAU
Northern Marianas (United States)
GUAM (United States)
MACAO (Portugal)
HAINAN (China)
NICOBAR ISLANDS (India)
ANDAMAN ISLANDS (India)
Inran Jaya (Indonesia)
New Guinea

Cities:
Shanghai, Ningbo, Suzhou, Huangzhou, Wuhan, Changsha, Hengyang, Guiyang, Chongqing, Nanning, Guangzhou, Hong Kong, Taipei, Okinawa (Japan), Koror, Manila, Cebu, Davao, Wewak, Jayapura, Lae, Port Moresby, Merauke, Yamdena, Kupang, Denpasar, Surabaya, Madura, Bali, Banjarmasin, Balikpapan, Samarinda, Manado, Pontianak, Bandar Seri Begawan, Singapore, Kuala Lumpur, Padang, Palembang, Jakarta, Bandung, Ho Chi Mihn City, Da Nang, Hue, Hai Phong, Hanoi, Vientiane, Bangkok, Phnom Penh, Mandalay, Myitkyina, Rangoon, Dhaka, Thimphu

Islands and geographic features:
Luzon, Mindoro, Panay, Samar, Mindanao, Palawan, Borneo, Sulawesi (Celebes), Maluku (Moluccas), Halmahera, Seram, Buru, Flores, Sumba, Sumbawa, Java, Sumatra, Nias, Siberut
Xi Jiang, Chang Jiang (Yangtze River), Mekong River

Asia–Southeast Asia.

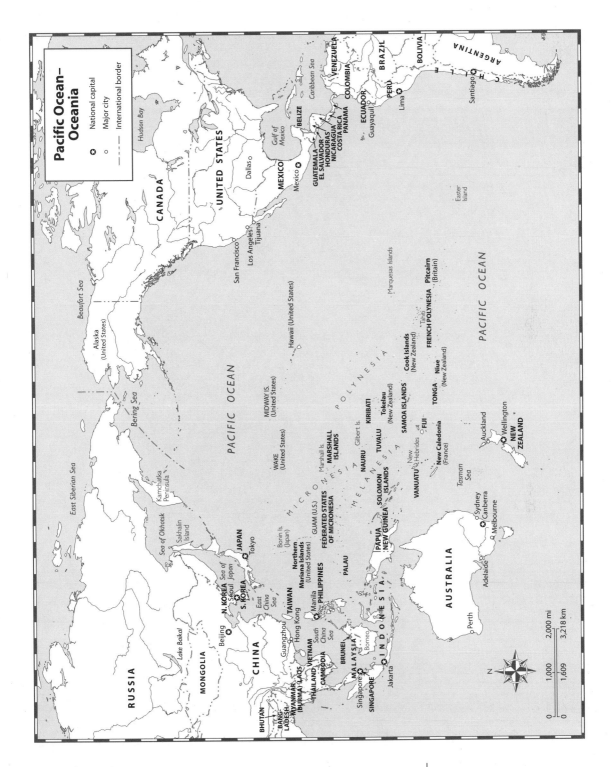

Pacific Ocean–Oceania

✪ National capital
○ Major city
–·–·– International border

RUSSIA

MONGOLIA

CHINA

Beijing ✪

Lake Baikal

East Siberian Sea

Bering Sea

Beaufort Sea

CANADA

Hudson Bay

UNITED STATES

Dallas

Gulf of Mexico

MEXICO ✪
Mexico

Caribbean Sea

BELIZE
GUATEMALA
EL SALVADOR
HONDURAS
NICARAGUA
COSTA RICA
PANAMA

VENEZUELA

COLOMBIA

ECUADOR
Guayaquil

PERU
Lima

BRAZIL

BOLIVIA

CHILE

ARGENTINA

Santiago ✪

Easter Island

Alaska (United States)

Kamchatka Peninsula

Sea of Okhotsk

Sakhalin Island

Sea of Japan

JAPAN ✪
Tokyo

Bonin Is. (Japan)

N. KOREA
Seoul ✪
S. KOREA

East China Sea

TAIWAN

Hong Kong

Guangzhou

South China Sea

PHILIPPINES
Manila ✪

PALAU

Northern Mariana Islands (United States)

GUAM (U.S.)

FEDERATED STATES OF MICRONESIA

Marshall Is.

MARSHALL ISLANDS

WAKE (United States)

MIDWAY IS. (United States)

Hawaii (United States)

San Francisco

Los Angeles ○
Tijuana

PACIFIC OCEAN

PACIFIC OCEAN

Marquesas Islands

FRENCH POLYNESIA
Tahiti

Pitcairn (Britain)

Cook Islands (New Zealand)

Niue (New Zealand)

TONGA

SAMOA ISLANDS
Tokelau (New Zealand)

KIRIBATI

Gilbert Is.

TUVALU

NAURU

FIJI

New Caledonia (France)

VANUATU
New Hebrides

SOLOMON ISLANDS

PAPUA NEW GUINEA

P O L Y N E S I A

M E L A N E S I A

M I C R O N E S I A

Auckland
Wellington ✪
NEW ZEALAND

Tasman Sea

AUSTRALIA

Sydney
Canberra ✪
Melbourne

Adelaide

Perth

I N D O N E S I A

Borneo

Jakarta ✪

SINGAPORE
Singapore ✪

MALAYSIA

BRUNEI

VIETNAM
CAMBODIA
LAOS
THAILAND
MYANMAR (BURMA)

BANG-LADESH

BHUTAN

N ↓

0   1,000   2,000 mi
0   1,609   3,218 km

Pacific Ocean–Oceanea.

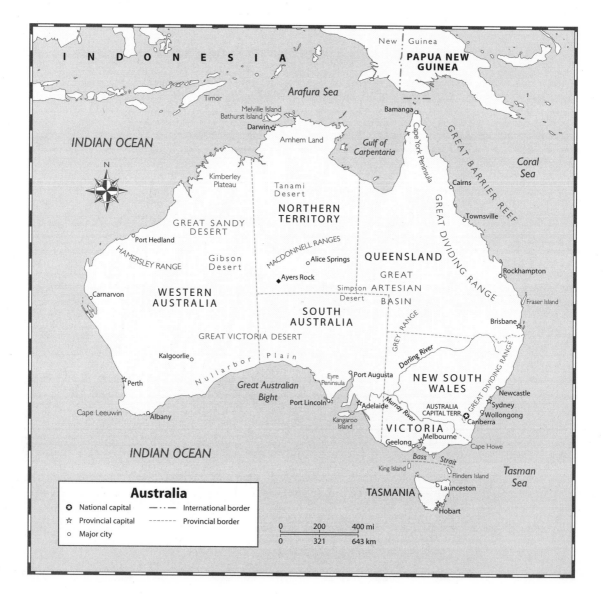

Australia

✪ National capital	▪▪▪ International border
★ Provincial capital	▪▪▪ Provincial border
○ Major city	

0	200	400 mi
0	321	643 km

INDONESIA

New Guinea

PAPUA NEW GUINEA

Arafura Sea

INDIAN OCEAN

N

Timor

Melville Island
Bathurst Island
Darwin ★

Bamanga

Arnhem Land

Gulf of Carpentaria

Cape York Peninsula

Coral Sea

GREAT BARRIER REEF

Kimberley Plateau

Tanami Desert

NORTHERN TERRITORY

GREAT DIVIDING RANGE

Cairns

GREAT SANDY DESERT

Port Hedland ○

HAMERSLEY RANGE

Gibson Desert

MACDONNELL RANGES

Alice Springs ○

QUEENSLAND

Townsville ○

Carnarvon ○

WESTERN AUSTRALIA

◆ Ayers Rock

Simpson Desert

GREAT ARTESIAN BASIN

Rockhampton ○

Fraser Island

SOUTH AUSTRALIA

Brisbane ★

GREAT VICTORIA DESERT

GREY RANGE

Kalgoorlie ○

Nullarbor Plain

Eyre Peninsula

Port Augusta ○

Darling River

NEW SOUTH WALES

Perth ★

Great Australian Bight

Port Lincoln ○

Newcastle ○

Cape Leeuwin

Albany ○

Kangaroo Island

Adelaide ★

Murray River

AUSTRALIA CAPITAL TERR.

Canberra ✪

Sydney ○
Wollongong ○

GREAT DIVIDING RANGE

VICTORIA

Geelong ○
Melbourne ★

Cape Howe

INDIAN OCEAN

Bass Strait

King Island

Flinders Island

Tasman Sea

TASMANIA

Launceston ○

Hobart ★

Pacific Ocean–Australia.

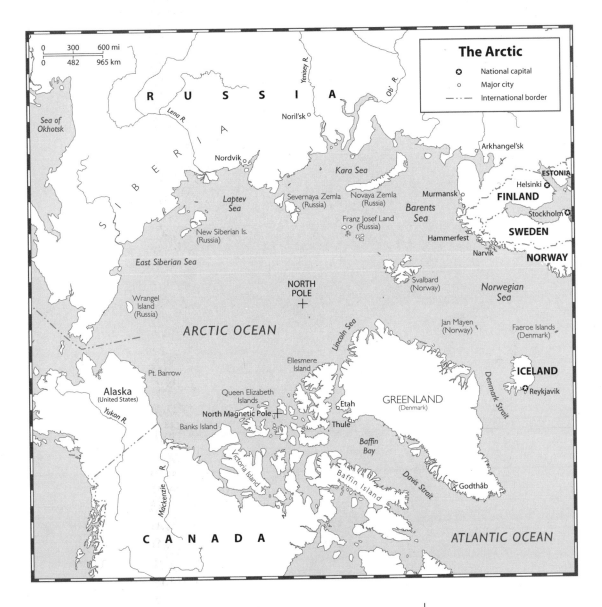

The Arctic

- ✪ National capital
- ○ Major city
- —·—·— International border

RUSSIA

Sea of Okhotsk

Yenisey R.

Ob' R.

Lena R.

Noril'sk

Arkhangel'sk

S I B E R I A

Nordvik

Kara Sea

ESTONIA

Helsinki

Laptev Sea

Severnaya Zemla (Russia)

Novaya Zemla (Russia)

Murmansk

FINLAND

Stockholm

New Siberian Is. (Russia)

Franz Josef Land (Russia)

Barents Sea

Hammerfest

SWEDEN

East Siberian Sea

Narvik

NORWAY

Wrangel Island (Russia)

NORTH POLE

Svalbard (Norway)

Norwegian Sea

ARCTIC OCEAN

Jan Mayen (Norway)

Faeroe Islands (Denmark)

Pt. Barrow

Lincoln Sea

Ellesmere Island

ICELAND

Reykjavik

Alaska (United States)

Queen Elizabeth Islands

North Magnetic Pole

Etah

GREENLAND (Denmark)

Denmark Strait

Yukon R.

Banks Island

Thule

Baffin Bay

Victoria Island

Baffin Island

Davis Strait

Godthåb

Mackenzie R.

C A N A D A

ATLANTIC OCEAN

0   300   600 mi
0   482   965 km

Arctic Region.

ATLANTIC OCEAN

INDIAN OCEAN

SOUTH ORKNEY ISLANDS
(United Kingdom)

SOUTH SHETLAND ISLANDS
(United Kingdom)

King
George
Island

Esparaza (Argentina)
Marambio (Argentina)

Farady (United Kingdom)

Palmer
(United States)

Adelaide
Island

Gen. San Martin
(Argentina)

Alexander Island

Weddell
Sea

Coats Land

Halley Bay
(United Kingdom)

Filchner
Ice Shelf

Berkner
Island

Ronne
Ice Shelf

Palmer
Land

Bellingshausen
Sea

Siple
(United States)

Ellsworth
Land

PETER I ISLAND
(Norway)

Thurston
Island

Amundsen
Sea

Siple Island

Walgreen Coast

Marie Byrd Land

PACIFIC OCEAN

LESSER
ANTARCTICA

Queen Maud Mtns.

Ross
Ice Shelf

Roosevelt Island

Scott (New Zealand)
McMurdo (United States)

Terra Nova
(Italy)

Ross Sea

Georg von Neumayer
(Germany)

Jutulsessen
(Norway)

Drescher
(Germany)

Princess Martha Coast

Maitri
(India)

Asuka (Japan)

Queen Maud Land

Syowa
(Japan)

Molodezhnaya (Russia)

Mawson (Australia)

Prince Charles Mtns

Amery Ice Shelf

Zhongshan (China)

Davis
(Australia)

GREATER
ANTARCTICA

SOUTH
POLE

Amundsen-Scott
(United States)

Mirnyy
(Russia)

Shackleton
Ice Shelf

Knox Coast

Casey
(Australia)

Wilkes Land

T R A N S A N T A R C T I C   M O U N T A I N S

Victoria Land

George V Land

Oates Land

Terre Adélie

Dumont d'Urville (France)

South Magnetic Pole

Commonwealth Bay
(Australia)

INDIAN OCEAN

Antarctica

○   Research station

········   Extent of ice shelf

0	300	600 mi
0	482	965 km

Antarctic Region.

EXPLORERS & DISCOVERERS

Pedro de Alvarado

Born in 1485, Badajoz, Extremadura, Spain
Died June 29, 1541, Guadalajara, Mexico

Pedro de Alvarado was born in the town of Badajoz, in Spain's west-central Extremadura region. Nothing is known about his early life until 1510, when he arrived in the West Indies with his four brothers. They settled in Santo Domingo (now the Dominican Republic), where Pedro helped run a plantation. He then lived in Cuba for a time. In 1518 he was given command of a ship in Juan de Grijalva's expedition, which explored along the coast of Mexico's Campeche Bay and the Yucatán Peninsula. Grijalva sent Alvarado back to Cuba with reports of a rich kingdom located in the center of Mexico: the Aztec civilization. Spanish governor Diego Velázquez sponsored an expedition led by conquistador Hernán Cortés to further explore the territory, the first Spanish expedition into Aztec country. In February of 1519 Alvarado sailed with Cortés as his lieutenant and second in command.

Cortés and his expedition were able to take over the Aztec capital of Tenochtitlán not long after their arrival. Their conquest was aided, in large part, by the fact that the Aztecs

Pedro de Alvarado was a Spanish conquistador who played a major role in the conquest of Mexico under Hernán Cortés. His conquest of the Mayans in Guatemala and El Salvador also led to Spanish domination in Central America.

thought their Spanish visitors were descendants of their god Quetzalcoatl. Within a few months, however, Cortés was forced to leave the city to fight another Spanish conquistador, Pánfilo de Narvaez, who was hoping to replace him and was approaching Tenochtitlán from the Gulf coast. During that time Alvarado was put in charge of the conquered capital city and its Spanish force of 140 soldiers.

Leads soldiers in Aztec slaughter

While Cortés was gone, the Aztec rulers celebrated an important religious ceremony in the city's main square. For reasons unknown, Alvarado ordered that the entrances to the square be blocked off, and he led his soldiers in an assault in which countless Aztecs were killed, including 200 nobles. It was said that Alvarado waged the attack because he was trying to stop the Aztec religious practice of human sacrifice, but he was also a military officer known for his boldness and cruelty. Afterward, he and his soldiers were set upon by an enraged mob and were forced to retreat to the palace of Axayácatl, where they were surrounded for a time.

When Cortés returned to Tenochtitlán he found its citizens preparing for a full-scale revolt against the Spanish. On the evening of June 30, 1520—called the "Sorrowful Night"— Cortés and his men were forced to leave the city. Hoping to trap the Spanish, the Aztecs had destroyed the causeways or bridges that crossed Lake Texcoco, which surrounded the city. But that did not stop Alvarado, who made an incredible leap across the water to safety. Later known as the "Salto de Alvarado," the feat would add to his reputation as a fearless fighter.

By the spring of 1521 Cortés began waging counterattacks to retake Tenochtitlán and gain control of Mexico. Alvarado played a major role in these efforts. On August 21, after a three-month siege, Cortés destroyed the city and captured the Aztec ruler Cuauhtémoc. He founded Mexico City on the ruins of the capital.

Subdues Indians of Central America

With much of Mexico firmly under control, Alvarado was sent to explore and conquer regions further south. In 1522

1541: Alvarado becomes involved in the Mixton War. During a battle, he is crushed when a horse falls on him.

In 1518, Alvarado commands a ship in Juan de Grijalva's expedition along Campeche Bay and the Yucatán Peninsula

Alvarado settles in Santo Domingo (now the Dominican Republic) in 1510

Alvarado dies on June 29, 1541

1519: Alvarado joins Cortés in the first Spanish expedition into Aztec country. The Spaniards take over the Aztec capital, Tenochtitlán, soon after their arrival. 1520: The Aztecs revolt, forcing the Spanish to leave the city. 1521: the Spanish return, destroy the city, capture the Aztec ruler, and found Mexico City on the ruins of the capital.

1522: Alvarado leads an expedition into the Oaxaca Valley, defeating the Mixtec and Zapotec Indians

1523: Alvarado travels to Central America, fighting several bloody battles with the Indian tribes there. After defeating the Atitláns, he founds the first capital of Guatemala.

After a difficult 6-month journey, Alvarado and his expedition arrive in Quito.

1534: Alvarado lands at Portoviejo, intending to travel inland to lay claim to wealth and territory controlled by the Inca empire.

UNITED STATES

Mexicali
Ciudad Juárez
Durango
MEXICO
Jalisco
Guadalajara
Tampico
Mexico City (Tenochtitlán)
Puebla
Sierra Madre del Sur
Acapulco
Gulf of Mexico
Bay of Campeche
Yucatán Peninsula
BELIZE
GUATEMALA
Guatemala City
HONDURAS
San Salvador
EL SALVADOR
NICARAGUA
Lake Managua
San José
COSTA RICA
PANAMÁ
Colón
Panamá
Gulf of Panamá
Medellín
COLOMBIA
Barranquilla
Cartagena
Maracaibo
VENEZUELA
ATLANTIC OCEAN
de Alvarado arrives from Spain
Havana
CUBA
BAHAMAS
HAITI
DOMINICAN REPUBLIC
PUERTO RICO
JAMAICA
Caribbean Sea
PACIFIC OCEAN
GALÁPAGOS ISLANDS
Portoviejo
Quito
Mt. Cotopaxi
ECUADOR
PERU
N

Modern-day political border

| 0 | 200 | 400 mi |
| 0 | 321 | 643 km |

he led an expedition along the Sierra Madre del Sur mountain range into Mexico's Oaxaca Valley, defeating the Mixtec and Zapotec Indians. A year later he traveled to the former Mayan territory of Guatemala in Central America. Over the next two years he fought several bloody battles with the Indian tribes there. His march across Guatemala ended when he reached the city of Tecpán, defeated the Atitlàns, and founded the first capital of Guatemala at the site of what is now Guatemala City. He then proceeded into the territory that comprises present-day El Salvador. There he traveled as far south as the capital of the Pipiles Indians, near what is now the city of San Salvador.

In 1526 Alvarado returned to Spain to report on his conquests. He was named governor and captain general of the new Spanish territories. He went back to Guatemala to take up his posts, and founded more Spanish settlements. But, missing the thrill of exploration, Alvarado was soon planning another expedition, this time hoping to sail a fleet of ships across the Pacific Ocean to Asia. His plans changed, however, when he heard about the experiences of conquistador Francisco Pizarro in Peru, whose conquest of the Incan empire had resulted in incredible wealth. Alvarado decided to sail his ships there instead, hoping to lay claim to territories not yet explored. He left Guatemala in 1533 with 500 Spanish soldiers, 3,000 Guatemalan slaves, and 227 horses.

Alvarado landed at the city of Portoviejo (in what is now Ecuador) on February 25, 1534. He pushed into the interior, hoping to reach the northern Incan city of Quito. Unfamiliar with the territory, Alvarado picked an unwise route to his destination. He and his party had to travel through thick jungles, where insects and disease plagued them and the damp heat caused their armor and weapons to rust. The men struggled to breathe when nearby Mount Cotopaxi erupted, filling the air with volcanic ash. Finally, when they had to make their way over the Andes Mountains, Alvarado chose one of the highest passes through which to cross. There the deep snow and freezing temperatures took a heavy toll. Eighty-five Spaniards died, along with most of the expedition's horses. And more than two thousand of the Guatemalans perished. Snatched from their tropical homelands, they quickly froze to death in the mountains. After six trying months, Alvarado and his expedition at last reached the Incan road that was to lead them to Quito. But they saw horses' tracks, and knew that Pizarro's forces had already come before them.

Narrowly avoids conquistador war

Alvarado and his expedition soon found themselves facing Pizarro's Quito forces, led by Lieutenant Diego de Almagro. It appeared that a conquistador war would take place. Alvarado had more men, and they were eager for battle and rewards after the terrible hardships they had endured. Almagro, on the other hand, represented the Christian establishment already in place in Quito. Both sides prepared for bloodshed. But the two Spanish forces also realized that if they did fight, they might become so weak that the conquered Incas could wage a counterattack. So a deal was struck instead. On August 26, 1534, Almagro paid Alvarado 100,000 gold pesos for his army and equipment, which would stay in Quito. Alvarado agreed to return to Guatemala. There he continued to rule as governor, adding Honduras to his territories in 1536.

In 1540 Alvarado again planned a sailing expedition east, this time to the Spice Islands (in what is now Indonesia). Intending to launch from Mexico's west coast, he was delayed by the country's viceroy (governor), who persuaded him to join the search for the legendary Seven Cities of Cíbola. Reportedly places of great wealth, the cities were thought to lie somewhere north of Mexico, in the American Southwest. Spanish explorer Francisco Vásquez de Coronado would lead the expedition. Alvarado agreed to the viceroy's request, but before his departure became involved in the Míxton War, an Indian uprising at Jalisco in central Mexico. Leading a cavalry attack against the Zacatecas, Alvarado was crushed when a horse fell on him. He was taken to the city of Guadalajara, where he died several days later, on June 29, 1541. For a brief time his widow, Dona Beatriz de la Cueva, succeeded him as governor of Guatemala. She is believed to be the only woman to hold such a high office during the Spanish colonial period in the Americas.

Sources

Baker, Daniel B., ed. *Explorers and Discoverers of the World*. Detroit: Gale Research, 1993.

Bohlander, Richard E., ed. *World Explorers and Discoverers*. New York: Macmillan, 1992.

Hemming, John. *The Conquest of the Inca*. Orlando, FL: Harcourt Brace & Co., 1970.

Waldman, Carl and Alan Wexler. *Who Was Who in World Exploration*. New York: Facts on File, 1992.

William Henry Ashley

Born in 1778, Powhatan County, Virginia
Died March 26, 1838, Cooper County, Missouri

Businessman William Henry Ashley was a leading figure in the American fur trade. On an expedition to the Green River, he and his trappers opened land routes that settlers would later travel when emigrating to the Far West.

In the early 1820s William Henry Ashley and his business partner, Andrew Henry, hoped to enter the beaver skin trade. The fur-trading business was just beginning in the newly opened lands of the Louisiana Purchase (which extended from the Mississippi River to the Rockies), and the mountains of the American West were a rich source of pelts. In 1822 they placed an ad in the St. Louis, Missouri, *Gazette and Public Advertiser,* calling for "Enterprising Young Men" to travel up the Missouri River as trappers and traders. The men were to sail the same route that explorers Meriwether Lewis and William Clark had opened across the North American continent almost twenty years before. But when hostile Indians stopped travel on the Missouri River, Ashley and the members of his Rocky Mountain Fur Company were forced to proceed west by land routes. The expeditions of these mountain men, as they were called, supplied information about the western wilderness that would prove invaluable to future explorers and settlers.

Ashley was born in 1778 in Powhatan County, Virginia. He moved west to the Missouri Territory sometime between 1803 and 1805, settling first in St. Genevieve and then in St. Louis. He entered the mining business and—along with his partner Henry—prospered selling saltpeter (an ingredient in gunpowder) to the U.S. Army during the War of 1812. Ashley also served in the Missouri territorial militia, eventually reaching the rank of general. In addition, he became involved in real estate and politics, and was elected lieutenant governor of Missouri when the territory became a state in 1821.

William Henry Ashley at the fur-trading summer rendezvous.

Establishes fur-trading business

Suffering a financial setback around this time, Ashley thought he could rebuild his fortune by fur trading on the upper Missouri River. He and Henry placed their advertisement for fur trappers in the newspaper, and undertook their first expedition in the spring of 1822. Accompanied by a small party of men, they sailed the Missouri north from St. Louis, to the mouth of the Yellowstone River in what is now far western North Dakota. There they set up a trading post, Fort Henry (later Fort Union). Their profit was small that trip, and Ashley planned to make a second expedition the following year.

Second Missouri mission meets with disaster

In the spring of 1823 a second party of Ashley's men were traveling the Missouri River near what is now the border between North and South Dakota. When they stopped at an Arikara Indian settlement to trade for supplies, they were met with a surprise attack. Up until the arrival of Ashley and his trappers, the Arikara had handled the fur trade for Indian tribes of the upper Missouri. They felt threatened by the white men's activities and looked to stop them. Pinned down by rifle fire and arrows against the sandy beach of the Arikara settlement, Ashley's men swam downstream to their keelboats (shallow riverboats) in a desperate attempt to escape. Fourteen trappers were killed.

While a military expedition led by Colonel Henry Leavenworth soon arrived and scattered the Arikara tribe north, other Indian attacks along the river continued. Water travel west appeared impossible, and Ashley was anxious not to miss a trapping season. He decided to send groups of trappers out from Fort Kiowa (in present-day South Dakota) overland to the Rocky Mountains.

One group—led by mountain man Jedediah Smith—went south, to the Green River in what is now western Wyoming. He sent word back to Ashley that the area was excellent for trapping, but that his men were in serious need of supplies. Ashley decided to lead a relief expedition there at once. He was now the sole owner of what had become the Rocky Mountain Fur Company, his partner having left the business. After the bad luck of his early expeditions, Ashley was more in debt than ever, and encouraged by the news of good trapping.

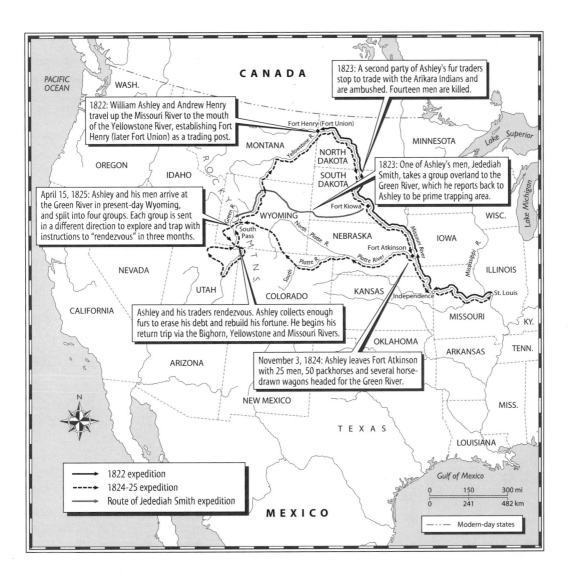

1823: A second party of Ashley's fur traders stop to trade with the Arikara Indians and are ambushed. Fourteen men are killed.

1822: William Ashley and Andrew Henry travel up the Missouri River to the mouth of the Yellowstone River, establishing Fort Henry (later Fort Union) as a trading post.

1823: One of Ashley's men, Jedediah Smith, takes a group overland to the Green River, which he reports back to Ashley to be prime trapping area.

April 15, 1825: Ashley and his men arrive at the Green River in present-day Wyoming, and split into four groups. Each group is sent in a different direction to explore and trap with instructions to "rendezvous" in three months.

Ashley and his traders rendezvous. Ashley collects enough furs to erase his debt and rebuild his fortune. He begins his return trip via the Bighorn, Yellowstone and Missouri Rivers.

November 3, 1824: Ashley leaves Fort Atkinson with 25 men, 50 packhorses and several horse-drawn wagons headed for the Green River.

→ 1822 expedition
---▶ 1824-25 expedition
→ Route of Jedediah Smith expedition

0   150   300 mi
0   241   482 km

----- Modern-day states

Leads expedition to Green River

On November 3, 1824, Ashley left Fort Atkinson, located on the Missouri River near present-day Omaha. He brought with him a party of twenty-five men, fifty pack horses, and several horse-drawn wagons. The expedition traveled west along the Platte River during the bitter prairie winter, and had to abandon the wagons and many of the horses along the way. The men would have died of starvation if not for the kindness of the Pawnee Indians of western

Nebraska, who offered them food and shelter. After resting a while in the Pawnee village, Ashley and his men went up the South Platte River and through the Wind River Range to the Rocky Mountains, which they quickly crossed. It was apparent that they had rediscovered the South Pass (found earlier in the century), the easiest route by which to cross the Rockies, located in what is now southwest Wyoming. The South Pass would later become the eastern end of the Oregon Trail, for years the gateway for emigrants traveling to the Far West.

Initiates "rendezvous" system of fur trading

Ashley and his men reached the Green River (which extends from western Wyoming into northern Utah) on April 15, 1825. There Ashley split his men into four groups. Three were sent in different directions to explore and trap. They were instructed to meet fifty miles down the Green River three months later. This "rendezvous" system of fur trapping was unique at the time, but would soon become a standard practice among mountain men and their suppliers in the American West. During the year trappers would collect furs, meeting at a selected spot every summer. There they would exchange their annual catch of beavers for money and supplies from a company trader. They would also visit with their fellow trappers for a time—drinking, gambling, and storytelling—before returning to their rugged and often solitary lives.

Ashley took the fourth group of men with him. They built boats from buffalo hides stretched across willow branches (bullboats) and became the first Westerners to sail down the Green River into present-day Utah. Ashley hoped that the water route would take them farther west. The waters of the Green were turbulent, and at one point the expedition leader and his boat were nearly sucked into one of the river's many whirlpools and drowned. The group had to carry boats and gear around the falls at Red Canyon, where Ashley wrote his name on the mountain wall. They continued down the Green River through Flaming Gorge, Lodore Canyon, and

Split Mountain Gorge—which are all national forest, recreation, or wilderness areas today.

On May 16 Ashley and his party came upon some French trappers who were traveling up from Taos, in what is now New Mexico. They informed the expedition that beaver hunting was poor farther south. After thirty-one days on the Green, Ashley changed his course, joining the Frenchmen as they traveled up the Uinta River (a northwestern tributary of the Green) to its source in the Uinta Mountains. There they traded for furs with the Ute Indians. They then traveled north by land to the "rendezvous" point near Henry's Fork on the Green River in southern Wyoming.

First rendezvous gathering a success

The first fur-trading rendezvous was a great success. Not only did Ashley's mountain men arrive with their pelts, but some French and British traders also came to the gathering—more than one hundred trappers in all. Ashley collected enough furs to erase his debt and rebuild his fortune. He headed north with his valuable cargo, traveling along the Bighorn and Yellowstone Rivers to the Missouri. On his way he was met by a U.S. Army expedition led by Colonel Leavenworth, which escorted him safely home to St. Louis.

The following year Ashley again traveled west for the annual rendezvous, this time held on the Cache River near the Great Salt Lake in what is now northwestern Utah. There he sold his business to Jedediah Smith and two of his partners. Ashley continued to supply them with goods and to market their furs, but he no longer traveled to the frontier, choosing instead to pursue a political career in Missouri. Ashley lost a race for governor of the state in 1824 and one for a senate seat in 1829. He was elected to the U.S. House of Representatives in 1831, however, serving in Congress for six years. During that time he was a member of the House Committee on Indian Affairs and strongly urged the government to adopt policies that would drive Native Americans from their lands. He retired in poor health in 1837 and returned to Missouri, where he died from pneumonia on March 26, 1838.

Sources

Baker, Daniel B., ed. *Explorers and Discoverers of the World*. Detroit: Gale Research, 1993.

Bohlander, Richard E., ed. *World Explorers and Discoverers*. New York: Macmillan, 1992.

Goetzmann, William H. *Exploration and Empire*. New York: William Morrow & Co., Inc., 1966.

Waldman, Carl, and Alan Wexler. *Who Was Who in World Exploration*. New York: Facts on File, 1992.

Willem Barents

Born c. 1550, Terschelling Island, The Netherlands
Died June 20, 1597, Barents Sea

During the sixteenth century the great maritime powers of Spain and Portugal largely controlled the trade routes to Africa and Asia. The country we now call the Netherlands was also a significant trading nation at that time, with a powerful merchant class and superb sailing vessels. Rather than force their way through established southern trade routes, the Dutch were interested in finding a northern water route that would take them to the Orient. Thus they began a series of journeys designed to sail north of Eurasia—into what was called the Northeast Passage—and then south into the Pacific Ocean, to China and India. Dutch navigator Willem Barents piloted three such expeditions during the 1590s. The hardships he and fellow crew members endured during their final journey discouraged all but the most hardy explorers from attempting such a passage, which was finally achieved by Swedish scientist Nils Adolf Erik Nordenskjöld some 275 years later.

Willem Barents was a Dutch navigator who piloted three expeditions in search of the Northeast Passage—a sailing route that ran north of Europe to the Orient. In his last attempt he discovered Bear Island and Spitsbergen, but died in the Arctic Ocean north of Russia.

*Willem Barents and his crew
build a wooden house in order
to spend the Arctic winter at
Ice Haven.*

Makes first attempt at Northeast Passage

Little is known about Barents's early life. He was a native of the island of Terschelling, off the coast of Friesland in the northern Netherlands. He moved to the bustling trade city of Amsterdam, where he became known as an accomplished sailor and navigator. In 1954 the Dutch government, along with a group of wealthy Amsterdam merchants, financed an expedition in search of the Northeast Passage and granted Barents command of one of its vessels; Jan van Linschoten, a major backer of the mission, captained another. On June 4 Barents left Holland and sailed through the North Sea, heading along the northern coast of Europe. He made his way around Norway's Cape North, and entered the expansive body of water later named in his honor—Barents Sea—before reaching the large island of Novaya Zemlya, off the northern

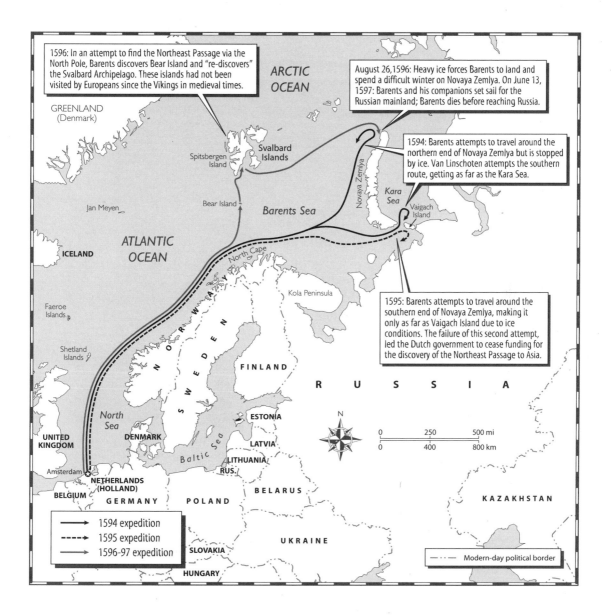

1596: In an attempt to find the Northeast Passage via the North Pole, Barents discovers Bear Island and "re-discovers" the Svalbard Archipelago. These islands had not been visited by Europeans since the Vikings in medieval times.

August 26, 1596: Heavy ice forces Barents to land and spend a difficult winter on Novaya Zemlya. On June 13, 1597: Barents and his companions set sail for the Russian mainland; Barents dies before reaching Russia.

1594: Barents attempts to travel around the northern end of Novaya Zemlya but is stopped by ice. Van Linschoten attempts the southern route, getting as far as the Kara Sea.

1595: Barents attempts to travel around the southern end of Novaya Zemlya, making it only as far as Vaigach Island due to ice conditions. The failure of this second attempt, led the Dutch government to cease funding for the discovery of the Northeast Passage to Asia.

ARCTIC OCEAN

GREENLAND (Denmark)

Svalbard Islands

Spitsbergen Island

Jan Meyen

Bear Island

Barents Sea

Novaya Zemlya

Kara Sea

Vaigach Island

ATLANTIC OCEAN

ICELAND

North Cape

N O R W A Y

Kola Peninsula

Faeroe Islands

Shetland Islands

S W E D E N

FINLAND

R U S S I A

North Sea

ESTONIA

DENMARK

LATVIA

Baltic Sea

LITHUANIA

Amsterdam

NETHERLANDS (HOLLAND)

RUS.

BELGIUM

GERMANY

POLAND

BELARUS

KAZAKHSTAN

UKRAINE

SLOVAKIA

HUNGARY

250   500 mi
400   800 km

→ 1594 expedition
--→ 1595 expedition
→ 1596-97 expedition

—·—·— Modern-day political border

coast of east Russia. He managed to travel to the island's northernmost point—which he named Ice Cape—before floating ice stopped his eastern progress.

During his return trip, Barents met up with van Linschoten, who had had better luck. Instead of taking Barents's more northerly route, he had sailed close to the European and Russian coast. He had passed Novaya Zemlya by sailing south of the island in ice-free waters, and had made it as far as the Kara Sea before turning back. Encouraged by van Linschoten's reports, the expedition's sponsors planned a second journey for the following year. Van Linschoten would command a seven-ship fleet, and Barents would serve as chief pilot. They would travel van Linschoten's southern route. The merchants were so confident of success that they filled the ships with goods to trade in the Far East.

Second try ends in failure

In the spring of 1595 the expedition set sail. But by August 19 the fleet had to abandon its mission, for the ice was particularly bad that year, and the travelers could make it only as far as Vaigach Island, located in the straits between Novaya Zemlya and mainland Russia. The trip was a dismal failure, and the Dutch government voted to spend no more public funds looking for the Northeast Passage.

But Barents convinced the merchants of Amsterdam to give the quest another try. On his third trip in search of the Northeast Passage, he served as expedition pilot for two ships. One was under the command of Jacob van Heemskerk; the other was captained by Jan Cornelizoon Rijp. Barents planned to direct the ships north, from the tip of Norway to the North Pole. This extreme route was based on an idea popular among European geographers at that time: that Arctic ice formed only in a wide band along the coast, and that farther north lay an open polar sea. If that were the case, the expedition would find a swift, smooth sailing route to the Pacific.

Explorers discover unknown Arctic islands

The expedition set sail on May 13, 1596. In June, when the explorers were north of Norway, they discovered Bear Island, so named after the fierce battle they had with a polar bear there. Not long after they came upon the island of Spitsbergen, part of the Svalbard Archipelago (a group of scattered islands), which they mistakenly thought was the east coast of Greenland. Barents and his companions were the first Europeans to sail that territory since the Vikings in medieval times. These island discoveries proved important, for the area soon became a profitable hunting ground for whale, seal, and walrus.

Icebergs kept the travelers from making their way farther north. In a disagreement over which route to take next, the two ships separated, with Rijp soon returning to Holland. Barents and van Heemskerk turned east, hoping to travel around Novaya Zemlya. But on the north coast of the island heavy ice set in, and the boat was forced to land in a bay that Barents called Ice Haven. On August 26, the crew abandoned ship as the advancing ice began to crush it. They would have to spend the Arctic winter on the island.

Stranded expedition endures polar winter

The seventeen expedition members built a cabin with driftwood and timber from the boat. They also used the wood for fuel, and kept a fire burning throughout the long winter. They nearly suffocated from the constant smoke, but the air was so cold that they could not do without the fire. Liquids froze before the men could drink them, and blankets froze to beds. The men had to be watchful of polar bear attacks. Yet foxes and walruses were plentiful in the area, and provided the crew with food. Miraculously, only two men died that winter.

When the summer thaw came Barents and his companions planned to set sail for the Russian mainland in two of the ship's remaining longboats. Before embarking on June 13, 1597, van Heemskerk made a copy of the expedition's log for each boat to carry. Barents wrote his own account of the ordeal, which he hid in the cabin's chimney. A few days into their sea journey, he died in the open boat, probably weakened by the harsh winter. The rest of the crew did manage to make their way through ice-filled waters to the mainland, where fishermen helped them reach a Dutch trading settlement on Russia's Kola Peninsula. There Rijp met them, sailing them safely back to Holland by November. The story of the expedition members' courage and endurance during the Arctic winter fascinated Europe. But the tale also emphasized the grave difficulty of traveling the Northeast Passage, and the Dutch made no further attempts. (Military victories against the Spanish would soon allow them to freely use the southern trade route to the Indies.)

The area along the Northeast Passage was so little traveled that it was not until 1871 that anyone revisited Novaya Zemlya's Ice Haven bay. Then, a Norwegian seal-hunting expedition led by Captain Elling Carlsen came upon the small cabin that Barents and his fellow crew members had built to face the Arctic winter so long ago. The place was little disturbed. In 1875 another explorer found part of Barents's secret journal. This and other artifacts of the expedition are now displayed at a museum in The Hague.

Sources

Baker, Daniel B., ed. *Explorers and Discoverers of the World*. Detroit: Gale Research, 1993.

Bohlander, Richard E., ed. *World Explorers and Discoverers*. New York: Macmillan, 1992.

Waldman, Carl, and Alan Wexler. *Who Was Who in World Exploration*. New York: Facts on File, 1992.

Vitus Bering

Born August 12, 1681, Horsens, Denmark
Died December 8, 1741, Bering Island, Russia

In 1725 Russian czar Peter the Great commissioned Danish navigator Vitus Bering to explore Siberia's Pacific Coast. During that time the Russian Empire was rapidly expanding east, and it was not yet known whether eastern Siberia and northwestern North America were connected. (Russia was also interested in opening an Arctic trade route to the Orient.) In the previous century cossack (Russian frontiersman) and sailor Semyon Ivanov Dezhnev had reported that the two continents were separated by a small strait, but his findings were unconfirmed. During Bering's two extensive expeditions into eastern Siberia and the northern Pacific Ocean, he proved without question that the two landmasses were separate. His many geographical discoveries in the area, including Alaska, introduced Russia to a region rich in furs of all kinds. This led to the Russian Empire's expansion overseas.

Bering was born August 12, 1681, in Horsens, Denmark. As a young man he sailed with a Dutch fleet to the East Indies, returning in 1703. Then he became one of the hundreds

Vitus Bering was a Danish navigator who sailed in the service of the Russian czar. His expeditions into the northern Pacific Ocean conclusively proved that the landmasses of Asia and North America were separated by a passage of water.

of foreigners recruited by Peter the Great to help modernize Russia. Bering entered the newly formed Russian Royal Navy as a sublieutenant, reaching the rank of captain in 1724. During those years he distinguished himself in the Great Northern War against Sweden, fighting in the Baltic, Black, and White Seas. Before his death in 1725, the czar commissioned Bering to lead an expedition to explore the eastern Siberian coast and the northern Pacific Ocean.

Leads first expedition to eastern Siberian coast

Leaving the Russian capital of St. Petersburg in February of 1725 (in what would be called the First Kamchatka Expedition), Bering and his party of some one hundred men traveled overland across Russia and Siberia, a distance of more than five thousand miles. They carried with them materials to build a boat, which they set about doing when they reached the settlement of Okhotsk on the southern Siberian coast in mid-1727. Called the *Fortune,* the boat was used to transport men and supplies across the Sea of Okhotsk to the Kamchatka Peninsula. Once there, it took nearly a year for the expedition members to sled across to the peninsula's east coast, from which they would launch their ocean explorations. But first the men had to build another sailing vessel.

Fog hides Alaska

On July 13, 1728, with the *St. Gabriel* complete, Bering and his crew at last set sail. He traveled north up the Siberian coast, reaching what would later be known as the Bering Strait, the narrow waterway that separates Asia and North America. The captain sighted St. Lawrence Island and the Diomede Islands but did not see the coast of Alaska because of heavy fog. When the Siberian mainland started to turn westward, he was convinced that he had come as far as the tip of Asia and that no land connected the two continents. Worsening ice stopped further progress, and he headed south for Kamchatka, where he spent the winter of 1728–29.

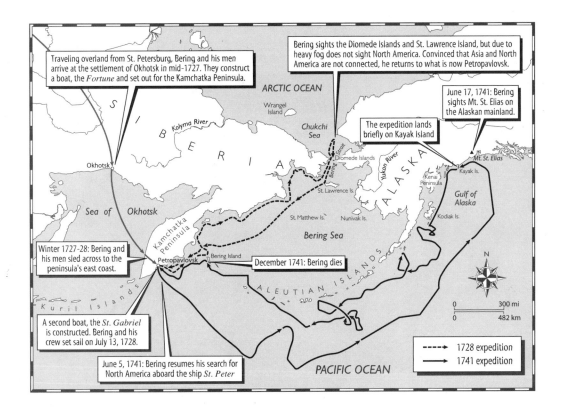

Traveling overland from St. Petersburg, Bering and his men arrive at the settlement of Okhotsk in mid-1727. They construct a boat, the *Fortune* and set out for the Kamchatka Peninsula.

Bering sights the Diomede Islands and St. Lawrence Island, but due to heavy fog does not sight North America. Convinced that Asia and North America are not connected, he returns to what is now Petropavlovsk.

June 17, 1741: Bering sights Mt. St. Elias on the Alaskan mainland.

The expedition lands briefly on Kayak Island

Winter 1727-28: Bering and his men sled across to the peninsula's east coast.

December 1741: Bering dies

A second boat, the *St. Gabriel* is constructed. Bering and his crew set sail on July 13, 1728.

June 5, 1741: Bering resumes his search for North America aboard the ship *St. Peter*

ARCTIC OCEAN

Wrangel Island

Chukchi Sea

S I B E R I A

Kolyma River

Okhotsk

Sea of Okhotsk

Kamchatka Peninsula

Petropavlovsk

Bering Island

Kuril Islands

Diomede Islands

St. Lawrence Is.

St. Matthew Is.   Nunivak Is.

Bering Sea

Yukon River

ALASKA

Mt. St. Elias

Kayak Is.

Kenai Peninsula

Gulf of Alaska

Kodiak Is.

A L E U T I A N   I S L A N D S

PACIFIC OCEAN

N

0   300 mi
0   482 km

------ 1728 expedition
——→ 1741 expedition

Heads Great Northern Expedition

By March 1, 1730, Bering and his men had made their way back to St. Petersburg. Empress Anna had ascended the Russian throne, and in 1733 she authorized another exploration. Bering was named commander of the Great Northern Expedition, which would not only investigate the landmass that lay east of Siberia in the Pacific Ocean (this effort was called the Second Kamchatka Expedition), but would trace a route from the Siberian coast to Japan. It would also include an overland exploration of the northern coast of Siberia, between the Ob and Lena Rivers. Preparations for the ambitious project were elaborate. The expedition included thirteen ships and several hundred crew members, as well landscape painters, surveyors, and more than two dozen scientists. The scientists brought with them hundreds of books and wagonloads of instruments. It took the enormous party eight years just to make its way to Okhotsk.

Vitus Bering and his crew discover Alaska.

From Okhotsk, Bering oversaw overland expeditions into the Lake Baikal region and the Amur River basin. Sailing expeditions were also made along the Arctic and Pacific coasts of Siberia, and southward to the Kuril Islands, which lay north of Japan. In September of 1740 Bering was finally able to turn his attention to the search for North America once again. He sailed his ship, the *St. Peter,* to Petropavlovsk, a new settlement on Kamchatka's Pacific coast. There he met one of his chief lieutenants, Alexei Ilyich Chirikov, who would command a companion ship, the *St. Paul,* as they made their way eastward. Waiting out the winter, the boats set sail on June 5, 1741.

The two ships soon became separated in a storm. Chirikov's boat managed to make it to the North American mainland, but the crew suffered greatly from scurvy (a disease caused by the lack of vitamin C, often seen in sailors who have no fruits or vegetables in their diet). They were lucky to make it back to Petropavlovsk by October, before the harsh northern winter set in.

Discovers Alaskan mainland and islands

Bering continued to sail east after the separation, entering the Gulf of Alaska. On July 17, 1741, he sighted Mount St. Elias on the Alaskan mainland and later landed briefly on Kayak Island off Alaska's southern coast. Although he was advised by his chief scientific officer to find a place nearby to wait out the coming winter, Bering ignored the suggestion, feeling there was still time to return to Petropavlovsk. On his voyage back he sighted Alaska's Kenai Peninsula and many of the Aleutian Islands. But storms made progress difficult and one finally dashed the *St. Peter* aground on a small island off the east coast of Kamchatka. Only three hundred miles from Petropavlovsk, the island would later be named Bering Island. The crew was forced to spend the winter there, and most members died from scurvy and exposure, including Bering himself on December 8, 1741.

When summer arrived the few survivors built a new boat from the wreckage of the *St. Peter* and sailed to Petropavlovsk, which they reached on August 27, 1742. Bering's chief lieutenants, Chirikov and Martin Spanberg, returned to St. Petersburg in 1743. The navigational charts they brought back proved that a strait separated Siberia and North America. Bering's explorations in the northern Pacific—now called the Bering Sea in his honor—formed the basis of Russian claims to mainland Alaska and its surrounding islands, which the empire later colonized.

Sources

Baker, Daniel B., ed. *Explorers and Discoverers of the World*. Detroit: Gale Research, 1993.

Bohlander, Richard E., ed. *World Explorers and Discoverers*. New York: Macmillan, 1992.

Waldman, Carl, and Alan Wexler. *Who Was Who in World Exploration*. New York: Facts on File, 1992.

Gregory Blaxland

Born June 17, 1778, Newington, Kent, England
Died January 1, 1853, North Parramatta, Australia

Gregory Blaxland, an Australian rancher, was the first person to find a way through the Blue Mountains, part of the Great Dividing Range that separates Australia's east coast from the rest of the continent.

The first British settlements in Australia were located in the colony of New South Wales, on the continent's fertile southeast coast. Explorers had tried to cross the Great Divide mountain range that separates that coast from the rest of Australia by traveling the canyons and passes that lay between the peaks and ridges. Their efforts had met with failure. Then in 1813 rancher Gregory Blaxland tried a different approach in his attempt to cross the mountains. With his farm—located near the main coastal settlement of Sydney—suffering from drought, he was looking for pasture land farther west. By traveling interconnecting ridges and not descending into the canyons, Blaxland and his party managed to cross much of the Blue Mountains, part of the Great Dividing Range. His trek encouraged further exploration and settlement of the interior of Australia, which took place rapidly over the next several decades.

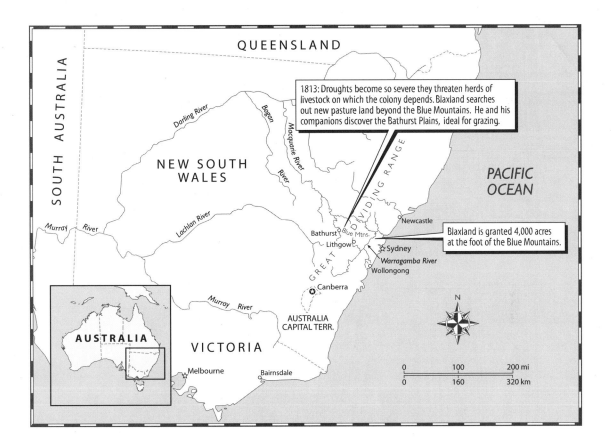

QUEENSLAND

SOUTH AUSTRALIA

NEW SOUTH WALES

Darling River

Bogan

Macquarie River

River

Lachlan River

Murray   River

GREAT DIVIDING RANGE

PACIFIC OCEAN

1813: Droughts become so severe they threaten herds of livestock on which the colony depends. Blaxland searches out new pasture land beyond the Blue Mountains. He and his companions discover the Bathurst Plains, ideal for grazing.

Blaxland is granted 4,000 acres at the foot of the Blue Mountains.

Newcastle

Bathurst   Blue Mtns.
Lithgow
☆ Sydney
Warragamba River
Wollongong

AUSTRALIA

Murray   River

☯ Canberra

AUSTRALIA CAPITAL TERR.

VICTORIA

Melbourne   Bairnsdale

N

0	100	200 mi
0	160	320 km

Becomes one of Australia's first free settlers

Blaxland was born in June of 1778 in the English town of Newington in the county of Kent. He was the son of a prosperous family—his father was a local mayor and large property owner. In 1799 Blaxland married the daughter of another prosperous farmer. Among their friends was Sir Joseph Banks, the British natural scientist who had explored Australia's Botany Bay with Captain James Cook in 1770. Banks encouraged the Blaxlands to be among the first wave of free emigrants to settle in New South Wales, which had served largely as a penal colony (populated by convicts) since its founding in 1788. The Blaxlands left England on September 1, 1805. Offering its encouragement, the British government granted Blaxland four thousand acres at the foot of the Blue Mountains, located northwest of Sydney, and forty convicts to work the land.

Leads expedition into Blue Mountains

Blaxland prospered, and added to his landholdings. He became one of New South Wales's most important citizens. But in 1810 his luck changed when a drought began. By 1813 it had become so severe that it was threatening to wipe out the herds of livestock on which the colony depended. Rather than stand by and watch his animals die, Blaxland decided to try to lead his sheep to new pastures. On May 11 he left his ranch at South Creek, near the present-day town of St. Mary, and followed the Warragamba River to the Blue Mountains. He was joined by surveyor William Lawson, fellow rancher William Charles Wentworth, and native guide James Burnes, as well as some convict servants.

Traveling with pack horses and a herd of sheep, the group progressed slowly through the Blue Mountains. They made their way by following the tops of the mountain ridges. On May 28 they reached Mount York, from which they could view the Bathurst Plains, a large fertile area fed by the plentiful waters of the Lett River. Recalling the sight, Blaxland would later remark that there lay "enough grass to support the stock of the colony for thirty years." He and his party entered the valley and camped on the river, a few miles south of the present town of Lithgow. There they feasted on kangaroo and fish, and the animals ate their fill of the lush vegetation. Then the expedition explored a bit farther—to what was later called Mount Blaxland—before making its way back to Sydney.

Discoveries spur further exploration

Believing that he had conquered the Blue Mountains, Blaxland reported the important news to the colonial governor. Governor Macquarie sent out his surveyor at once, to retrace Blaxland's route. Surveyor George William Evans discovered that the Bathurst Plains were not located on the western side of the mountain range but, instead, lay in an isolated valley. He continued his explorations west until he did cross the Blue Mountains, locating the Fish River on the other side. So while Blaxland did not, in fact, make it over the mountains, he did discover the method by which the feat could be achieved. And the route Blaxland pioneered would become the Great Western Highway, the main road between Sydney and all lands west.

Less than two years after Blaxland's expedition, convict laborers built a road into the newly established settlement of Bathurst in the Blue Mountains. Blaxland received no compensation or profit from the lands he discovered, and lost of much of his wealth in the continuing drought. Embittered, he became a harsh critic of the colonial government. In 1829 he traveled to London on a mission sponsored by a group of New South Wales settlers, petitioning for a more representative government for the colony. They wanted the same rights enjoyed by other British subjects, such as trial by jury and participation in government policy making.

Blaxland published an account of his expedition in 1823. Besides his anti-government activities, he spent his time conducting agricultural experiments on his farm. He had great success growing grapes, and was awarded a silver medal in England for one of his wines. His wife died in 1826, and he spent his later years quietly, on his property in what is now the Sydney suburb of North Parramatta. Suffering from depression, Blaxland hanged himself on January 1, 1853.

Sources

Baker, Daniel B., ed. *Explorers and Discoverers of the World*. Detroit: Gale Research, 1993.

Bohlander, Richard E., ed. *World Explorers and Discoverers*. New York: Macmillan, 1992.

Waldman, Carl, and Alan Wexler. *Who Was Who in World Exploration*. New York: Facts on File, 1992.

Jean-Baptiste Charcot

Born July 15, 1867, Neuilly-sur-Seine, France
Died September 16, 1936, at sea off Iceland

Jean-Baptiste Charcot was a French physician and scientist who led two expeditions to unexplored parts of the Antarctic coast. He also led several expeditions to the North Atlantic.

In the late nineteenth and early twentieth centuries, explorers turned their attention to the icy continent of Antarctica. Seal and whale hunters had long visited the polar region, but by the 1890s many countries were sending scientific expeditions there. French physician Jean-Baptiste Charcot was anxious for his country to join these exploratory efforts. He was the driving force behind two French Antarctic expeditions that discovered and charted new coasts and islands in the frigid territory.

Charcot was born in the Paris suburb of Neuilly-sur-Seine, the son of famous neurologist Jean Martin Charcot. Like his father, Jean-Baptiste also became a physician, working at a Paris hospital. But the young man was drawn to sailing and the sea. He owned large boats that he navigated with great skill. In 1901 he sailed to the Faeroe Islands in the North Atlantic and carried out scientific research there. He returned in the summer of 1902 to study Jan Mayen Island. Captivated by the news of ongoing expeditions to the continent of

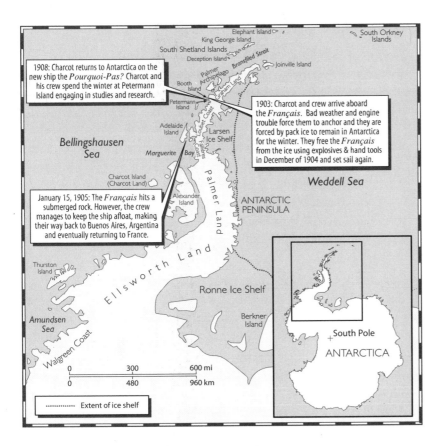

Elephant Island
King George Island
South Shetland Islands
Deception Island
Palmer Archipelago
Booth Island
Petermann Island
Adelaide Island
Larsen Ice Shelf
Graham Land
Joinville Island
Bransfield Strait

South Orkney Islands

1908: Charcot returns to Antarctica on the new ship the *Pourquoi-Pas?* Charcot and his crew spend the winter at Petermann Island engaging in studies and research.

1903: Charcot and crew arrive aboard the *Français.* Bad weather and engine trouble force them to anchor and they are forced by pack ice to remain in Antarctica for the winter. They free the *Français* from the ice using explosives & hand tools in December of 1904 and set sail again.

Bellingshausen Sea

Marguerite Bay

Charcot Island (Charcot Land)

January 15, 1905: The *Français* hits a submerged rock. However, the crew manages to keep the ship afloat, making their way back to Buenos Aires, Argentina and eventually returning to France.

Alexander Island

Palmer Land

ANTARCTIC PENINSULA

Weddell Sea

Thurston Island

Ellsworth Land

Ronne Ice Shelf

Berkner Island

Amundsen Sea

Walgreen Coast

South Pole
ANTARCTICA

0   300   600 mi
0   480   960 km

.... Extent of ice shelf

Antarctica, Charcot began to plan a polar expedition of his own, northward to Greenland.

When his father died Jean-Baptiste inherited a large fortune, which he used to build a ship suited especially for travel in icy waters. Named the *Français,* the 150-foot-long, three-masted schooner-steamer was constructed entirely of oak—with a reinforced hull—and weighed 245 tons. Charcot had to sell a valuable painting he inherited to pay for the ship's scientific laboratory and instruments.

Plans rescue of missing Antarctic expedition

With the *Français* ready to set sail, Charcot suddenly changed his plans. In the spring of 1903 word reached Europe that the Antarctic expedition led by Swedish explorer Otto Nordenskjöld appeared to be missing. Charcot decided to sail south in his newly completed ship and to join in the search for the lost explorers. But the Frenchman needed funding for the journey. He received the support of scientific organizations like the French Academy of Science, the Geographical Society, and the Museum of Natural History, as well as the approval of the French president. But most of the expedition's funds were raised when the Paris newspaper *Le Matin* asked for contributions from the public. The patriotic French people responded generously. Besides searching for the missing expedition, Charcot and his party hoped to chart the western coastline of the Antarctic Peninsula. They also hoped to make botanical, zoological, and other scientific studies.

On August 15, 1903, Charcot and his party of twenty scientists and seamen set sail from the French port of Le Havre. They returned within minutes after a crew member was killed by a broken piece of equipment. They departed again on August 27. After a two-month voyage they reached the continent of South America. When the *Français* stopped at Buenos Aires in Argentina, Charcot learned that missing explorer Nordenskjöld and his expedition had been rescued. Nonetheless, the Frenchman and his crew continued on their way to Antarctica.

Crew endures polar winter

The *Français* reached the west coast of the Antarctic Peninsula and Charcot and his party began explorations there. But by March bad weather and constant engine trouble forced them to set anchor in a shallow bay on the north coast of Wandel (now Booth) Island and wait out the winter. Some very long, cold months lay ahead. The first thing they did was stretch a chain across the mouth of the bay to deep drifting ice from crushing the ship. Charcot and his fellow expedition members spent many hours conducting scientific investigations. But the commander also went to great lengths to keep the hardships and boredom of an Arctic winter from overtaking his crew. Lectures were given, old newspaper articles were read again and again, and music was played on a gramophone. At one point the expedition even went ashore for a picnic, with the food they brought so frozen that it had to be chopped with axes.

During that time Charcot and his party also made exploratory visits to nearby areas. He charted the Palmer Archipelago in great detail. He also discovered a mountainous section of the coast of Graham Land, which he named the Loubet Coast in honor of French president Emile Loubet. He explored the area around Adelaide Island. Altogether almost 620 miles of new coasts and islands were sketched and charted. Finally, in December of 1904, after using explosives, icesaws, picks, and crowbars, the crew of the *Français* was able to free the ship from its icy harbor and set sail once again. But after traveling north for a few weeks, disaster struck. On January 15, 1905, the boat hit a submerged rock. Water began pouring in. In order to keep the ship afloat the pumps had to be run day and night, with crew members' fingers becoming so cold that they sometimes froze to the pump handles.

Fortunately, the pumps of the *Français* managed to keep ahead of the flooding waters. In February Charcot and his crew made it to Buenos Aires, where they received a warm welcome. The Argentine government offered to buy the damaged ship, a deal that its French commander accepted. On May 5, 1905, Charcot and his party returned to France with seventy-five crates filled with the results of their expedition.

Prepares for second Antarctic expedition

After the great success of his first Antarctic trip, Charcot planned another. This time he did not have to struggle with financing, for the French government paid for most of the journey and scientific organizations provided additional support. Charcot built a second three-masted schooner-steamer and named it *Pourquoi-Pas?* which means "Why Not?" in French. Much grander than the *Français,* it weighed 800 tons, its hull reinforced with iron plates. It had three laboratories, and a powerful generator that would provide the boat with electricity. Its new engine was four times more powerful than the troublesome second-hand engine Charcot had been forced to use for the *Français.* Other modern features aboard included a motor launch, searchlight, and telephones. The ship had a library of 1,500 books.

The second French Antarctic Expedition set out from Le Havre on August 15, 1908, with twenty-two crew members on board. After stops in South America, it reached western Antarctica by way of the Strait of Magellan in December. Charcot and his party stopped at Deception Island (one of the South Shetland Islands), where they came upon a colony of Norwegian whalers. To look for new whaling sites, the fishermen were using copies of a map Charcot had made during his earlier expedition. On Christmas Day the *Pourquoi-Pas?* sailed on to Petermann Island, where its crew found an excellent natural harbor. Naming it Port Circumcision, Charcot and his party made it their home base and spent their second Antarctic winter there.

During an exploration of the Palmer Archipelago, the *Pourquoi-Pas?* hit a rock, which did serious damage to its keel (bottom). The boat was so well designed, however, that crew members were able to make enough repairs to keep the ship operable. Sailing beyond the Antarctic Circle, Charcot and his crew explored the coast of Adelaide Island, proving that it was not eight miles long—as was previously thought—but a full seventy miles long. They also mapped and named the huge bay to its south, Marguerite Bay.

At the end of January, the expedition had to stop its explorations because of the coming winter. Again the crew stretched heavy chain across the mouth of their inlet to protect the *Pourquoi-Pas?* from advancing ice. Occupying themselves with studies on water, weather, and magnetism, the explorers also fought off boredom by competing against one another in ski and sledge (heavy sled) races. In addition, they passed the time by helping one of the ship's officers write a romantic novel called *L'Amant de la Dactylographe,* or *The Typist's Lover.*

Makes more important geographical discoveries

Although Charcot feared that the *Pourquoi-Pas?* might be too heavily damaged to continue explorations, he could not make himself return home after the winter had passed. He wanted to discover more territory for the glory of France. So on January 7, 1910, he turned his ship southward, exploring a section of coastline on Marguerite Bay that he named the Fallières Coast. He also sighted a unknown landmass far in the distance—through his binoculars—and claimed it for France. He called it Charcot Land in memory of his father. The commander tried to reach the headland by ship but there was too much ice in his way, and he could not risk further damaging the ship. Finally, in late January, Charcot decided to end his second polar expedition. He headed his boat toward South America and then home.

By early June the *Pourquoi-Pas?* had crossed the Atlantic Ocean and was sailing up the Seine River toward the French city of Rouen. The explorers received a naval escort and passed riverbanks lined with cheering people. The second French Antarctic Expedition had charted and mapped some 1,250 miles of coastline and new territories. The men had brought back three thousand photographs of their trip and scientific records that filled more than two dozen volumes. Largely due to Charcot's efforts, France would later be granted rulership of Antarctica's Adelie Land.

Over the next twenty-five years, Charcot continued his scientific sailing expeditions on the *Pourquoi-Pas?* mainly in the Atlantic and Arctic Oceans. (During World War I he served as an auxiliary lieutenant in the French navy, working on ways to stop German submarines.) He made a voyage every summer. In 1921 he went to Rockall, a small island northwest of Ireland, to study its geology. He traveled to Scoresby Sound, an inlet on the northeastern coast of Greenland, to rescue a troubled Danish expedition there in 1926. He would later help establish a French scientific base at that location, visiting frequently. In 1929, when Italian aviator Umberto Nobile crash-landed in the Arctic, Charcot led one of the expeditions sent to find him.

In the late summer of 1936, while on its way to Scoresby Sound, the *Pourquoi-Pas?* met with a terrible storm off the coast of Iceland. The vessel was bashed against the rocks and in the early morning of September 16, it sank. Charcot and all but one crew member drowned.

Sources

Antarctica: Great Stories from the Frozen Continent. New York: Reader's Digest, 1988.

Baker, Daniel B., ed. *Explorers and Discoverers of the World.* Detroit: Gale Research, 1993.

Bohlander, Richard E., ed. *World Explorers and Discoverers.* New York: Macmillan, 1992.

Waldman, Carl, and Alan Wexler. *Who Was Who in World Exploration.* New York: Facts on File, 1992.

Evelyn Cheesman

Born in 1881, Westwell, Kent, England
Died April 15, 1969, London, England

Remembering her childhood years, Lucy Evelyn Cheesman (who rarely used the name "Lucy") described them as "care-free happy days soaking in wildlife." She and her brothers and sisters lived a comfortable country life in a small village in Kent, their father a member of England's privileged class. They spent much of their time outdoors, collecting its treasures—snails, worms, plants, and flowers.

Evelyn was particularly drawn to the natural and biological sciences, and hoped to become a veterinarian. But at that time the veterinary college she wanted to attend did not admit women. So she began to educate herself while working at other jobs, reading about animal anatomy and helping as a nurse in a dog hospital.

Discovers the science of insects

During World War I Cheesman served as an office clerk for the government. She then worked as a secretary at the Im-

Evelyn Cheesman was a British scientist who traveled to remote islands in the South Pacific collecting insect specimens.

perial College of Science, a job that led to a position at the London Zoo. There she was put in charge of the Insect House. She took a course in entomology (the study of insects), which she found she truly loved. She excelled at her new job, happily arranging exhibits, conducting school tours, and writing several books about insects for young people.

In 1923 Cheesman was asked to keep records for a government research expedition to the South Pacific. She was excited because this part of the world had always fascinated her. The expedition stopped at Madeira, Trinidad, Martinique, and Panama. It then went on to the Galapagos Islands, the Marquesas islands, and the Tuamotu Archipelago (islands made of coral reefs). Cheesman managed to break away from the group from time to time to do some collecting of her own, relying on directions from the native inhabitants.

Decides to do field studies alone

While the expedition was in Tahiti, Cheesman received a large sum of money from her brother, which allowed her to resign her government position. She wanted to choose her own sites of exploration and to remain at each as long as she liked. An old sea captain on the island allowed Cheesman to live in a one-room hut he owned and gave her a few supplies. From her home base in Tahiti she explored other islands in French Polynesia, including Bora Bora. She stayed with Europeans she had met or native villagers during these excursions. She ate what she could find, and when there was no trail to where she wanted to go, she cleared one. After several months in Tahiti, Cheesman returned to England with a collection of five hundred insect specimens, which she donated to the British Museum of Natural History.

Impressed by her work, the British Museum gave Cheesman a grant in 1928 to collect insects in the South Pacific island group of the New Hebrides (now called Vanuatu). She was the first natural scientist to go there, and she was warned that some of the natives of the islands could be dangerous, especially the Big Nambas of Malekula, reported to be cannibals. But when Cheesman visited with King Ringapat of the Nambas in his inland village, she felt so safe and com-

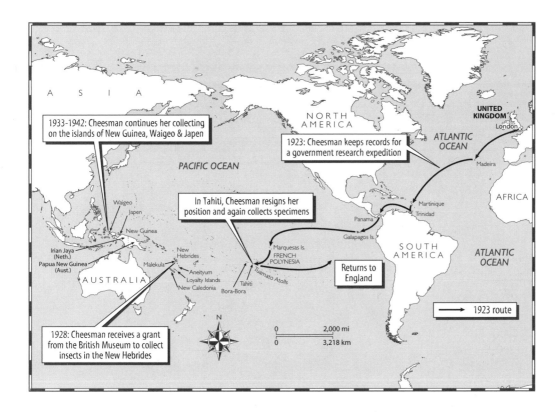

1933-1942: Cheesman continues her collecting on the islands of New Guinea, Waigeo & Japen

1923: Cheesman keeps records for a government research expedition

In Tahiti, Cheesman resigns her position and again collects specimens

Returns to England

1928: Cheesman receives a grant from the British Museum to collect insects in the New Hebrides

1923 route

fortable that she decided to stay for a while, collecting. King Ringapat later gave her a gift to take to her king: a fourteen-foot spear (which eventually ended up in the British Museum). Cheesman spent two years collecting in the northern and southern islands of the New Hebrides, staying with various tribes. During a trip to the small island of Aneityum, however, a serious illness cut her trip short, forcing her to leave for Australia to recuperate.

Cheesman's next goal was to gather insect specimens in New Guinea, hoping to figure out through them the connection of that island group with others in the Pacific. She left for the Australian colony of Papua New Guinea in 1933. Setting up permanent camps for her heavy equipment, she then wandered about for days with her butterfly net and killing bottle. At night she placed a light under a screen, and in the morning the screen was covered with new insect specimens attracted to the glow. The natives there came to know the scientist well, and she, likewise, became their friend and took an interest in their way of life. Next, Cheesman traveled to the Cyclops Mountains, located in the little-known Dutch-ruled western half of the island. A rugged year in the nearby Waigeo and Japen islands followed. On Japen Cheesman collected unusual animal skins for the museum, including those of tree kangaroos and rock wallabies.

Island knowledge helps during war

When the Japanese invaded New Guinea in 1942, Cheesman was on the last boat to leave the island. She returned to England, where she helped with the war effort in many ways, including entertaining the troops with accounts of her exotic travels. Her most important contribution, though, was her knowledge of the South Pacific islands. Especially valuable were her notes on the relative heights of the mountains there, critical information for airplane pilots.

Near the end of the war, Cheesman was injured in a railway accident, and for a while she was unable to walk. She recovered enough to make a trip to the South Pacific island of New Caledonia, however, where she climbed its long central mountain chain, collecting specimens. She also visited Lifou, one of the Loyalty islands, where she was adopted into a Polynesian family. But pain from her injury continued to worsen and, unable to do much collecting, she returned to England. Cheesman feared that her traveling days were over.

Then in 1953 she had her damaged hip replaced with an artificial one, and she was able to walk comfortably again. Now more than seventy years old, Cheesman wasted no time in resuming her travels—by the following year she was once again collecting specimens on the island of Aneityum. She was often alone on the island, but still quite content with her rugged way of life. She was forced to leave when boats would no longer make regular stops there.

An "honorary associate" of the British Museum, Cheesman never received a salary for her work; she lived off the income she earned from lectures and books she wrote about her expeditions. In 1953, though, the government awarded her the Order of the British Empire and a small pension, recognizing her life of service to science. She lived out her last years quietly in London, until her death on April 15, 1969, at the age of eighty-eight.

Sources

Baker, Daniel B., ed. *Explorers and Discoverers of the World.* Detroit: Gale Research, 1993.

Tinling, Marion. *Women Into the Unknown: A Sourcebook on Women Explorers and Travelers.* Westport, CT: Greenwood Press, 1989.

Nicholas Clapp

Born 1936

Nicholas Clapp is an American documentary filmmaker who led an expedition into the Omani desert, discovering the buried ruins of the legendary city of Ubar. It was a major center on the ancient frankincense trade route.

In ancient times the southern rim of the Arabian peninsula was a major trade center. Ships brought spices and fabric from India, silk from China, and gold from Ethiopia. These treasures were then transported by camel caravan to places like Egypt, Persia, Syria, and even Rome. Two locally grown products were also among the prized far-ranging cargo: frankincense and myrrh. Myrrh, a clear gummy sap produced by the myrrha tree, was an ingredient used in cosmetics and perfumes. The fragrant sap of the scrubby frankincense tree was required by the Egyptians for embalming. It was also used nearly everywhere in religious ceremonies and cremations as an incense, to mask the smell of burning flesh. In the ancient world, these products were as valuable as gold. In fact, the Bible says that when the three Wise Men visited the baby Jesus, the gifts they carried were gold, frankincense, and myrrh.

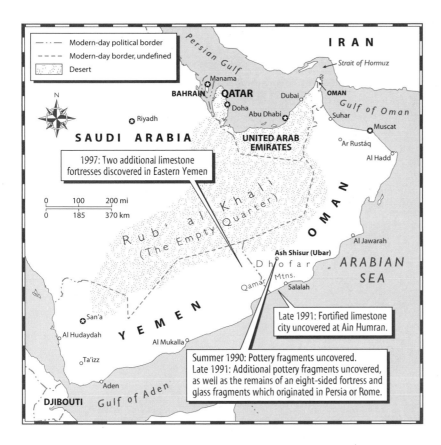

Legend:
- ·—·—· Modern-day political border
- - - - - Modern-day border, undefined
- Desert

IRAN

Strait of Hormuz

Persian Gulf

Manama
BAHRAIN QATAR
Doha
Dubai
OMAN
Abu Dhabi
Suhar
Gulf of Oman
Riyadh
SAUDI ARABIA
UNITED ARAB EMIRATES
Muscat
Ar Rustáq
Al Hadd

1997: Two additional limestone fortresses discovered in Eastern Yemen

0   100   200 mi
0   185   370 km

Rub' al Khali (The Empty Quarter)

OMAN

Al Jawarah

Ash Shisur (Ubar)
Dhofar Mtns.
ARABIAN SEA
Qamar
Salalah

Late 1991: Fortified limestone city uncovered at Ain Humran.

San'a
YEMEN
Al Hudaydah
Al Mukalla
Ta'izz

Summer 1990: Pottery fragments uncovered. Late 1991: Additional pottery fragments uncovered, as well as the remains of an eight-sided fortress and glass fragments which originated in Persia or Rome.

Aden
DJIBOUTI *Gulf of Aden*

The legendary city of Ubar

Large trade centers—often walled to protect the riches gathered there—were built up along the caravan routes. One such fortified city was called Ubar. It thrived for three thousand years until sometime between the first and fourth centuries A.D., when it disappeared beneath the desert sands. Its destruction was discussed in Islamic writings like the *Arabian Nights* and the Koran. According to them, Allah (God) buried the city because its inhabitants had become sinful and greedy as a result of their great wealth. The Koran also stated that anyone who attempted to find the ruins would be cursed.

But that did not keep explorers from trying. During the 1930s British soldier and adventurer T. E. Lawrence (Lawrence of Arabia) had planned a search for this "Atlantis of the Sands," but died before it began. A decade before him, British explorer Bertram Thomas had found and crudely mapped a faint road that he discovered between giant sand dunes—many over six hundred feet high—on the edge of Arabia's southern desert Rub al Khali, or "Empty Quarter." He believed that this was the route the ancient frankincense traders had used. Thomas wrote about his discovery in the book *Arabia Felix*.

Lost city becomes filmmaker's obsession

Emmy Award-winning documentary filmmaker Nicholas Clapp also fell under the spell of the lost city of Ubar. He first learned about the legendary city in 1981, while on a trip to the sultanate of Oman, a small country on the south coast of the Arabian Peninsula. When he returned home, he read everything he could about that area of the world, including ancient maps and texts, because he thought that a search for Ubar would make an excellent documentary. Eventually his research would fill more than fifty notebooks. Of particular interest was a map drawn by Ptolemy, an Egyptian astronomer and geographer who lived during the second century A.D. The mapmaker had used latitude and longitude to plot geographical places. On his map of Arabia was a spot labeled Omanum Emporium (Omani Marketplace), located in the land of the Ubarites. Clapp wondered: Could that marketplace be the lost city of Ubar?

In a old issue of *Science* magazine Clapp read about how radar from a space shuttle had helped scientists find extinct riverbeds in deserts in the Middle East. He wondered if the technology might also work on ancient roads buried beneath the sand. He contacted one of the authors of the magazine article, Ron Blom, a geologist specializing in space remote-sensing who worked at the Jet Propulsion Laboratory (JPL) of the National Aeronautics and Space Administration (NASA). Before long Clapp had Blom and other scientists at JPL hard at work on the project. In October 1984 the space shuttle *Challenger* used Shuttle Imaging Radar (SIR) to scan the southern Arabia Peninsula, particularly Oman. For it was only there, on the desert side of the Dhofar Mountains, that frankincense trees grew. A second shuttle radar flight followed.

When the images were analyzed, faint traces of ancient roads were visible. Still, clearer pictures were needed.

Satellite pictures reveal ancient trade routes

Blom and his colleagues at JPL decided to use satellite imaging in their efforts. They combined pictures from the French SPOT satellite, and from the U.S. *Landsat 5,* which used reflected light in the visible and near-infrared range of the spectrum to locate features in the terrain. The caravan trails became even more clear, for—unlike the undisturbed sand surrounding them—they reflected light differently, their bases ground down over the centuries by countless donkey and camel hooves. The satellite images also provided a view of a wider area, so that the roads could be tracked more plainly over a large distance. Some of the trails disappeared under massive sand dunes in the Rub al Khali, indicating that they had been around for a very long time. But most exciting of all was the fact that all the roads seemed to lead to the area that Ptolemy had marked Omanum Emporium on his ancient map.

With such clear evidence that the legendary city of Ubar had really existed, Clapp decided that it was time to launch an expedition to Oman. He began to gather other experts to help in the search. George Hedges, a Los Angeles attorney with a background in archaeology, joined the team. He helped Clapp finance the expedition and took care of the group's business concerns. Dr. Juris Zarins, a professor of anthropology at Southwest Missouri State University, was an expert in Arabian history who had worked on projects in the Middle East. He became the team's chief archaeologist. Completing the group was British explorer Ranulph Fiennes, famous for his expeditions to the polar regions. He had also spent many years in Oman, at one time assisting its sultan during the Dhofar War. Thus, the Omani ruler gave the expedition his full support, even offering the explorers military air and ground support.

First expedition to Oman

In the summer of 1990 the group traveled to Oman on a fact-finding trip, to check out possible sites for later excavation. Clapp's wife, Kay, and Blom also made the trek. Struggling with the blazing heat, they visited several sites that looked promising on their satellite maps, located in the Empty Quarter. They found artifacts, but nothing old enough to be associated with the ancient trade routes or the lost city of Ubar. A sandstorm forced them to take refuge at the small oasis town of Ash Shisur. The village was built near the ruins of a three-hundred-year-old fortress, which had been described and then ignored by other explorers. But Zarins found a piece of pottery there that did not resemble those they had already collected. He was further intrigued by the ancient well in the town. He wondered if Shisur shouldn't be at the top of their list of sites to excavate when they returned later that year. Maybe they were looking too far out into the desert for Ubar. Maybe they needed to shift their focus, in the direction of the frankincense mountains.

A return trip to Oman was planned for November of 1990. But the Gulf War struck the Middle East and all plans were stalled. During that time Zarins concluded that the odd piece of pottery he had found was at least two thousand years old. Another *Landsat* image was ordered of the region, this time concentrating on the area around Shisur. What the JPL scientists found was a network of ancient roads, all gathering around the small oasis town.

The team returned to Oman in late 1991, this time with the addition of Ron's wife, Kristine, a technologist at JPL. Clapp brought his movie equipment, planning to record their excavations for his documentary. After quick digs at several sites without success, the group moved on to Shisur. A second look at the area around the oasis revealed numerous old pottery fragments. The region had obviously been a gathering spot long ago. But what the explorers really needed to find were artifacts from other parts of the world—India, China, Rome—to show that here had been a center of worldwide trade.

Team discovers ancient ruins

Kristine Blom used a subsurface radar device to measure the depth of the rubble in the area around Shisur. It extended far underground, indicating that there were probably buried ruins. Zarins led an excavation of the site, aided by archaeology students from his university and local volunteers. Painstakingly moving one bucketful of earth at a time, the diggers uncovered, over the course of three weeks, the remains of an eight-sided fortress with limestone walls ten to twelve feet high, built as early as 1000 B.C. At each corner were towers that reached some thirty feet high. Inside was an open court with a well in the center, probably the marketplace. Buildings ringed the courtyard; some still contained the tools used for processing frankincense resin (sap) into incense. Frankincense burners were also found. The diggers were especially excited when they came upon pieces of glass made in either ancient Persia or Rome. They also found two thousand-year-old Persian pottery. These artifacts were proof that the site they were excavating was indeed a worldwide trade center—and almost certainly the lost city of Ubar.

Northeast of the Ubar site, Zarins also discovered small firepits, flint tools, and pieces of pottery near an ancient riverbed. Most likely caravans had stopped and rested there while their members conducted business inside the city. Some of the artifacts dated back as far as 5000 B.C.

More discoveries along the frankincense trade route

In addition to Ubar, Clapp's team discovered the ruins of what appeared to be a similar fortified limestone city at Ain Humran, on Oman's coast. Zarins made a later expedition to this second archaeological site. In 1997 a third expedition, headed by George Hedges and including other members of the original Ubar team, made its way into eastern Yemen, a region only recently opened to Westerners. Following the same far-reaching caravan trails mapped from space, the team found the ruins of two more limestone fortresses that in all respects resembled those found in Oman. They also found what appeared to be stone caravan route markers—called triliths because they stood in groups of three—between the forts and elsewhere in the region.

In the first century A.D. Roman scholar Pliny the Elder wrote that the frankincense region could be reached by following a trail that was marked by eight fortresses or rest stations. It is assumed that the sites in Oman are the last two on the route, and now it appears that Hedges and his team have found more along the way. Further explorations are planned.

Mystery of city's disappearance solved

Clapp and his expedition also thought that they had discovered the cause of the city's violent end. Ubar appeared to have been built over an underground limestone cavern that probably collapsed when the water that filled it was drained by countless caravanners through the central well. An earthquake may have triggered the final collapse. Blowing sand helped bury the rubble.

On February 4, 1992, Clapp and other members of his team held a press conference to share their findings. Their discovery made headlines around the world. In the years since, Clapp has completed his documentary film about uncovering the lost city of Ubar.

Sources

Crabb, Charlene. "Frankincense." *Discover*. January 1993: 56.

The Not-So-Lost City of Ubar. [Online] Available http://www-dial.jpl.nasa.gov/kidsat/explorations/Explorations TEAM/Russell_Moffitt/ubarpage/index.html, March 12, 1997.

Public Information Office. Jet Propulsion Laboratory. [Online] Available http://www2.jpl.nasa.gov/files/releases/arabia.text, July 19, 1997.

Welzenbach, Michael. "Search for the Lost City." *Reader's Digest*. October 1995: 84–89.

Wilford, John Noble. "Ruins in Yemeni Desert Mark Route of Frankincense Trade." *The New York Times*. January 28, 1997: B9–B10.

Barry Clifford

Born 1946

For the past few centuries, pirates have been portrayed as romantic figures. In books and movies they have been shown as both fiercely cruel and dashingly brave, skillful fighters whose adventurous, treasure-stealing lives defied the rules of a civilized world. Yet few historical clues have been left behind to support these ideas. In 1984 salvager Barry Clifford discovered the pirate ship *Whydah* off the coast of Cape Cod, Massachusetts. The more than 100,000 artifacts recovered from the vessel, shipwrecked in 1717, would reveal that pirates' lives were quite different than imagined.

Clifford grew up in the town of Brewster on Cape Cod, and was attracted to the outdoor life. He enjoyed hunting and fishing in the woods and marshes around his home. He was fascinated by the tales of sea adventure told by his Uncle Bill, especially those about the *Whydah,* the sailing ship commanded by pirate captain Black Sam Bellamy. According to local legend, Bellamy was returning to Cape Cod for his mistress, Goody Hallett, when he and most of his crew met their

Barry Clifford is a treasure hunter who discovered the sunken eighteenth-century pirate vessel Whydah. *Its salvaged artifacts have provided valuable information about the way pirates really lived.*

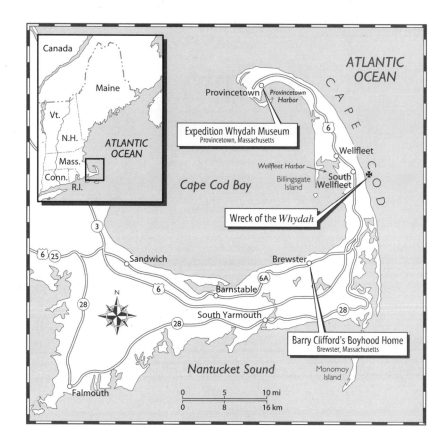

deaths by storm. She was condemned as a witch, and her spirit is still said to walk the cliffs of Wellfleet, where the ship went down.

Finds legendary shipwreck

Clifford began doing salvage work (recovering lost or sunken valuables) while he researched the *Whydah*. He learned that when Bellamy captured the one-hundred-foot ship in the Caribbean (a place where the pirate was said to have raided more than fifty other ships in 1716 and early 1717), it had been a new vessel built to carry black slaves and African gold. Towing behind his own boat an electronic device that could detect large concentrations of metal, Clifford came upon the ship's broken hull in shallow water. He and a team of divers hauled up cannons, ammunition, ship's instruments, pewter tableware,

silver and gold coins, and gold bars and dust. They recovered the ship's bronze bell, inscribed "The Whydah Gally—1716." The vessel was perhaps named for the African whydah (pronounced WID-da) or "widow bird."

The ship also yielded a huge collection of gold jewelry. The objects were considered by experts to be among the finest examples of art from Akan peoples of the west coast of Africa, in what is now Ghana and the Côte d'Ivoire (Ivory Coast). They were also rare proof of the thriving European-African gold trade that had gone on for more than five centuries. The *Whydah* treasures were worth several million dollars.

A real look at pirate life

But what did these finds reveal about pirate life? Clifford and his crew found that much of the gold jewelry had been

Barry Clifford points out the words "The Whydah" on the bell recovered from the wreck of the pirate ship.

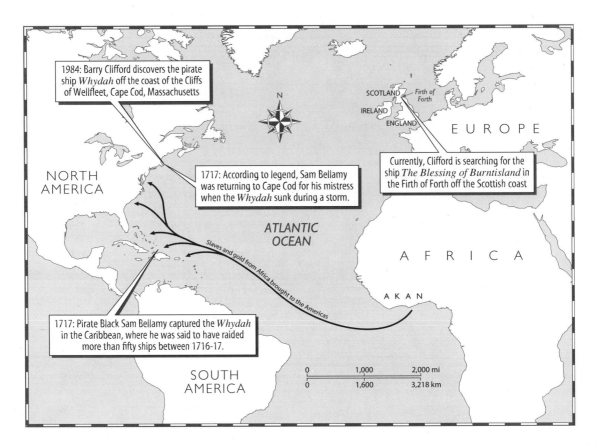

1984: Barry Clifford discovers the pirate ship *Whydah* off the coast of the Cliffs of Wellfleet, Cape Cod, Massachusetts

1717: According to legend, Sam Bellamy was returning to Cape Cod for his mistress when the *Whydah* sunk during a storm.

Currently, Clifford is searching for the ship *The Blessing of Burntisland* in the Firth of Forth off the Scottish coast

1717: Pirate Black Sam Bellamy captured the *Whydah* in the Caribbean, where he was said to have raided more than fifty ships between 1716-17.

Slaves and gold from Africa brought to the Americas

NORTH AMERICA

SOUTH AMERICA

EUROPE

SCOTLAND   *Firth of Forth*

IRELAND

ENGLAND

AFRICA

AKAN

ATLANTIC OCEAN

N

| 0 | 1,000 | 2,000 mi |
| 0 | 1,600 | 3,218 km |

hacked into pieces so that it could be shared equally among the sailors. This showed that there was a democratic distribution of stolen goods on the ship, and that the image of an all-controlling pirate captain was probably a myth (save for exceptions like the terrifying Blackbeard). The treasure hunters also found twenty-seven cannons but very few cannonballs; in some cases the large guns were packed with sacks of musket balls. This indicated that the pirates had no desire to blast ships until they sank; the raiders were more interested in subduing the crews of opposing vessels so that they could go aboard. Also found were dozens of hand grenades—hollow balls filled with gunpowder—that seemed to be made more for frightening than killing. Altogether, it appeared that the pirates intended to bluff and bully their victims into surrendering without a fight. The raiders were not the bloodthirsty villains they were thought to be, and few of their opponents ever "walked the plank" to their deaths.

A selection of the ship's artifacts is on display at Expedition Whydah, a museum in Provincetown, Massachusetts, dedicated to the preservation of the wreck. Clifford estimates that only 10 to 15 percent of the sunken vessel has been excavated so far. He hopes to use sonar (sound waves) to uncover more treasures on the cape's sandy bottom, where he believes four or five tons of gold and silver still remain.

Searches for more sunken treasures

While actively excavating the *Whydah,* Clifford became a celebrity of sorts, his efforts covered by television, newspapers, and magazines. He also wrote about them in his autobiography, *The Pirate Prince: Discovering the Priceless Treasure of the Sunken Ship Whydah.* He participated in other treasure hunts—expeditions in the United States, Central America's Belize (British Honduras) and Panama, and the Philippines—that concluded without success. Still, his work brought him to the attention of a group of Scottish treasure hunters who were convinced that in the cold, dark Firth of Forth—the forty-eight-mile-long waterway between eastern Scotland's River Forth and the North Sea—lay one of Britain's greatest sunken treasures. Archive research had convinced group members that *The Blessing of Burntisland,* a baggage ferry carrying the belongings of King Charles I of Great Britain as he made a coronation tour of the region, had sunk during a gale on its way from Burntisland to Leith (now part of Edinburgh) in July of 1633. Among the ferry's valuable royal cargo was a 280-piece silver banquet service made for Henry VIII. Estimates of the entire treasure's worth topped $400 million.

With such a prize before him, Clifford has methodically waged his search. Working from a sonar-generated map of the Firth of Forth's bottom, he and his small diving team regularly leave the docks of Burntisland, a former shipyard, and check one promising blip after another. They dive in standard cold-water scuba gear. It is tough going, for the water is blackened by drifting silt and visibility is extremely poor. The water is filled with debris in which the divers can easily become entan-

A look at piracy

Piracy—armed robbery on the high seas—can be traced to ancient times. Records from the first century B.C., for instance, show that the inhabitants of Rome nearly starved because pirates so actively raided their grain shipments. The great age of piracy took place between A.D. 1650 and 1725, when transport of precious metals and spices from colonial lands and the development of the slave trade made the practice especially profitable. Thousands of men (and a few women) took to the seas in an attempt to make their fortunes by stealing. Not every ship carried precious cargo, however, and more often than not, the pirates' spoils would be less than glamorous: a few bales of cloth, tobacco, some spare sails.

Not all pirates were Europeans during this time. It is estimated that nearly a quarter of them were black slaves who had escaped from captivity or who had been freed by pirate gangs, which they joined. The development of national navies eventually put an end to widespread piracy.

Blackbeard (Edward Teach, or Thatch) was one of history's most feared pirates, famous for his cruelty to victims and crew members alike. Between 1716 and 1718 he terrorized shipping and coastal settlements of the West Indies and on the Atlantic coast of North America. The English pirate's vessel was a stolen French merchant ship, which he equipped with forty guns and renamed *Queen Anne's Revenge*. He was killed by British forces in the American colonies in 1718.

gled. Furthermore, the waterway—used as a shipping lane for centuries—is the site of at least five hundred boat sinkings since 1830, vessels downed by accidents, war, and consistently violent winds. Trying to find *The Blessing of Burntisland* in the Firth of Forth is like trying to find a needle in a haystack. But as Clifford knows, in treasure hunting there are no guarantees.

Sources

Broad, William J. "Archeologists Revise Portrait of Buccaneers as Monsters." *The New York Times*. March 11, 1997: C1.

Heard, Alex. "For the Low, Low Price of $50,000 You, Too, Can Own a Share of Henry VIII's Sunken Flatward." *Outside*. October, 1995.

PROVINCETOWN:Whydah. [Online] Available http:// www.province town.com/village/pt-history/whydah/whydah.html, March 31, 1997.

Fa-Hsien

Born c. 374, Wu-yang, Shansi, China
Died c. 462, Hupei, China

Fa-Hsien was a Chinese Buddhist monk who made an epic fifteen-year journey to and from India in search of religious texts.

Fa-Hsien was born in the village of Wu-yang in China's Shansi province. Because his three older brothers had all died in childhood, his father dedicated him to a Buddhist society in hopes of safeguarding his life. Thus he went to live in a Buddhist monastery at the age of three.

When Fa-Hsien was ten his father died, and his uncle urged him to return home. But the boy decided to continue the religious life his father had chosen for him. Fa-Hsien became a full monk at the age of twenty.

Plans trip to recover Buddhist texts

Also a scholar, Fa-Hsien felt that the Chinese translations of the Buddhist texts he used were of poor quality. He wished to make his own translations from the original texts, which were written in Sanskrit, the ancient holy language of India. In A.D. 399, when he was about twenty-five years old, he set off on a quest to discover authentic Buddhist writings.

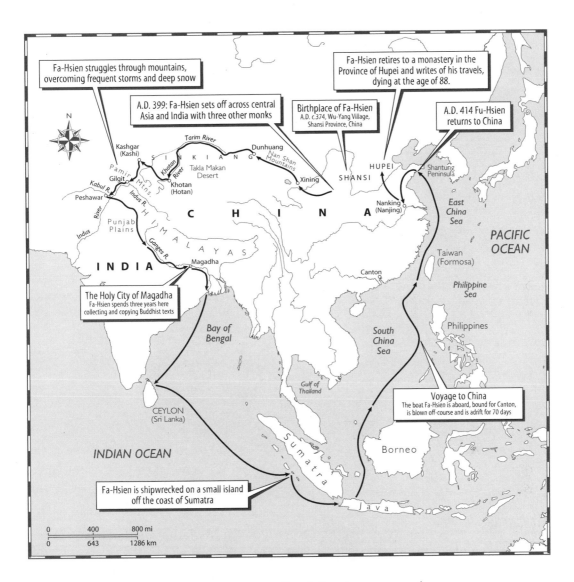

Fa-Hsien struggles through mountains, overcoming frequent storms and deep snow

A.D. 399: Fa-Hsien sets off across central Asia and India with three other monks

Fa-Hsien retires to a monastery in the Province of Hupei and writes of his travels, dying at the age of 88.

Birthplace of Fa-Hsien
A.D. c.374, Wu-Yang Village, Shansi Province, China

A.D. 414 Fu-Hsien returns to China

The Holy City of Magadha
Fa-Hsien spends three years here collecting and copying Buddhist texts

Voyage to China
The boat Fa-Hsien is aboard, bound for Canton, is blown off-course and is adrift for 70 days

Fa-Hsien is shipwrecked on a small island off the coast of Sumatra

| 0 | 400 | 800 mi |
| 0 | 643 | 1286 km |

He planned to cross central Asia into India, following an ancient spice trading route.

Traveling with three other monks, Fa-Hsien began his journey in northern China. He made his way to Xining, at that time the country's westernmost city. He then went along the south side of the Nan Shan Mountains to Dunhuang. Afterwards he followed the Tarim and Khotan Rivers around the great Takla Makan Desert and stopped at the oasis town of Khotan, located in what is now the Chinese province of

The life of Buddha

Buddha was an Indian philosopher and the founder of Buddhism. He probably lived from 563 to 483 B.C. He was born at Kapilavastu, in the Himalayan foothills of what is now southern Nepal. The son of a Sakya chief, he was named Siddhartha Gautama. According to legend, he grew up in great luxury, married, and had a son. But growing weary of palace life and wishing to see more of the world, he left home at the age of twenty-nine and traveled around northern India. Siddhartha observed that human suffering and death were inescapable. Still, he knew that there were ways that man could make his life meaningful, and find inner peace. To discover those ways, he used yoga meditation. He also fasted and put himself through extreme punishments in an effort to become enlightened. Finally, at the age of thirty-five, the keys to man's spiritual happiness came to him as he sat motionless under a pipal tree at Buddh Gaya. Thus he took the title Buddha—or the Enlightened One. For the next forty-five years he taught up and down the Ganges River valley, sharing all he had learned. He established a community of monks, the sangha, to continue his work. He died in Kusinagara, not far from his birthplace.

Sinkiang. Khotan was an oasis town on the southern part of the "Silk Road" trading route that ran between China and India, thus facilitating the spread of Buddhism into China.

Struggles through mountain passes

Fa-Hsien traveled to the city of Kashgar, located on the western edge of what is now Chinese Turkestan. He then passed with difficulty through the Pamir Mountains on his way to the Indus River. A second mountain range (probably the northwest Himalayas) gave the travelers even more trouble, for it had frequent storms and was deep with snow. Later, in his memoirs, Fa-Hsien would write of the mountains: "There are also among them venomous dragons, which, when provoked, spit forth poisonous winds, and cause showers of snow and storms of sand and gravel. Not one in ten thousand of those who encounter these dangers escapes with his life."

Fa-Hsien and his party managed to reach Gilgit and then traveled down the Kabul River to the great city of Peshawar, in what is now Pakistan. Close to his destination, he crossed the Punjab plains into northern India. In the holy city of Magadha (near modern-day Patna), he spent the next three years collecting and copying Buddhist texts. During that time he also visited many shrines and holy sites where important events in Buddha's life had taken place. Traveling down the Ganges River, Fa-Hsien reached the port of Tamralipti, where he spent another two years.

Leaving India, Fa-Hsien sailed to the nearby island of Ceylon (now Sri Lanka), which was an important center of Buddhism. He spent two more years there. At that point, he had been abroad for more than a decade. In about 413 the monk began his journey back to China by sea. It would not be an easy trip.

Disasters threaten journey home

Heading eastward across the Indian Ocean, Fa-Hsien's ship was wrecked on a small island off the coast of Sumatra in Indonesia. He managed to make it to the nearby island of Java, where he spent the next five months waiting for a second ship to China. That boat, which was headed for the south Chinese city of Canton, got blown off its course and was adrift for seventy days. Finally, it touched land on the Shantung Peninsula in northern China. The year was 414.

Upon his return, Fa-Hsien went to Nanking (Nanjing), then China's capital city. He spent the next several years working on Chinese translations of the Sanskrit texts he had brought back. He then retired to a monastery in the province of Hupei, where he wrote the story of his travels. Entitled *Fo-Kwe-Ki* (Memoirs of the Buddhist Realms), it told future Chinese pilgrims of the way to India over land and by sea. Fa-Hsien stayed at the monastery until his death at the age of eighty-eight.

Sources

Baker, Daniel B., ed. *Explorers and Discoverers of the World*. Detroit: Gale Research, 1993.

Basic Teachings and Philosophical Doctrines of Buddhism. [Online] Available http://www.friesian.com/buddhism.htm, March 25, 1997.

Faxian Fa-Hsien. [Online] Available http://acc6.its.brooklyn.cuny.edu/~phalsall/texts/faxian.html, July 19, 1997.

Waldman, Carl, and Alan Wexler. *Who Was Who in World Exploration*. New York: Facts on File, 1992.

John Forrest

Born August 22, 1847, Bunbury, Western Australia
Died September 3, 1918, at sea, off the coast of
Sierra Leone, Africa

John Forrest was an Australian surveyor who made expeditions into the little-known interior of Australia. He became the first person to cross the western half of the continent from west to east.

John Forrest was born in the port city of Bunbury, Western Australia, on August 22, 1847. His parents were Scottish immigrants who had come to Australia as servants and had saved enough money to buy a farm. Forrest went to school in Bunbury until he was thirteen, when he attended a private school in the capital city of Perth. In 1863 he began an apprenticeship as a surveyor. Three years later he joined Western Australia's Survey Department.

Leads first expedition into interior

In 1869 Forrest was put in charge of an expedition into the interior of Western Australia, in search of the remains of German explorer Friedrich Wilhelm Ludwig Leichhardt, who had disappeared with his party some twenty years earlier while trying to cross the continent. Forrest was to examine the skeletal remains that Aborigines (Australia's native inhabitants) had recently come upon. Leaving from Perth in April, the surveyor and his group traveled in a northeasterly direc-

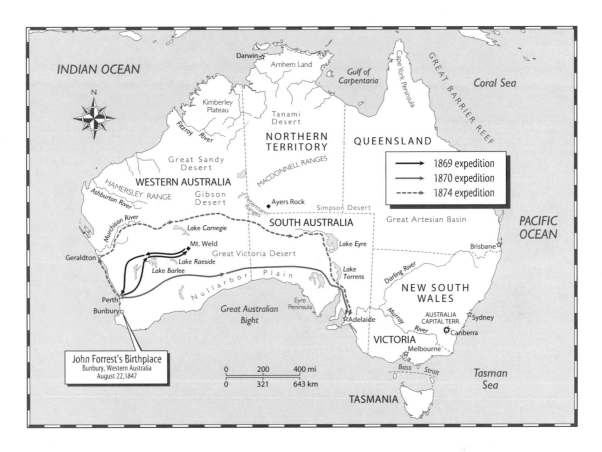

tion as far as Lake Raeside. He found no traces of the doomed expedition, and the bones the Aborigines had found turned out to be those of runaway horses from an 1854 exploration. Still, Forrest continued his expedition, going as far as Mount Weld on the western edge of the Great Victoria Desert. He crossed more than two thousand miles of territory, some of which had never been mapped. Among his discoveries were areas suitable for raising livestock, a growing source of wealth for the colony. Forrest returned to Perth in August.

In March of the following year, Forrest undertook a second expedition, this time to survey the coast of Australia's southern bay—the Great Australian Bight—from Perth to the South Australia city of Adelaide. He and his party followed a route similar to the one taken by English adventurer Edward John Eyre in 1841, only they were crossing in the opposite direction: from west to east. Forrest arrived in Adelaide in August. Like Eyre before him, he found that most of the country was barren desert, although he did come upon some good grazing land. Later, in 1877, the route he mapped would be chosen for a transcontinental telegraph line. (The present-day highway across Australia's Nullarbor Plain also follows Forrest's course.)

Survives desert crossing into central Australia

After these successes, Forrest was put in charge of all surveying in the northern part of Western Australia. Thus he undertook a third expedition in March of 1874, hoping to make a complete crossing of Western Australia and then proceed into the continent's largely unknown central region. Sailing from Perth to Geraldton, up Australia's west coast, he and five others (including his brother Alexander) headed north, their provisions carried by twenty packhorses. They looked for the source of Western Australia's Murchison River, which flowed into the Indian Ocean. They also explored the vast area bordered by the Gibson Desert on the north and the Great Victoria Desert on the south. Traveling through the barren land was difficult, and the men almost died from lack of water. At times Aborigines attacked them.

Continuing eastward, Forrest and his men explored the mountain ranges of central Australia: the Petermanns in the Northern Territory and the Tomkinsons in South Australia. They then proceeded to South Australia's Alberga River and followed it to Lake Eyre. From there they knew they could find the new Central Overland Telegraph line, which stretched between the north coastal city of Darwin and Adelaide on Australia's south shore. The weary travelers followed the line to the southern city, where they received a warm welcome in November of 1874. Only four of the expedition's horses made it through. A year later Forrest published a book about his cross-country journey, titled *Explorations in Australia*.

As a reward for his efforts, Forrest received a land grant of five thousand acres. In 1876 he was named deputy surveyor general. Soon after, he led an expedition to survey Western Australia's Ashburton River. Four years later he led another expedition to the Fitzroy River region that lay farther north. In 1883 he was appointed surveyor general of Western Australia.

Holds important political posts

After that, Forrest began an active political career. From 1890 to 1901, he served as Western Australia's first premier. During much of that time, Australia's separate colonies were drawing up plans to form a central government. Forrest played an important role in the difficult process. After Britain's Parliament approved Australia's new constitution in 1901, he held a number of posts in the national government. He became postmaster general of the Commonwealth in 1901. He served as the Commonwealth minister of defense (1901–03), minister of home affairs (1903–04), and treasurer (1905–07, 1909–10, 1913–14, and 1917–18). Forrest made several attempts to become the country's prime minister as well, but those efforts ended in disappointment.

In 1918 Forrest became the first native-born Australian to become British nobility. In recognition of his lifelong service to his country, Britain's King George V honored him with the title First Baron Forrest of Bunbury. The statesman traveled to England for the royal ceremony. Suffering from cancer, he died on September 3, 1918, as he sailed back to Australia.

Sources

Baker, Daniel B., ed. *Explorers and Discoverers of the World.* Detroit: Gale Research, 1993.

Explorers of Australia: John Forrest. [Online] Available http://werner. ira.uka.de/~maier/australia/explore/forrest.html, March 25, 1997.

Waldman, Carl, and Alan Wexler. *Who Was Who in World Exploration.* New York: Facts on File, 1992.

Steve Fossett

Born 1945

Steve Fossett is a millionaire adventurer who has broken sailing and aviation records. His next goal is to circle the globe in a balloon.

Steve Fossett is drawn to adventure. The fifty-two-year-old Chicago-based investor and self-made millionaire has swum the English Channel and competed in Alaska's 1,165-mile Iditarod dogsled race. He is the only man to have crossed the Atlantic and Pacific Oceans by both balloon and sailboat. And he has twice attempted to circle the world in a balloon. Like many other aeronauts (balloonists), he is obsessed with this last great feat of aviation, racing to become the world's first. All balloonists agree that it is a goal unlikely to be reached without using the fierce currents of the jet stream high in the atmosphere, where the air is thin and the temperatures are freezing.

Breaks ballooning and sailing records

Fossett began breaking records in 1995. He ballooned across the Pacific Ocean in February of that year, the first person to do so alone. Taking off from Seoul, South Korea, he

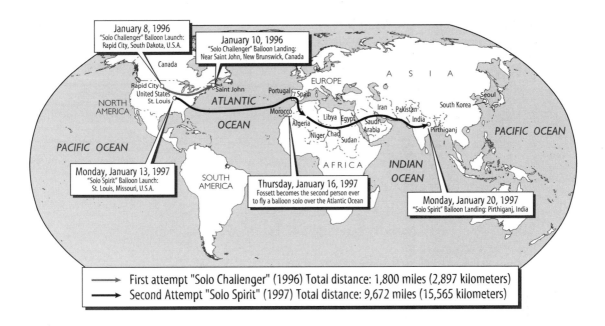

January 8, 1996
"Solo Challenger" Balloon Launch:
Rapid City, South Dakota, U.S.A.

January 10, 1996
"Solo Challenger" Balloon Landing:
Near Saint John, New Brunswick, Canada

Monday, January 13, 1997
"Solo Spirit" Balloon Launch:
St. Louis, Missouri, U.S.A.

Thursday, January 16, 1997
Fossett becomes the second person ever
to fly a balloon solo over the Atlantic Ocean

Monday, January 20, 1997
"Solo Spirit" Balloon Landing: Pirthiganj, India

First attempt "Solo Challenger" (1996) Total distance: 1,800 miles (2,897 kilometers)
Second Attempt "Solo Spirit" (1997) Total distance: 9,672 miles (15,565 kilometers)

landed in a farm field in the Canadian province of Saskatchewan and set the distance record: 5,438.08 miles. Later, in August, he sailed his trimaran (a sailboat with three hulls, side by side) with a crew of three from Yokohama, Japan, to San Francisco, California. The trip took sixteen days, seventeen hours. It broke the Pacific Ocean sailing record by more than four days, set by a clipper ship 110 years before.

The adventurer made his first attempt at circling the globe in early 1996. He expected his journey to take from sixteen to twenty-one days. He wanted to beat Dutchman Henk Frink and British airline tycoon Richard Branson to the takeoff, two men who were also planning to circumnavigate (circle) the world that year in balloons. But unlike his competitors, Fossett intended to sail alone, without flight crews, which would make sleeping difficult. His competitors also planned to travel in pressurized cabins that would protect them from weather changes and thin air. Fossett, on the other hand, would sail in a small gondola capsule about four feet wide and six feet high, equipped with a bunk and a sleeping bag. A bucket would serve as his toilet. Solar power—and a backup propane generator—would provide the electricity he needed. A space heater would help him fight off the cold, for temperatures outside his cabin were likely to reach 40 degrees below zero. An oxygen mask would be used for high altitudes, although he planned to travel lower and at slower speeds that his better-equipped competition. Three global positioning systems would help him figure his location from satellites, and he would have electronic and radio contact with the ground. He expected to fly at 18,000 to 24,000 feet, averaging about 35 miles per hour (mph) over land and 50 mph over sea.

First globe-circling attempt ends in disappointment

Fossett's "Solo Challenger" was a silvery mylar balloon 150 feet tall and 50 feet wide. A Rozier type (a balloon that gets its lift mostly from helium, but is supplemented as needed by hot air), it held two helium balloons, heated by a hot air envelope. In the early morning on January 8, he launched from the Stratobowl, a low riverbed surrounded by sheltering cliffs, located twelve miles southwest of Rapid City, South Dakota. The takeoff was trouble-free and the wind was blowing him along his planned route, a southeasterly path that would take him over South Dakota, Nebraska, Iowa, Missouri, Illinois, Kentucky, the Carolinas, and then out over the Atlantic Ocean. Europe, China, Japan, and the Pacific Ocean would follow, with a landing in either western Canada or the United States. On his first day he averaged 41 mph. The following day, however, weather changes shifted his course. Then Fossett got caught in a low-pressure system that carried him up the Atlantic coast to Maine and into Canada. Thick clouds reduced the solar panels' ability to produce electricity and the backup generator wouldn't work, so the balloon's burners could not produce enough hot air. Fossett was having trouble staying aloft. He tried throwing two of his fuel tanks into the Bay of Fundy (between the Canadian provinces of New Brunswick and Nova Scotia) to gain altitude, but that didn't work. Finally, after a journey of 1,800 miles, he was forced to land in a snow-covered Canadian pasture near St. John, New Brunswick, his balloon ripped to shreds. "I'm rather disappointed and embarrassed that I didn't do better on this," he remarked, admitting that he had underestimated the difficulty of the trip.

But in January of 1997, Fossett was attempting his goal again. (Two other balloonists had already made unsuccessful round-the-world tries earlier that month.) He launched a new balloon, the silver "Solo Spirit," from Busch Stadium in St. Louis, Missouri, on January 13. While he had originally planned to cross the Atlantic into Scandinavia, air currents pushed him on a speedy southerly course toward Spain and Portugal. Just sixty-four hours after takeoff, Fossett was gliding over Europe, traveling at speeds of about 100 mph and at altitudes of nearly 24,000 feet. With the challenge of the ocean crossing behind him, he was now faced with the problem of getting permission from various countries to cross their airspace. This "military risk" was the part of the trip that Fossett feared most, for in 1995 two American competitors in a yearly distance contest—the Gordon Bennett Balloon Race—had been shot down and killed by combat aircraft over Belarus.

Political problems lead to low fuel

Fossett's support team at Loyola University in Chicago worked day and night to get permits from several nations for flyovers. At the same time they looked for winds that he could use to avoid those countries that might refuse him passage. With currents blowing Fossett south toward North Africa, Libya threatened to become a problem. The nation at first denied him airspace, and Fossett had to burn extra fuel while trying to guide his balloon away from the country. While Libya later granted him clearance, his fuel supply had already been drained. Altogether, forty-three nations allowed Fossett to fly over their territories.

He landed safely in Pirthiganj, a northern Indian village, on January 20, his $400,000 balloon snagging in a tree. The traveler had run out of fuel well short of his goal. Still, the journey was considered a great success, for several records had been broken. Fossett had made the longest trip in a balloon: six days, two hours, and fifty-four minutes. He had trav-

Balloon aviation

An aerial balloon is a craft that is lifted by inflating one or more containers with a gas that is lighter than air (like hydrogen or helium) or with heated air; its flight is directed by the wind. The passenger vessel attached to a balloon is usually called a gondola.

Ballooning is the oldest form of aviation. In 1783 Frenchman Pilatre de Rozier made one of man's first ascents, rising in a hot-air balloon (anchored by a rope to prevent free flight) to a height of eighty-four feet. Other pioneers followed, experimenting with ballooning materials, heights and distances. Frenchman J. A. C. Charles, for instance, traveled in the first hydrogen-filled balloon in 1783 for a distance of twenty-seven miles. French balloonist J. P. Blanchard and Dr. John Jeffries, an American physician, made the first sea voyage by balloon, crossing the English Channel in 1784. Swedish engineer S. A. Andree failed in his attempt to reach the North Pole by balloon in 1897. And in 1932 Belgian physicist Auguste Piccard rose to the height of 55,000 feet in a sealed gondola. Heights exceeding 100,000 feet would eventually be reached. Today balloon racing is a popular sport, with helium replacing hydrogen because it is nonflammable.

eled 9,672 miles, breaking his own distance record. And he had been the first balloonist to cross the skies of Niger, Chad, Libya, and Iran.

Encouraged, Fossett told reporters at a National Geographic Society gathering that he would attempt to circle the world again. He would try as early as the coming November, the start of the three-month period best suited for long-distance ballooning. In the meantime, the adventurer and his team were looking for ways to fix problems that he had run up against on the last trip: his heater had not worked at high altitudes, for instance, and he had spent most of the journey freezing. "This flight, we didn't know all the answers when I started off," Fossett related. "We knew things would go wrong and I would need to respond to that during the flight. In this sense, this was true adventure."

Sources

Around-the-world flight planned again. [Online] Available http://www.freep.com/news/nw/qtrek28.htm, January 28, 1997.

Balloon-Steve Fossett. [Online] Available http://www.discovery.com:80/DCO/doc/1012/world/exploration/balloon/balloon1.3.3.html, March 30, 1997.

Browne, Malcolm W. "U.S. Balloonist Trying a Circumnavigation Conquers Atlantic." *The New York Times.* January 17, 1997: A11.

"Early Balloon Landing." *Maclean's.* February 3, 1997: 37.

Fossett up, up and away with hopes of circling the globe. [Online] Available http://www.caller.com:80/newsarch/news3124.html, January 15, 1997.

Hot News. [Online] Available http://www.u-net.com/icarus/hot.air.ballooning/hotnews, March 24, 1997.

John Mills, KMOV-T ... dUPI in St. Louis. [Online] Available http://www.trucom.com/ppages/jmills/balloon.htm, May 5, 1997.

"Riding the World's Winds." *Time for Kids.* January 24, 1997: 3.

Solo Spirit: Transglobal Balloon Flight. [Online] Available http://www.luc.edu:88/solo/, July 5, 1997.

Charles Francis Hall

Born 1821, Rochester, New Hampshire
Died November 8, 1871, northwestern Greenland

Charles Francis Hall was an American adventurer who led two expeditions into the Canadian Arctic in search of the lost explorer Sir John Franklin. He also led a disastrous expedition that tried to reach the North Pole.

British military officer Sir John Franklin led an expedition into the Canadian Arctic in 1845 in search of the Northwest Passage: a northern water route connecting the Atlantic and Pacific Oceans. When he and his men were never heard from again, several expeditions were sent out to learn their fate. The search parties would indirectly produce more discoveries about the Canadian Arctic. One such searcher was American Charles Francis Hall, whose polar journeys would lead him to sail farther north than any explorer before him. Hall's adoption of Inuit (Eskimo) ways would also show future Arctic expeditions how to better survive the frigid region.

Hall was born in 1821 in Rochester, New Hampshire, the son of a blacksmith. Before finishing high school, he moved west, settling in Cincinnati, Ohio. There he worked in the newspaper business, first as an engraver and then as a journalist. He ran a small newspaper called the *Cincinnati News*. He married and had two children.

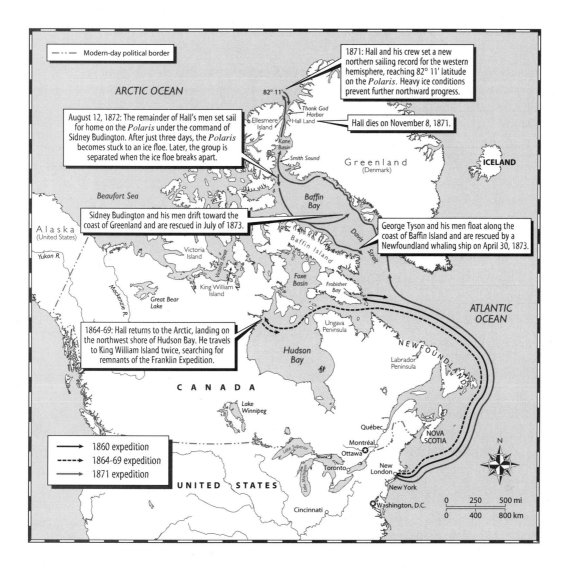

- - - Modern-day political border

1871: Hall and his crew set a new northern sailing record for the western hemisphere, reaching 82° 11' latitude on the *Polaris*. Heavy ice conditions prevent further northward progress.

ARCTIC OCEAN

82° 11'

Thank God Harbor
Hall Land
Hall dies on November 8, 1871.

Ellesmere Island

August 12, 1872: The remainder of Hall's men set sail for home on the *Polaris* under the command of Sidney Budington. After just three days, the *Polaris* becomes stuck to an ice floe. Later, the group is separated when the ice floe breaks apart.

Kane Basin

Smith Sound

G r e e n l a n d
(Denmark)

ICELAND

Beaufort Sea

Baffin Bay

A l a s k a
(United States)

Yukon R.

Victoria Island

Sidney Budington and his men drift toward the coast of Greenland and are rescued in July of 1873.

Baffin Island

Davis Strait

George Tyson and his men float along the coast of Baffin Island and are rescued by a Newfoundland whaling ship on April 30, 1873.

Victoria Strait

Mackenzie R.

King William Island

Great Bear Lake

Foxe Basin

Frobisher Bay

ATLANTIC OCEAN

1864-69: Hall returns to the Arctic, landing on the northwest shore of Hudson Bay. He travels to King William Island twice, searching for remnants of the Franklin Expedition.

Ungava Peninsula

Hudson Bay

N E W F O U N D L A N D

Labrador Peninsula

C A N A D A

Lake Winnipeg

Québec

Montréal

NOVA SCOTIA

Ottawa

Lake Superior

New London

Toronto

Lake Michigan

New York

N

→ 1860 expedition
⇢ 1864-69 expedition
→ 1871 expedition

U N I T E D   S T A T E S

Cincinnati

Washington, D.C.

0	250	500 mi
0	400	800 km

Obsessed with finding lost explorer

Hall closely followed news of expeditions sent out to look for Franklin. He too wanted to participate in the quest, and tried, without success, to join the search parties of Edwin Jesse de Haven and British military officer Sir Francis Leopold McClintock. When McClintock eventually found what was believed to be remains of the lost expedition in 1859, Hall was nonetheless convinced that some survivors still remained in the Arctic. After more than ten years there, he reasoned, they would have to take on the Inuit way of life.

Learns Inuit ways

After receiving the financial sponsorship of a wealthy New York merchant, Henry Grinnell, Hall prepared for a trip to the Arctic. He sold his newspaper, left his family, and on May 29, 1860, set sail from New London, Connecticut, on a northbound whaling ship. He traveled to the southeast coast of Baffin Island, where he hoped to live with the Inuit people for a while. He was convinced that learning their language and secrets of survival in the bleak environment would help him greatly in his explorations. He was especially fortunate to meet an Inuit couple there who had once been taken to England by whalers and had learned his language. Tookolito (called "Hannah") and Ebierbing (called "Joe") would serve as Hall's guides and companions for the rest of his life.

Discovers traces of earliest European expedition

Ebierbing's grandmother told Hall a story about white men who had come to Baffin Island long ago. He realized that she was referring to British explorer Sir Martin Frobisher, who was one of the first Europeans to look for the Northwest Passage, during the late 1570s. The Inuit led him to the spot where Frobisher had set up a gold mine. Because Hall was unable to find a ship that would take him to King William Island—where evidence of Franklin's expedition had been found—he spent the rest of his time in the Arctic exploring the territory around Baffin Island's Frobisher Bay. There he came upon the remains of a house built by the British explorer and his men and other valuable artifacts from the three-hundred-year-old expedition (which have since mysteriously disappeared).

Hall returned to the United States with Tookolito and Ebierbing in 1862. He immediately began a lecture tour about living with the Inuit, accompanied by his friends, who wore fancy native costumes. He also published a book about his life on Baffin Island, *Arctic Researches and Life Among the Esquimaux,* in 1864. The explorer was hoping to raise money for another expedition, for he was still obsessed with finding out more about Franklin and his men. Because the United States was in the middle of the Civil War, Hall had difficulty raising funds. Finally, on July 1, 1864, he and his Inuit companions caught another whaling ship headed north. The trio landed on the northwest shore of Hudson Bay. Hall would remain in the Arctic region for nearly five years.

Finds artifacts of doomed explorers

The explorer stayed at various locations in the Arctic, managing to travel to King William Island twice, in 1866 and 1869. On both visits he heard Inuit accounts of how the remaining 79 Franklin Expedition members (the group had started out with 129) had died of starvation and exposure after leaving their ship (originally there had been two vessels, the *Erebus* and the *Terror*). With their boat surrounded by ice in Victoria Strait, the party had headed down the coast on foot, hoping to reach the mainland. The Inuit also led Hall to artifacts of the unlucky expedition. These included silverware and the skeleton of one of Franklin's officers.

Hall left the Arctic on a whaling ship on August 13, 1869, and returned to the United States with Tookolito and Ebierbing. Realizing that he had probably found out as much about Franklin's expedition as he ever would, the explorer changed his goals. He wanted to be the first man to reach the North Pole. Hall asked Congress to sponsor the polar expedition, and was granted money for the trip. He was also given a U.S. Navy ship—altered for travel through icy waters—which was named the *Polaris*.

Polar expedition sets Arctic distance record

Setting sail from New London on July 3, 1871, Hall and his expedition made their way to the west coast of Greenland. They continued through Smith Sound to Kane Basin, named for the United States's first Arctic explorer, Elisha Kent Kane.

Hall traveled two hundred miles farther than Kane and set a new northern sailing record for the western hemisphere: 82°11' latitude. But heavy ice prevented the *Polaris* from continuing north, and in late August the expedition turned south to winter at a small port on the Greenland coast called Thank God Harbor. While there, Hall traveled by sledge (heavy sled) to areas farther north, to the edge of the Greenland ice sheet. There he discovered what would become known as Hall Land, a large iceless area where plants and wildlife were plentiful.

Hall dies mysteriously

In late October, after returning from a sledge trip, Hall fell violently ill after drinking a cup of coffee. Suffering from bouts of fever and hallucinations, he died on the morning of November 8, 1871. The U.S. Navy later ruled that—although mysterious—the explorer's death was the result of a stroke. In 1968 Hall's biographer, Chauncey Loomis, traveled to Thank God Harbor and had the explorer's remains dug up and examined. A fatal amount of arsenic was found in Hall's body. Although arsenic was frequently used during the nineteenth century to treat medical problems, the possibility that the explorer was murdered is strong. Suspects included Sidney Budington, captain of the *Polaris,* who was an alcoholic and cared little for Hall or his mission; and Dr. Emil Bessels, the expedition's chief scientist. Bessels and nearly half the ship's crew were German, and had trouble getting along with their American shipmates. Bessels had especially hated Hall.

Crew stranded on ice flow

Without Hall's presence and purpose, the polar expedition fell apart. Both Budington and first officer George Tyson were said to be drunk most of the time. Discipline deteriorated among the crew and regular shipboard routines were abandoned. The *Polaris* was not able to leave Thank God Harbor until August 12, 1872. Three days later Budington ran the ship into heavy ice, and it became stuck on a floe that carried it south for two months. On October 13, when a fierce storm pounded the ice into the ship's hull and seawater began to leak

How the *Polaris* castaways survived

Polaris first officer George Tyson was stranded on an ice floe with nine crew members and nine Inuit passengers that included women and children. Among the Eskimos were Tookolito and Ebierbing and Hans Hendrik, who was a veteran of many polar expeditions. The stranded party had some food, a handful of dogs, two lifeboats, and two kayaks (Inuit canoes made from animal skins) on the floe, which measured about a mile across. At first, the group tried to row to Greenland's shore in the lifeboats, but the water was so full of thick ice that they had to give up.

The Inuit built a complex of igloos to house the party. The group had plenty of drinking water from the snow that covered the ice floe. The dogs were eaten within the first few days. Then the hunting skills of Ebierbing and Hendrik were relied upon, and the castaways' diet consisted entirely of seals. The group members drank the animals' blood and ate the flesh and organs. They even ate the bristly skin and intestines, and the eyes were considered a real treat.

As spring and warmer weather approached, the floe disintegrated rapidly. On April 1 the group piled into the remaining lifeboat (one had been used for firewood) and moved to a larger floe. So cramped was their boat that they had to leave stores of seal meat and ammunition behind. Disastrously, their new floe soon broke apart, and they were left to survive on an even smaller chunk of ice than before.

Bad weather caused seawater to flood the floe, contaminating the group's drinking water. Seals were becoming scarce. A violent gale threatened to sweep all of the castaways into the sea.

Rescue finally came at the end of April. Spotting a sealing ship, the group burned pans of blubber to signal their location. The first vessel did not spot them. Tyson fired guns into the air to alert a second ship, but it could not penetrate the ice to reach them. A third boat went by. Finally, on the morning of April 30, a fourth vessel approached. Tyson had Hendrik paddle his kayak out to meet it. The castaways were taken aboard the *Tigress,* a Newfoundland sealing ship. Surviving an Arctic winter, the party had drifted nearly fifteen hundred miles south, from near Littleton Island to the Labrador Peninsula.

in, the crew moved lifeboats and supplies overboard onto firmer ice a distance away. Suddenly the ice broke apart, and Tyson and eighteen others were stranded and adrift on an ice floe, with the *Polaris* disappearing from sight.

Tyson's party floated south along the east coast of Baffin Island for many months. Although its members suffered countless hardships, all managed to survive, thanks to the hunting and survival skills of the Inuit among them. They were picked up by a Newfoundland seal-hunting ship on April 30, 1873, after being at sea for nearly seven months. The *Polaris* crew members who had been left on the leaking ship had soon abandoned it and made their way to Greenland's shore, where they were eventually rescued in July of 1873.

So all members of the expedition returned safely home except its commander. Hall's achievements were overshadowed by naval inquiries into his mysterious death and into the behavior of his shipboard crew, who—it seemed—had made little attempt to rescue their mates adrift on the ice. Four years after Hall's death, however, a British polar expedition led by Sir George Strong Nares raised an American flag over the adventurer's grave. The explorers also left an honorary plaque that told how Hall had sacrificed his life for the sake of science, and how they, "following in his footsteps, have profited by his experience."

Sources

Baker, Daniel B., ed. *Explorers and Discoverers of the World.* Detroit: Gale Research, 1993.

Bohlander, Richard E., ed. *World Explorers and Discoverers.* New York: Macmillan, 1992.

Maxtone-Graham, John. *Safe Return Doubtful: The Heroic Age of Polar Exploration.* New York: Scribner, 1988.

Neatby, Leslie H. *Conquest of the Last Frontier.* Athens: Ohio University Press, 1966.

Waldman, Carl, and Alan Wexler. *Who Was Who in World Exploration.* New York: Facts on File, 1992.

Ahmad Ibn Fadlan

Tenth Century

A hmad Ibn Fadlan lived near the city of Baghdad (in what is now Iraq) during the early 900s. Although not an Arab himself, Ibn Fadlan was an Islamic scholar, and he served the caliph (the Islamic ruler) of the city, which was a center of commercial and religious importance. In 921–22 Ibn Fadlan was the religious advisor of a diplomatic mission sent by the Abbasid Caliph al-Muktadir to the king of the Volga Bulgars, a Turkish tribe then living on the east bank of the Volga River, in what is now Russia. One of the purposes of the journey was to explain the laws of Islam to the Bulgars, who had recently converted to the religion. Ibn Fadlan would later write the only account of this trip to the north, describing the peoples he encountered and their extraordinary beliefs and customs.

Ahmad Ibn Fadlan, an Islamic theologian in the service of the caliph of Baghdad, made one of the first recorded trips into early medieval Russia.

Travelers meet inhabitants of central Eurasia

Leaving Baghdad on June 21, 921, the mission traveled by well-known caravan routes into western Persia (now Iran). Its

Ibn Fadlan narrates a bestselling modern novel

In 1976 blockbuster author Michael Crichton (whose works include *Jurassic Park*) published the inventive novel *Eaters of the Dead*. Its narrator is none other than Ibn Fadlan, a representative of the caliph of Baghdad, sent to the valley of the Volga River on a diplomatic mission in the year 922. Before he arrives there he meets Buliwyf, a powerful Viking chieftain who must return home to save his countrymen, who are being attacked by dark, hairy monsters that come during the misty nights and devour their victims' flesh. Ibn Fadlan abandons his diplomatic mission, accompanying Buliwyf to Scandinavia instead. He records their incredible experiences.

Crichton explained that *Eaters of the Dead* was based on the old English epic *Beowulf,* which relates the adventures of a heroic Norse (Scandinavian) warrior who slays a water monster that roams the land at night in search of human flesh. The author remembered Ibn Fadlan's tenth-century eyewitness accounts of Viking life and culture, and felt that the historical figure would make a perfect narrator for his recreation of the story of Beowulf. As an outsider, Ibn Fadlan could objectively report on events as they occurred. The first three chapters of *Eaters of the Dead* consist of Ibn Fadlan's actual accounts as he approaches the Volga Bulgar capital. After that, Crichton supplies the Islamic diplomat's voice as he continues on his then-fictional journey.

members then turned north toward the Caucasus region—which lies west of the Caspian Sea—before heading into eastern Europe. The expedition met many peoples along the way: the Oghuz Turks, ancestors of the modern Turkomans that live east of the Caspian Sea; the Petchenegs, a Turkish tribe living along the Ural River; and the Bashkirs, Turks who now live in central Russia. Ibn Fadlan also wrote about the Khazars, a Turkish tribe on the southern end of the Volga River that had converted to Judaism at the beginning of the ninth century. Ibn Fadlan's accounts of these peoples are among the earliest written, and they provide valuable information about the history of different ethnic groups in central Eurasia.

The Arab diplomatic mission arrived at the capital of the Bulgars on May 12, 922. When presented to the king, Ibn Fadlan gave him the gifts the caliph had sent, and read a letter he himself had written celebrating the occasion. While visiting the Bulgars, the travelers met members of the Rus, Vikings from the Baltic region who were settling in the area. They were the ancestors of modern Russians. The Rus had trading posts along the Volga River. They had not yet converted to Christianity, and Ibn Fadlan wrote very disapprovingly about their pagan ways, which included idol worship and animal sacrifices.

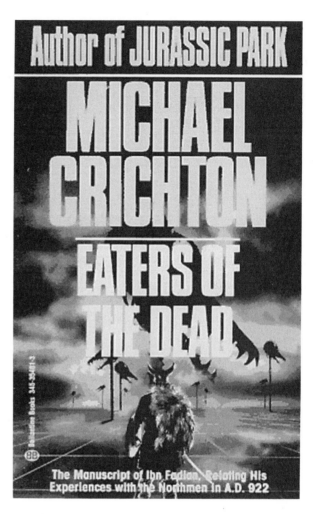

Author of JURASSIC PARK

MICHAEL CRICHTON

EATERS OF THE DEAD

The Manuscript of Ibn Fadlan, Relating His Experiences with the Northmen in A.D. 922

Visitors witness Viking funeral

In the best-known passages of Ibn Fadlan's written account, he describes the burial of a Viking chief. The man's property was divided into three parts, with one portion kept by the family and the rest sold to finance the funeral. The ceremony involved the sacrifice of a female slave who was first forced to take part in a ritual orgy. She was then stabbed to death and placed alongside the dead chief on a Viking boat, which was set afire and launched into the river.

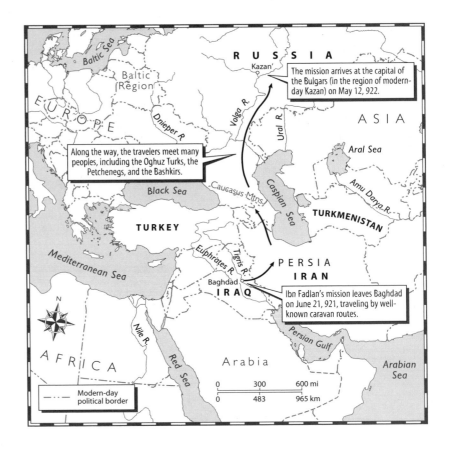

The mission arrives at the capital of the Bulgars (in the region of modern-day Kazan) on May 12, 922.

Along the way, the travelers meet many peoples, including the Oghuz Turks, the Petchenegs, and the Bashkirs.

Ibn Fadlan's mission leaves Baghdad on June 21, 921, traveling by well-known caravan routes.

Modern-day political border

Ibn Fadlan's account of his travels—which he simply entitled *Kitab,* or "Book"—contained many such descriptions of foreign customs and rituals. They must have seemed especially strange to the Islamic scholar from Baghdad, which was one of the world's most wealthy and civilized cities at that time. Ibn Fadlan also related some miraculous stories in his book, like the account of the legendary giants Gog and Magog, but he was always careful to point out that he had not witnessed the fantastic things himself; he was merely relating what was told to him.

It is unfortunate that the last part of Ibn Fadlan's text was lost, and that we know nothing about how the mission returned to Baghdad or of the author's own fate. The text, in fact, was not known in Europe until 1823, when a Russian scholar, C. M. Fraehn, translated it from Arabic into German. It then became an important historical document about the

early Russians and the Turkic people of eastern Europe and
west-central Asia.

Sources

Baker, Daniel B., ed. *Explorers and Discoverers of the World.* Detroit:
Gale Research, 1993.

Crichton, Michael. *Eaters of the Dead.* New York: Ballantine, 1976.

Waldman, Carl, and Alan Wexler. *Who Was Who in World Exploration.* New York: Facts on File, 1992.

Mae Jemison

Born October 17, 1956, Decatur, Alabama

American Mae Jemison was the first black female astronaut in space.

When the National Space and Aeronautics Administration's space shuttle *Endeavour* was launched on September 12, 1992, Mae Jemison—one of the seven-member crew—became the first black woman to travel in space. A mission specialist or "science astronaut" on the eight-day mission, she used her medical training to perform many experiments while in orbit. On her return she was treated as something of a celebrity and held up as a role model for black youths. Overcoming the discrimination that women and minorities often face in the United States, she had fulfilled her childhood dreams. Jemison hoped that her historic journey would encourage other blacks to pursue careers in space exploration, science, and technology.

Jemison was born October 17, 1956, in Decatur, Alabama. The daughter of a maintenance worker and an elementary schoolteacher, she moved with her family to Chicago when she was three. She remembers being encouraged to spend hours in the library, reading about astronomy and other sciences. Jemison especially liked to read books about space travel and novels of science fiction. She was also a big fan of the science fiction television program *Star Trek*. The show's black female officer, Lieutenant Uhura, was her particular favorite. Jemison always believed that one day she, too, would travel in space, although at that time there were no black or female astronauts.

Completes medical training

Following high school graduation, Jemison attended Stanford University in California on a scholarship. She earned degrees in chemical engineering and Afro-American studies in 1977. She was also the first female leader of the Black Student Union there. She then enrolled at Cornell University's Medical College in New York City. Her interest in seeing the world and helping other people led her to volunteer during summer school as a medical worker at a Cambodian refugee camp in Thailand. A grant program also allowed her to conduct health studies in the east African country of Kenya, in 1979. She earned her medical degree from Cornell in 1981.

Jemison served in the Peace Corps from 1983 to 1985. A medical officer in the west African countries of Sierra Leone and Liberia, she was in charge of the health and safety of Peace Corps volunteers and State Department employees. She also ran disease research projects. After her return to the United States, she worked as a doctor in private practice in Los Angeles, California. While there she took graduate classes in engineering and applied to NASA for admission to the astronaut program. Her first application was not accepted. But in 1987, after a second application, Jemison became one of fifteen people selected out of nearly two thousand astronaut hopefuls. She was the program's first black woman.

Prepares for first space flight

Jemison spent the next year becoming a mission specialist. This required learning about the space shuttle and how it operated, and practicing how to maneuver in a weightless en-

Mae Jemison performs a pre-flight switch check in the crew module of the space shuttle Atlantis.

vironment: conducting experiments, launching payloads or satellites, and walking in space. She then worked as an astronaut office representative at the Kennedy Space Center at Cape Canaveral, Florida, which involved preparing space shuttles for launch. Jemison's first flight assignment came in 1992, when she was selected to join the crew of the *Endeavour*. Set to launch on September 12, the flight was a joint mission in which NASA and the National Space Development Agency of Japan (NASDA) would conduct microgravity experiments using a manned Spacelab module. For the first time, a Japanese astronaut traveled aboard a U.S. shuttle.

Conducts weightlessness experiments

More than forty experiments were conducted around-the-clock on the mission, with the crew divided into two teams. Among the projects were those investigating the effect of no gravity on living things. Test subjects included the crew, Japanese koi fish, chicken embryos, fruit flies, plant seeds, and frogs and frog eggs. Jemison was in charge of the frog embryology experiment. She fertilized the eggs of South African frogs to see if they would develop normally in space. The tadpoles looked normal.

As a medical doctor, Jemison was also in charge of the motion sickness experiment. She was the only member of the crew who did not take medicine to help combat the nausea and other symptoms that astronauts usually experience during their first days in space. Jemison was trained in biofeedback—using the conscious mind to control unconscious bodily processes, like breathing—and used meditation and relaxation to bring her pulse and temperature back to normal when she felt sick. Her other medical experiments involving weightlessness included measuring its effect on tissue growth and the loss of bone calcium.

Talks to children from shuttle

At one point during the eight-day flight, Jemison gave a fifteen-minute talk that was transmitted live to sixty children gathered at the Museum of Science and Industry in Chicago. "I'm closer to the stars," she told them, "somewhere I've always dreamed to be." On the shuttle mission she brought a number of items that held special meaning for her, including a proclamation from the Chicago public school system, where she had taken her first steps toward outer space. Also among her things was a flag from the Organization of African Unity. As a student of African history, the astronaut knew that many black people had explored the heavens before her. "Ancient African empires—Mali, Songhai, Egypt—had scientists, astronomers," she said in a published report. "The fact is that space and its resources belong to all of us, not to any one group."

The shuttle *Endeavour* landed on the runway of the Kennedy Space Center on September 20, 1992. It had orbited the earth 127 times and had traveled 3,271,844 miles.

Jemison left NASA in 1993 to pursue her interest in promoting science education for minorities. She was also interested in bringing advanced technologies to underdeveloped countries. She founded a company called the Jemison Group, which develops and sells such advanced technologies. The former astronaut lives in Houston, Texas, with her cat, Sneeze.

Sources

Astronaut Speaks In Honor of Dr. King. [Online] Available http://ccf.arc.nasa.gov/dx/archives/astronauts/astronaut_speaks.html, January 11, 1989.

Engelbert, Phillis. *Astronomy & Space: From the Big Bang to the Big Crunch.* Detroit: U•X•L, 1997.

"The Fifty Most Beautiful People in the World." *People.* May 3, 1993: 145.

Mae C. Jemison: Astronaut, Physician. [Online] Available http://www.lib.lsu.edu/lib/chem/display/jemison.html, February 2, 1997.

Mae C. Jemison Academy. [Online] Available http://www.gsu.edu/~usgacmx/jemison_info.html, May 1, 1997.

Mae Jemison. [Online] Available http://sun3.lib.uci.edu/~afrexh/Jemison.html, July 8, 1997.

STS 47. [Online] Available http://vib.kuaero.kyoto-u.ac.jp/space_and_aeronautics/USA/sts-47.html, July 3, 1995.

Charles-Marie de La Condamine

Born January 27, 1701, Paris, France
Died February 4, 1774, Paris, France

During the eighteenth century scientists debated the shape of the earth. Was it a sphere, swollen in the center and flattened at the poles, as English mathematician Sir Isaac Newton had suggested? Or was it more oval in shape, slimmer in the middle and longer at the poles, as proposed by French-Italian mathematician Jacques Cassini? The controversy needed to be resolved so that locations could be accurately mapped around the world. French scientists were especially interested in proving the theory of their countryman correct. The king of France proposed sending out two expeditions to test the theories. One went to measure the curvature of the earth in Lapland, near the North Pole. The other, headed by Charles-Marie de La Condamine, went to Quito in South America to measure the earth at the equator.

La Condamine was born in Paris on January 27, 1701, into a wealthy, aristocratic family. He entered the French army when he was eighteen and fought in the War of Spanish Succession. But drawn to mathematics, astronomy, and natural

Charles-Marie de La Condamine was a French mathematician and scientist who led an expedition to South America to measure the curvature of the earth at the equator. He also led the first scientific voyage down the Amazon.

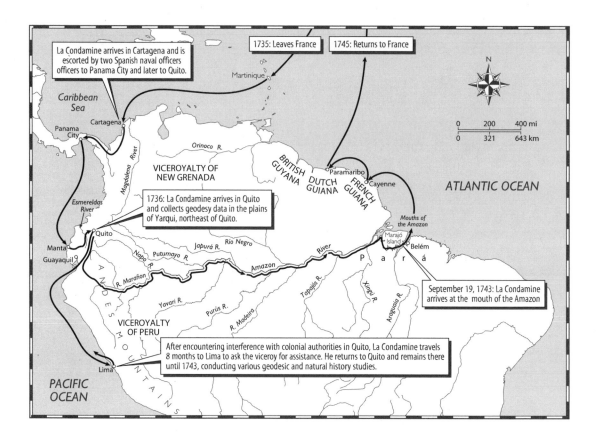

La Condamine arrives in Cartagena and is escorted by two Spanish naval officers to Panama City and later to Quito.

1735: Leaves France

1745: Returns to France

Martinique

Caribbean Sea

Cartagena

Panama City

Orinoco R.

VICEROYALTY OF NEW GRENADA

BRITISH GUYANA

DUTCH GUIANA

FRENCH GUIANA

Paramaribo

Cayenne

ATLANTIC OCEAN

Magdalena River

Esmereldas River

1736: La Condamine arrives in Quito and collects geodesy data in the plains of Yarqui, northeast of Quito.

Quito

Manta

Guayaquil

Napo R.

Putumayo R.

Japurá R.

Rio Negro

River

Mouths of the Amazon

Marajó Island

Belém

R. Marañón

Amazon

P a r á

Yavari R.

Purús R.

R. Madeira

Tapajós R.

Xingú R.

Araguaia R.

September 19, 1743: La Condamine arrives at the mouth of the Amazon

VICEROYALTY OF PERU

A N D E S   M O U N T A I N S

After encountering interference with colonial authorities in Quito, La Condamine travels 8 months to Lima to ask the viceroy for assistance. He returns to Quito and remains there until 1743, conducting various geodesic and natural history studies.

Lima

PACIFIC OCEAN

N

| 0 | 200 | 400 mi |
| 0 | 321 | 643 km |

history, he left the army to pursue a career in science. La Condamine became a member of major scientific circles in Paris, and at the age of twenty-nine was elected to the French Academy of Sciences, a considerable honor for one so young. In 1731 he went on his first scientific expedition, to the African coast of the Red Sea and to Constantinople (now Istanbul, Turkey), where he further distinguished himself with his mathematical and astronomical studies.

Heads expedition to equator

La Condamine was also interested in geodesy—earth measurement. In order to determine the true shape of the earth, a single degree of latitude would have to be measured at different geographical locations in the world. One had already been measured in France. Measurements at places far north and far south would be needed for comparison. France's Royal Academy of Science sponsored the two expeditions in 1735. Pierre Moreau de Maupertius was chosen to head the exploration into Lapland above the Arctic Circle. La Condamine was selected to lead the French Equatorial Expedition to the Spanish colonial city of Quito (now Ecuador's capital) in South America, considered to be the most approachable place near the equator. Permission from the king of Spain was obtained, making La Condamine and his party the first non-Spanish/non-Portuguese Europeans to freely explore the continent in 250 years.

With a group of fellow scientists, La Condamine left the French port of La Rochelle on May 16, 1735. They sailed to the French Caribbean island of Martinique, then on to the city of Cartagena in what is now Colombia. There they were joined by two Spanish naval officers, who were sent to watch over them. They proceeded on land for 230 miles, crossing the Isthmus of Panama to Panama City. From there they set sail again, down South America's Pacific coast to the city of Manta, in what is now Ecuador. La Condamine went ashore there, choosing to take an interior route to Quito with Pedro Vicente Maldonado, the local colonial governor. Most of the group continued by ship down the coast to the large seaport of Guayaquil. It had taken them a year to reach their destination.

Discovers rubber trees

La Condamine and his small party traveled along the Esmeraldas River on their way to Quito. The scientist was fascinated by his jungle surroundings, which had cockroaches as big as mice. He was also intrigued by an elastic material called "caoutchouc" that was removed from certain trees. He made a sack out of it to protect some of his delicate scientific instruments from wear and water. The mysterious new substance he discovered was natural rubber, and when he returned home he brought news of its wonderful characteristics. This led to a thriving rubber industry in the Amazon in the following century.

In early June of 1736 La Condamine and his party reached Quito after a final trek through the Andes Mountains. He rejoined his scientific team and they immediately began the long and complicated process of measuring a degree of latitude at the equator. The chosen area was located in the plains of Yarqui, a few miles northeast of Quito. Measuring the land proved a challenge to the scientists, delaying their progress significantly. The windswept, semidesert plain was eight thousand feet up, blazing hot during the day and freezing cold when the sun went down. At times steep mountain outcroppings forced the scientists to make treacherous climbs to gather data. In addition, political problems further delayed their scientific mission: Spanish colonial authorities in Quito interfered with the expedition so much that La Condamine had to travel all the way to Peru's capital city of Lima—a journey of more than eight months—to ask the Spanish viceroy there (who oversaw Quito) to fix the problem.

Soon after his return to Quito, La Condamine received word that the Lapland expedition had completed its mission. The team had returned to France with measurements that proved without a doubt that Newton's theory was right: the earth was indeed shaped like a sphere that flattened at the poles. Although the data of the equatorial team was no longer needed to settle the controversy, La Condamine and his group continued their work, their findings adding further information about the true shape of the earth. The scientist remained in Ecuador until 1743, conducting various geodesic and natural history studies.

Makes scientific expedition down Amazon River

When La Condamine decided to return to Europe, he planned to sail down the Amazon River, crossing the South American continent from coast to coast. Maldonado would again be his traveling companion. Leaving Quito in June, they headed through the Andes, crossing deep canyons and mountain passes by way of dizzying rope bridges. The travelers headed south until they came to the Marañón River (in what is now Peru). There they boarded canoes and, despite some dangerous rapids, made their way to the Amazon. Although La Condamine was not the first European to sail down the great river, he was the first *scientist* to do so, and he noted everything with a scientist's keen eye. He logged the Amazon's volume, depth, width, and rate of flow—and until the twentieth century his map remained the most accurate for navigating the river. He also investigated its tributaries and islands.

In addition, La Condamine took notes on the Indian tribes he met along the way. He puzzled over the Omaguas, who squeezed the heads of their newborn babies between two boards to make the infants' faces more round. He also noted the tribe's use of the seeds of the curupa plant, which they ground into a powder and sometimes inhaled through a reed for an intoxicating effect. He observed that other tribes tipped their hunting arrows with a poison called curare, probably from the same plant. And La Condamine wondered how the Indians protected themselves from insects in a place that was swarming with them. He suspected that another plant extract gave the natives relief.

La Condamine completed his Amazon journey, arriving in Pará on the north coast of Brazil, on September 19, 1743. After a brief stay in which he conducted scientific experiments (he determined that the nearby island group of Marajó was actually a single island, for example), he traveled up the coast to Cayenne in French Guiana. There he engaged in more scientific studies. He finally set sail for Europe from Paramaribo, a port in Dutch Guiana. With a stopover in the Netherlands, he returned to Paris in early 1745—a full ten years after his departure.

Once home, La Condamine worked on his map of the Amazon and wrote about his discoveries there. His observations would prompt others to explore the region. He also wrote a book about his scientific efforts in Quito, published in 1751 as the *Journal of a Voyage by Order of the King to the Equator.* He later campaigned for a vaccination against smallpox, a disease he had suffered from when young. In 1760 he was elected to the prestigious Académie Française (the French Academy), a learned society.

Stricken by ill health, La Condamine spent the last decade of his life nearly deaf and paralyzed because of a crippling disease. He died in Paris on February 4, 1774.

Sources

Baker, Daniel B., ed. *Explorers and Discoverers of the World*. Detroit: Gale Research, 1993.

Bohlander, Richard E., ed. *World Explorers and Discoverers*. New York: Macmillan, 1992.

Goodman, Edward J. *The Explorers of South America*. New York: Macmillan, 1972.

Waldman, Carl, and Alan Wexler. *Who Was Who in World Exploration*. New York: Facts on File, 1992.

Louis S. B. Leakey

Born August 7, 1903, Kabete (near Nairobi), Kenya
Died October 1, 1972, London, England

Mary Leakey

Born February 6, 1913, London, England
Died December 9, 1996, Nairobi, Kenya

Richard Leakey

Born December 19, 1944, Nairobi, Kenya

Louis Leakey ⟶

When Louis Leakey told his university professors that he wanted to explore East Africa for human fossils, they told him that he was wasting his time. "If you really want to spend your life studying early man," one of them said, "do it in Asia." Turn-of-the-century discoveries of 500,000-year-old Peking Man and Java Man had pointed to Asia as the place of man's origins. But Leakey, who had grown up in Africa and had stumbled upon primitive stone arrowheads and tools during his boyhood wanderings through the Kenyan countryside, felt that he knew better. In time he and his archaeologist wife, Mary, would prove them wrong about man's Asian beginnings, their discoveries placing man's birthplace in East Africa some 3.5 million years ago.

Leakey was born near Nairobi in 1903, the oldest child of British missionaries sent to live among the Kikuyu, Kenya's largest tribe. He learned the tribal language before he could understand English and his playmates were Kikuyu children. When he was thirteen, he was made a member of the

The Leakeys are a family of scientists whose fossil finds in East Africa have shaped our ideas about the course of human evolution.

Mary Leakey.

tribe, and given the name Wakaruigi, or Son of the Sparrow Hawk, because of his love of birdwatching. Tutored by his parents until he was sixteen, Leakey left for England to continue his education. It was while recovering from a sports injury at Cambridge University that he settled on his future career, joining an archaeological expedition to Tanganyika (now Tanzania) headed by the well-known Canadian paleontologist W. E. Cutler. It was from him that Leakey learned many of his digging methods and skills.

A hardworking team

Leakey earned a doctorate in archaeology and anthropology from Cambridge; in breaks from his teaching duties there he led fossil-hunting expeditions to East Africa. In 1933 he met a young archaeologist and artist named Mary Nicol at one of his lectures, and asked her to illustrate his upcoming book, *Adam's Ancestors*. She agreed, and in a short time the pair became close companions, although Leakey was already married and the father of two children. Louis and Mary planned to marry as soon as Leakey could get a divorce; in the meantime, she joined him in the field in Tanzania. Mary fell in love with the wild and beautiful country. After their marriage in 1936 she often worked on their digging projects alone, as Louis was called off for research, or to aid British intelligence during World War II, or to work at the Coryndon Memorial Museum in Nairobi, where he served as a curator for nearly twenty years. The couple had three children, and it was not unusual to see young Jonathan, Richard, and Philip scraping about in the dusty earth beside their mother, with tiny picks, brushes, and sieves.

The Leakeys' early years of work in Africa went largely unnoticed. That is, until Mary came upon the skull of a primitive ape-like creature while she and Louis were excavating on the island of Rusinga in Lake Victoria, Kenya, in 1948. Named

Proconsul africanus, the animal was considered by most experts to be a common ancestor of both mankind and the apes and higher primates, living from twenty-five to forty million years ago. Mary painstakingly pieced together the more than thirty fragments of the skull and took her find to England for analysis. The discovery finally brought world attention to the Leakeys, and planted the idea that East Africa could, indeed, be the birthplace of mankind. (The Leakeys would find yet another link between ape and early man, *Kenyapithecus,* at Fort Ternan, near Lake Victoria, in 1962.)

Incredible fossil finds

But it was at the Olduvai Gorge in northern Tanzania that the Leakeys concentrated most of their digging efforts. The thirty-five-mile-long ravine sliced through three hundred feet of sediment that once covered the bed of a prehistoric lake. The sides of the gorge revealed layer after layer of the earth's history, and the couple was sure that hidden there were fossils of creatures that had lived up to one million years ago. In their early years at the gorge the Leakeys unearthed nearly one hundred forms of extinct animal life. Some of their incredible finds included a prehistoric pig as large as a rhinoceros, a sheep that stood six feet high at the shoulders and had a horn span of fourteen feet, and a short-necked giraffe. *Simopthecus jonathani,* a giant prehistoric baboon, was named after Jonathan Leakey, who found its jawbone in 1957. The fossil of a giant ostrich was discovered by Philip two years later. In addition, the archaeologists located crude stone tools that suggested the presence of a human ancestor, although no bodily remains were found.

The Leakeys were still convinced that they would find the fossil remains of early man there, however. And on July 17, 1959, while Louis rested at camp with a fever, Mary continued

Richard Leakey.

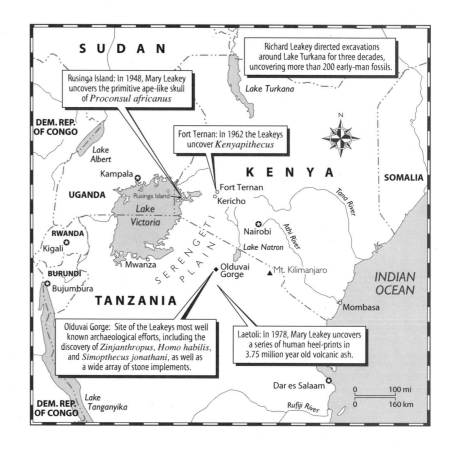

Richard Leakey directed excavations around Lake Turkana for three decades, uncovering more than 200 early-man fossils.

Rusinga Island: In 1948, Mary Leakey uncovers the primitive ape-like skull of *Proconsul africanus*

Fort Ternan: In 1962 the Leakeys uncover *Kenyapithecus*

Olduvai Gorge: Site of the Leakeys most well known archaeological efforts, including the discovery of *Zinjanthropus*, *Homo habilis*, and *Simopthecus jonathani*, as well as a wide array of stone implements.

Laetoli: In 1978, Mary Leakey uncovers a series of human heel-prints in 3.75 million year old volcanic ash.

their search. Soon she came upon an incredible sight: embedded in a spot on the cliff were two large human-looking teeth. She rushed back to get her husband, and the two painstakingly unearthed a full upper jaw and set of teeth by using dental picks and artists' paintbrushes. They eventually collected four hundred other bone fragments in the earth nearby, and pieced together the skull of a near-man, some 1.75 million years old. He was named *Zinjanthropus*. Over the next few months, Mary found more *Zinj* bones and 164 stone tools, including choppers, scrapers, anvils, and hammerstones. From their finds the archaeologists guessed that the creature had possessed a brain about half the size of modern man's. Around five feet tall, he had walked upright on spindly legs. His chest and shoulder muscles had been very large and his forehead sloped, with no brow. He had lived on nuts and meat. (Their discovery came to be called "Nutcracker Man," because of his diet.)

New ideas about human evolution

After this important discovery, the Leakeys no longer had to worry much about funding for their excavations. The National Geographic Society became a full sponsor. The fame of the archaeologists skyrocketed, and the outgoing Louis was in demand the world over as a teacher and lecturer. While at first thinking that his *Zinjanthropus* was the missing link between *Australopithecus africanus,* the extinct near-man found in South Africa in 1924, and modern man, Louis later decided that his discovery was just a different kind of australopithecine species outside the mainstream of human evolution. This was because he and Mary had found a second near-human skull in the same earth layer in which *Zinj* had been found, and this second skull clearly housed a much bigger brain. They named this creature *Homo habilis,* or "able man," because it was clearly he who had made and used the stone tools that they had earlier thought belonged to *Zinjanthropus.* The idea that two kinds of human-like creatures could have lived in the same place at the same time was a shocking one at that time, for the development of man was thought to be linear, with one stage following another. Yet the Leakeys' ideas on human evolution would eventually take hold among scientists. (And findings by their son Richard in excavations in the Lake Turkana region of Nairobi over the next few decades would further stretch their ideas.)

While Louis became swept up in a celebrity's life, Mary remained at the permanent camp at Olduvai Gorge. She became more independent both personally and professionally, and in 1968 the two separated. After her husband's death in 1972, the usually shy Mary took on a more public role, lecturing and fundraising so that excavation efforts in East Africa could continue. In 1978, at Laetoli, on the Serengeti Plain some thirty miles south of Olduvai, she made what she considered to be her most important discovery. Preserved in hardened volcanic ash some 3.75 million years before was what appeared to be a human heelprint. Further investigation revealed that it was part of a seventy-five-foot-long trail of clear footprints made by three human-like creatures. At one point, it appeared that one of the smaller figures had playfully stepped into the footprints of the largest companion; later, one of them seemed to pause and turn left briefly before continuing north. To Mary, these "intensely human" actions brought the footprints to life. And because areas surrounding the prints—while filled with human and animal fossils—held no tools, she theorized that bipedalism (walking on two feet) came before the making of tools in man's development. Her discovery also showed that early man had walked upright much sooner than scientists had ever imagined.

Mary Leakey died December 9, 1996, in Nairobi. Son Jonathan became a herpetologist (a scientist who studies reptiles and amphibians); Philip became a politician, the only white member of the Kenyan parliament; and Richard followed most closely in his parents' footsteps. While lacking formal schooling in paleontology and anthropology, he went on to organize some of the most successful African fossil expeditions of this century. For nearly three decades he ran excavations in the Lake Turkana region of northern Kenya, with his team of scientists unearthing more than two hundred early-man fossils—an extraordinary number for a single site. The quality of the specimens was also unusually fine: the collection contained a dozen skulls, many nearly complete jaws, and some partial skeletons; the best of the finds was an almost complete *Homo erectus* skeleton that was thought to be 1.6 million years old.

More branches on man's family tree

The Turkana finds forced scientists to rethink their ideas about human evolution. The remains in the collection suggested that three different kinds of early humans all lived roughly during the same time span (between 2.5 and 1 million years ago). When Leakey's colleague Alan Walker discovered a fourth man-like species of the same approximate age in 1985, it became clear that the human family tree was much more complicated than scientists had ever imagined. In addition to his archaeological work, Richard Leakey has been active in protecting Africa's wildlife. Serving as director of the

Kenya Wildlife Service from 1989 to 1994, he worked to have Africa's elephants declared an endangered species. The proposal was adopted by over one hundred nations in 1989, and all international trade in elephant products became illegal. Leakey has also worked hard to get Western governments and other organizations to donate money for wildlife conservation. Knowing that most African countries are too poor to do the job alone, he believes that wealthier countries from the industrialized world have an equal responsibility in preserving Earth's wild creatures.

Sources

Begley, Sharon. "Witness to the Creation: Mary Leakey, 1913–1996." *Newsweek*. December 23, 1996: 23.

Current Biography. New York: H. W. Wilson, 1966, 1985, 1995.

Kaufman, Michael T. "Dr. Louis Leakey Dead; Discovered Earliest Man." *The New York Times*. October 2, 1972: 40.

Ella Maillart

Born February 20, 1903, Geneva, Switzerland
Died March 27, 1997, Chandolin, Switzerland

Ella Maillart was a Swiss adventurer who explored places not often visited by Westerners. In 1935 she made a 3,500-mile journey through forbidden regions of central Asia with English journalist Peter Fleming.

During the 1930s Japan, the Soviet Union, and China were battling for power in central Asia. China's last dynasty had been overthrown in 1912, ending some thirty centuries of imperial rule, and the country was suffering from unrest and civil war. It disintegrated into regions ruled by warlords—independent military leaders—and was fought over by rival political parties, particularly the Communists and the Chinese Nationalists, or Kuomintang. Japan, rising rapidly as a world power, tried to take advantage of the turmoil by seizing territories under Chinese control. The Soviet Union, too, after its communist revolution in 1917, looked to spread its new socialized way of life across its borders. Into this unsettled region ventured wealthy Swiss adventurer Ella Maillart (pronounced "mayAHR"). Her seven-month, 3,500-mile journey from Peking (Beijing) to Kashmir through Chinese Turkestan allowed her to witness the last days of an ancient civilization.

Maillart was born in Geneva, Switzerland, on February 20, 1903. Her father was a wealthy Swiss fur dealer and her mother was from Denmark. Like her mother, Maillart was very athletic, and excelled at swimming, sailing, rowing, skiing, and playing field hockey. In the 1924 Olympics, she was a member of the Swiss sailing team. She also founded Switzerland's first women's field hockey club and organized a ski racing team there.

Multi-talented and restless, Maillart had trouble settling on a single occupation as she grew older. She worked as a winter sports correspondent for a Geneva newspaper; she taught French at an English girls' school and English to private students in Berlin, where she had a brief film career in 1930; she spent several months in Crete, excavating the remains of a primitive village; and she was an excellent photographer.

Restless sportswoman turns to travel

Maillart had been horrified by World War I and was later disgusted by the feeble efforts of European powers "to establish a real peace." It awakened in her a desire to travel and experience other ways of life. Of special interest was the Soviet Union, with its revolutionary thinking about the evils of private ownership and the power of its workers.

Maillart traveled to Moscow to study Russian filmmaking. While there she made a trip with a group of workers and students to the Caucasus Mountains, considered by many to be the boundary between Europe and Asia. She was fascinated by the different villages they passed along the way. Especially interesting was Free Svanetia in the upper Ingur valley, a village cut off from the rest of the world except during the three months of summer. The Russian Revolution had not yet touched these primitive people, who traveled by ox-pulled sleds and cooked on heated stone slabs. Maillart wished to remain longer with the Svanes to study their customs and way of life, but was forced to move on with her group, which eventually reached the Black Sea. Yet, feeling drawn to the eastern world, the adventurer set her mind to return there soon.

Journeys into Asian territories

When Maillart returned to Geneva she wrote an article about her Russian experiences. The piece sold, and she used

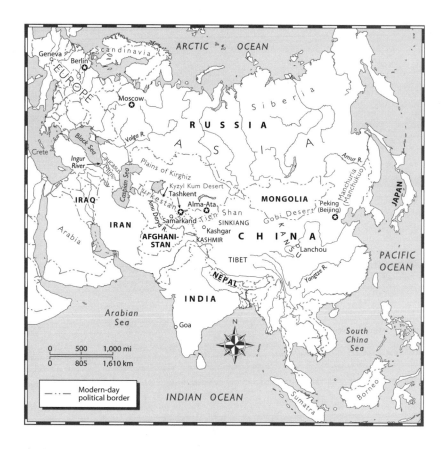

the money for a second eastern journey, this time to Russian Turkestan in central Asia. Leaving in the spring of 1932, she and four Russian traveling companions visited the mountain range of Tien Shan. They then crossed the plains of Kirghiz and were graciously received by its inhabitants, who gave a banquet in their honor. The visitors feasted on lamb and koumiss (fermented mare's milk) and stayed in a yurt (a round felt tent). Later, when from a mountain pass she viewed the distant Gobi Desert, Maillart knew that she would travel further east one day, into China's unknown regions.

At the city of Alma-Ata Maillart parted with her Russian friends, who planned to return to Moscow. She continued traveling through Turkestan alone, taking only what she could carry. Like the inhabitants of the poor region in which she traveled, she often lacked food or a comfortable place to sleep. Such hardships did little to dull her enthusiasm, however, as she visited Tashkent, Samarkand, Bukhara, and Turk-tol. Her adventures included a barge ride on the Amu Darya River and crossing the Kyzyl Kum Desert by two-wheeled cart and camel. Throughout her travels she interviewed many refugees she saw along the way, trying to get a true picture of how Soviet policies—like collective farms (run by govern-ment-appointed groups instead of individual owners)—were affecting the people. Maillart wrote a book about her journey, translated as *Turkestan Solo,* soon after her return home.

Meets traveling partner Peter Fleming

Still dreaming of traveling through China, Maillart con-vinced the editor of *Petite Parisien* to finance her trip to the city of Manchukuo, to report on Japan's military takeover of Manchuria. While there she ran into Peter Fleming, a journal-ist for the London *Times* whom she had met earlier in Eng-land. He shared her love of travel and the two of them made short trips together into northern China. When she told him about her plans to cross central China into India, he informed her that he too was considering a similar route for his return to Europe. The two decided to make the journey together, al-though the Chinese region of Sinkiang, through which they needed to pass, had been closed to foreigners for four years due to civil wars. Getting passports to travel to the troubled area would be all but impossible.

Yet through some sneaky maneuvering, the pair man-aged to get passports and permits, and hurriedly prepared to leave the Chinese capital of Peking. Traveling with them was a Russian couple who were returning to their home in Tsaidam in west central China. They would be able to guide Maillart and Fleming at least half the way. Among the travel-ers' provisions were presents for people they would meet, on whose help their lives might very well depend. They carried little money with them, but had a bar of gold from which pieces could be cut. The travelers also had special cards printed with their names spelled out in Chinese characters. Fleming was Fu Lei-ming, the Learned Engraver on Stone; Maillart was Ma Na-ya, the Horse of International Goodwill.

Chinese officials turn back guides

Traveling mostly by train, the group made it as far as Lanchou in the province of Kansu before trouble struck. Officials there took their passports and kept them for several days. When the documents were finally returned, only Maillart and Fleming were allowed to proceed. Without their Russian guides, the two were doubtful that they could continue.

But they decided to carry on. From her earlier travels, Maillart was used to harsh conditions. She could make up a tent, cook outdoors, wash and mend their few clothes, and tend to their ailments. Fleming was an expert hunter, and could shoot their food if necessary. He also knew a bit of Chinese, and could deal with officials when they needed permission to proceed, or to hire guides or pack animals. Sometimes they journeyed alone. At other times they joined fellow travelers. Once they rode with a caravan of some 250 camels led by the prince of Dzun.

While Fleming wanted them to travel as fast as they could, Maillart liked to proceed slowly, so that she could observe the people and their way of life and record what she saw in photographs. She was especially moved by the sight of Chinese women struggling to walk after having their feet bound as children (because small, tapered feet were admired in females) and by young girls whose feet were still tied up. By June Maillart and Fleming had traveled well into the forbidden region of Sinkiang and were relieved to find that the area was quite peaceful. When they reached the western city of Kashgar they stayed with its British vice-consul for a while and enjoyed good food, hot baths, and clean beds. Despite seven trying months, they were in good health and high spirits, and considered their trip a success. Still, the pair had three mountain passes to cross before they ended their journey in Kashmir, British India.

Pair writes books about journey

After reaching their destination, Fleming returned to London. Maillart stayed for a while before flying to Lebanon and then on to Paris. Both wrote well-received books about their trip. Fleming's was entitled *News From Tartary*. Maillart's was translated as *Forbidden Journey*. Her photographs of the trip were later shown in a Paris exhibition.

In 1939 Maillart again turned to Asia in an attempt to forget her worries about Europe, which was on the brink of another war. This time she traveled through Afghanistan by automobile, taking along a sick friend as a companion. Unfortunately, the woman's problems ruined Maillart's usual enjoyment of her exotic surroundings. After her companion returned home, the world traveler managed to spend time in India and Tibet. Later, she visited Iran and lived for a time at a Hindu retreat in southern India. When the kingdom of Nepal opened its borders to travelers in 1949, she was among its first visitors, writing about it in *The Land of the Sherpas.*

Maillart was made a fellow of Britain's Royal Geographical Society. She continued to travel for enjoyment until she was well into her eighties. Her last trip abroad was a visit to Goa, India, in 1994. She died in her mountain home in Chandolin, Switzerland, on March 27, 1997.

Sources

Biography.com Find. [Online] Available http://www.biography.com/cgi-bin/biography/biography-request.pl?page=/biography/data/M/M.9135.txt.html, July 19, 1997.

Heroine. [Online] Available http://humpc61.murdoch.edu.au/~cntinuum/Richo/Heroine.html, May 21, 1997.

Thomas, Robert. "Ella Maillart, a Swiss Writer and Adventurer, Is Dead at 94." *The New York Times*. March 31, 1997: B5.

Tinling, Marion. *Women Into the Unknown: A Sourcebook on Women Explorers and Travelers*. Westport, CT: Greenwood Press, 1989.

Jacques Marquette

Born June 10, 1637, Laon, France
Died May 18, 1675, territory of Illinois Indians,
North America

Jacques Marquette was a French Jesuit who founded missions in the Great Lakes area of North America. He also accompanied French-Canadian explorer Louis Jolliet on the expedition that led to the discovery of the Mississippi River.

In 1672 Louis Jolliet was chosen to lead a French-Canadian expedition to explore the Mississippi River and to discover whether it emptied into the Gulf of Mexico or the Pacific Ocean. French Jesuit missionary Jacques Marquette was chosen to go along as the expedition's interpreter, for he spoke several Indian languages fluently. The information he learned from Native Americans proved invaluable to the explorers as they made their way into the unknown. In addition—when Jolliet's account of the expedition was lost in a canoe accident—Marquette's journal became the only first-person record of the historic trip.

Marquette was born on June 10, 1637, in the northern French town of Laon. The son of a distinguished family, he entered the Jesuit order in 1654, studying to become a priest. During that time he wrote to a religious superior, asking to be sent out to foreign lands as a missionary. In 1666 he got his wish when he was ordained a missionary priest and sent to French Canada to teach and convert Native Americans. He ar-

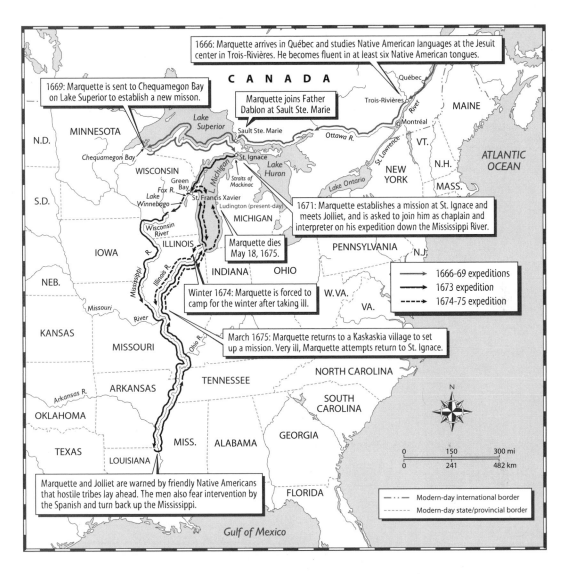

1666: Marquette arrives in Québec and studies Native American languages at the Jesuit center in Trois-Rivières. He becomes fluent in at least six Native American tongues.

1669: Marquette is sent to Chequamegon Bay on Lake Superior to establish a new misson.

Marquette joins Father Dablon at Sault Ste. Marie

1671: Marquette establishes a mission at St. Ignace and meets Jolliet, and is asked to join him as chaplain and interpreter on his expedition down the Mississippi River.

Marquette dies May 18, 1675.

Winter 1674: Marquette is forced to camp for the winter after taking ill.

March 1675: Marquette returns to a Kaskaskia village to set up a mission. Very ill, Marquette attempts return to St. Ignace.

Marquette and Jolliet are warned by friendly Native Americans that hostile tribes lay ahead. The men also fear intervention by the Spanish and turn back up the Mississippi.

CANADA

Québec
Trois-Rivières
Montréal
MAINE
VT.
N.H.
ATLANTIC OCEAN
MASS.
NEW YORK
N.J.
PENNSYLVANIA
OHIO
W. VA.
VA.
NORTH CAROLINA
SOUTH CAROLINA
GEORGIA
FLORIDA
Gulf of Mexico
LOUISIANA
MISS.
ALABAMA
TEXAS
OKLAHOMA
ARKANSAS
TENNESSEE
KANSAS
MISSOURI
NEB.
IOWA
ILLINOIS
INDIANA
MICHIGAN
WISCONSIN
MINNESOTA
N.D.
S.D.

Lake Superior
Chequamegon Bay
Sault Ste. Marie
Ottawa R.
St. Lawrence River
Lake Huron
Lake Ontario
St. Ignace
Straits of Mackinac
L. Michigan
Green Bay
Fox R.
Lake Winnebago
St. Francis Xavier
Ludington (present-day)
Wisconsin River
Mississippi R.
Illinois R.
Missouri River
Ohio R.
Arkansas R.

1666-69 expeditions
1673 expedition
1674-75 expedition

N

0   150   300 mi
0   241   482 km

- · - · - Modern-day international border
- - - - - Modern-day state/provincial border

rived in the city of Québec in September. Studying Indian languages for a time at the Jesuit center in Trois-Riviéres on the St. Lawrence River, he showed great ability, and became fluent in at least six Native American tongues.

Founds missions in Great Lakes area

Marquette next joined his Jesuit superior, Father Dablon, at the Ottawa Indian mission located near Sault Ste. Marie (between Lakes Superior and Huron). Then in September of

1669 he was sent out to found a new mission on Chequamegon Bay, at the western end of Lake Superior. Indian hostilities eventually drove Marquette to set up a second mission, however, on the north shore of the Straits of Mackinac (connecting Lakes Michigan and Huron) in 1671. Called St. Ignace, the mission was where the Jesuit first met the explorer and fur trader Jolliet, who had been sent by the French-Canadian colonial government to travel the great south-flowing river—what would become known as the Mississippi—that Indians in the region had often spoken about.

Joins Jolliet in Mississippi expedition

Marquette was asked to accompany Jolliet on his expedition, as its chaplain and interpreter. His Jesuit superiors saw the trip as a wonderful opportunity to introduce Christianity to the Native American tribes met along the way. Marquette, too, was eager for the chance: in his journal he wrote, "because the salvation of souls was at stake ... I would be willing to give my life." In May of 1673 the expedition of seven men set off from St. Ignace, paddling in birchbark canoes. They traveled westward along the north shore of Lake Michigan to Green Bay, then up the Fox River. Carrying their gear overland to the Wisconsin River, they reached the Mississippi in mid-June. They were warmly greeted by members of the Illinois Indian tribe, who gave the party a calumet, or peace pipe. The expedition members would use it for the rest of their trip, when meeting other Native Americans for the first time.

As the expedition continued down the Mississippi, it became obvious to the explorers that the river flowed south—into the Gulf of Mexico—and not west. They did pass the mouth of the Missouri River as it rushed into the Mississippi, though, and both Jolliet and Marquette felt sure that this great waterway was the one that headed west. Traveling as far south as the border of present-day Arkansas and Louisiana, the expedition cut short its mission after local Indians warned the men of danger. On their way to the mouth of the great river, the travelers were told, they would likely meet hostile tribes that possessed guns. Spanish forces were also said to be approaching the area from the west. Rather than risk warfare or capture, the explorers turned back just days short of their destination. They had traveled more than twenty-five hundred miles in four months.

On July 17, 1673, the expedition headed north up the Mississippi. Paddling against the strong current made progress difficult. Told by Indians about an easier route, the group traveled up the Illinois River and crossed overland to the Chicago River, which carried them to Lake Michigan by September. Jolliet and Marquette split up at St. Francis Xavier mission at Green Bay. The explorer went on to Montreal in French Canada to report on his discoveries. Marquette fell ill, and stayed at a mission near present-day De Pere, Wisconsin, for some time.

Preaches before Indian gathering

By mid-1674 Marquette had recovered and resumed his missionary work. Wishing to fulfill a promise he had made to a Kaskaskia Indian tribe he met on the expedition, he headed for their village to set up a mission. Before reaching his destination, however, ill health returned, forcing him to winter at a camp in what is now suburban Chicago. Continuing his journey in March of 1675, Marquette finally made it to the Kaskaskia village on the Illinois River during Holy Week, a few days before Easter. There he preached a sermon to a gathering of two thousand Illinois Indians, including five hundred chiefs. By this time, Marquette was terribly sick. He headed north for the mission of St. Ignace, but his ailing body could not withstand the journey, and he died along the way, on May 18, 1675. He was buried at the mouth of a river that now bears his name, located near the present town of Ludington on Lake Michigan's eastern shore.

Journal sparks controversy

During his time in North America, Marquette sent regular reports about his activities to his superiors in France. Among those documents is one entitled *Récit,* which is believed to be the Jesuit's first-person account of the 1673 Mississippi expedition. But starting in 1928, with the writings of Franciscan friar Francis Borgia Steck, historians have questioned the authorship of the narration. A number believe the that the journal was really written by Father Dablon from the recollections of Jolliet and the notes of Marquette. (After Jolliet lost all of his papers when his canoe overturned, he did write another report entirely from memory, and it corresponds very closely with *Récit*.) It is unlikely that the controversy will ever be resolved. Regardless, Marquette—who is one of two Wisconsin figures represented in the Statuary Hall of the U.S. Capitol—remains celebrated for his religious dedication and adventurous spirit.

Sources

Baker, Daniel B., ed. *Explorers and Discoverers of the World*. Detroit: Gale Research, 1993.

Bohlander, Richard E., ed. *World Explorers and Discoverers*. New York: Macmillan, 1992.

Saari, Peggy and Daniel B. Baker. "Louis Jolliet." *Explorers and Discoverers*. Detroit: U•X•L, 1995.

Waldman, Carl, and Alan Wexler. *Who Was Who in World Exploration*. New York: Facts on File, 1992.

Mir space station

Launched February 1986

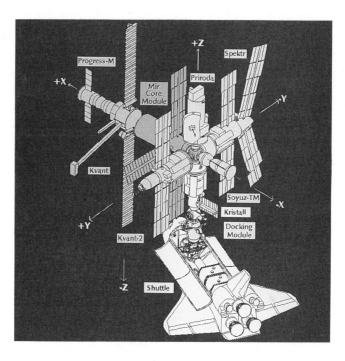

The International Space Station

The United States, Russia, Japan, Canada, and fourteen member countries of the European Space Agency (ESA) are hard at work on the International Space Station (ISS), an Earth-orbiting space research facility scheduled to be completed in mid-2002 and operated by a full-time international crew. Phase I of the project is known as the *Mir*/Shuttle rendezvous program, in which the National Aeronautics and Space Administration (NASA) is launching eleven space shuttle flights over a four-year period, most docking with the Russian space station *Mir*. During docking, new crew members—including American astronauts—come aboard the station for stays that usually last four months, while veteran crew members return to Earth. On board *Mir,* its two or three resident astronauts and cosmonauts (Russian astronauts) perform scientific experiments and research, along with daily tasks and routine space station maintenance. In the process, the

Mir is a Russian space station that has been orbiting Earth since 1986. From March 1995 to May 1998, it is serving as a host station to NASA astronauts in Phase I of a global effort to build an International Space Station.

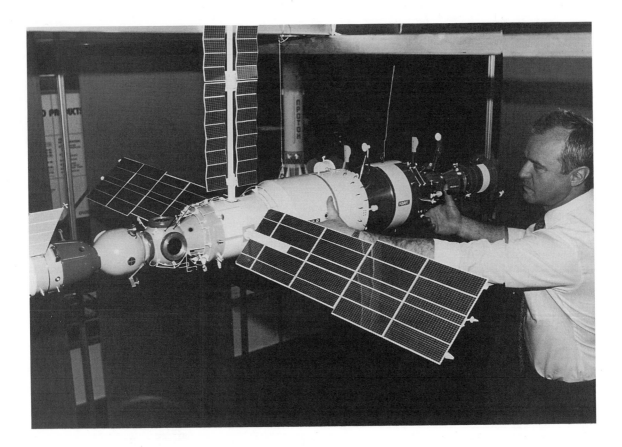

A scale model of the Mir *space station.*

American and Russian crew members acquire valuable knowledge about living and working together in space—good training for life on the International Space Station.

How *Mir* is built

Mir is a collection of modules put together like building blocks. The central Core Module provides basic services, such as living quarters, life support, and power. The Russians have added three expansion modules (launched by rockets) at separate times, each modernizing and increasing *Mir*'s capabilities. The Kvant Module, for instance, carries powerful telescopes that have allowed the crew to conduct special Earth and space observations. The Kristall Module added a docking mechanism able to receive heavy (up to 100-ton) spacecraft. Beginning in 1995, the United States added three modules of its own, carrying additional scientific equipment. For example, its Priroda Module brought a bioreactor that American astronaut John Blaha used to study the effects of microgravity on the growth of cartilage cells. Now complete with seven modules, *Mir* has a mass of 100 tons. This modular method of station assembly will be used when building the ISS, and much valuable information has been learned about the process on *Mir*.

Life in orbit

What is it like to call *Mir* home? Even though there is no gravity in the space station, the work and living areas in the Core Module are made to look like they have floors, ceilings, and walls. The "floors" have carpeting and the "ceilings" have fluorescent lamps. Equipment is also arranged in a top-to-bottom way, because the crew prefers this "normal" arrangement of things. The living section is painted in soft pastel colors, to make it feel more like a home. It contains an eating area with a table, cooking equipment, and trash storage. Each cabin has a porthole, hinged chairs, and a sleeping bag. There is a shared personal hygiene area with a toilet, sink, and shower. In the event of visitors, *Mir* can accommodate six people for up to one month. Temperatures range from 70 to 86 degrees Fahrenheit in different parts of the space station and the humidity is around 70 percent. The sun shines every twenty-five to forty-five minutes, each time *Mir* orbits the globe.

Food, clothes, and equipment are received every six weeks or so, on a resupply vehicle that hooks up to one of *Mir*'s six docking ports. According to American astronaut Shannon Lucid (who broke the U.S. spaceflight duration record on *Mir* at six months and also became the world's female spaceflight record holder), the first few days after the supply ship comes are an exciting time. Crew members read mail sent by friends and family members, who may include little gifts like books and candy. And the space dwellers eat their fill of fresh fruits and vegetables, a supply that sadly dwindles as the weeks go by.

Russian commander Yuri Onufrienko (bottom left), astronauts Shannon Lucid (bottom right), Linda Godwin (top left), and Atlantis commander Kevin Chilton in a televised image from the space station Mir.

Special astronaut training

NASA astronauts receive special training before living aboard *Mir.* They must first undergo cosmonaut certification training in Star City, Russia. They also learn to speak Russian so that they can live and work easily with their fellow space dwellers. In addition, they are trained to perform the scientific experiments assigned to them during their *Mir* stays. Many of the studies involve weightlessness: its effect on the biological processes of plants, animals, and humans (especially over long periods of time), and on a variety of space operations. American astronaut Michael Foale, for instance, reported that the turnip seeds he planted in the space station's greenhouse seemed to be developing more slowly than they would on Earth, possibly due to a lack of gravity. Other research activities include testing new space technologies; Earth observa-

How safe is *Mir*?

Since February 1997 the eleven-year old Russian space station, which was originally designed to last five years, has been plagued by serious problems, including a flash fire, leaking antifreeze fumes, broken oxygen generators, and difficulties with the carbon dioxide removal system. The latest in *Mir*'s disasters, which NASA describes as "very serious," is a collision that took place on June 25 between an unmanned cargo ship and the space station. During a practice docking, the remote-controlled cargo vessel veered off course and crashed into Spektr, *Mir*'s laboratory module. A small gash was made in Spektr's thin aluminum hull, but *Mir* crew members—cosmonauts Vasily Tsibilyev and Alexander Lazutkin and U.S. astronaut Michael Foale—were quickly able to seal off the depressurizing module from the rest of the station before too much air escaped. (A fully depressurized *Mir* could fall out of orbit.)

Most of the science experiments aboard Spektr were destroyed by the collision when the module lost air pressure. In addition, Spektr's exterior solar arrays—panels connected to *Mir*'s batteries that supply the space station with nearly half of its power—were damaged. The men have since worked in darkness, much of their equipment turned off to save energy. Their life-support systems may become threatened if power is not restored soon. (*Mir* is equipped with an escape spacecraft, the "lifeboat" *Soyuz*.)

In Star City, the cosmonaut training center outside of Moscow, Russian and U.S. space experts have been trying to figure out ways for *Mir*'s crew members to repair the damaged solar arrays. The scientists have been working on an underwater model of the spacecraft in order to simulate the effects of weightlessness. The cosmonauts will be required to wear heavy spacesuits and enter the deadly vacuum inside Spektr to reconnect power cables, with *Mir*'s hatch sealed behind them. The main problem is the bulkiness of the space gloves the men must wear. The electrical connections are very close together, and will be difficult to work on through the gloves. But the repair was eventually simulated on Earth, and Russian and U.S. support teams are optimistic that the same process will succeed in space. (Spectr's gash, however, might take months to fix.)

Mir's crew has since been practicing emergency repair procedures. On July 5 Russia launched a spacecraft filled with repair equipment and fuel, scheduled to rendezvous with the space station. The fate of future Russian/U.S. space projects may well depend on the success of the restoration mission.

tion—studying its atmosphere, oceans, and land surface; and examinations of the universe's galaxies, quasars, and neutron stars using *Mir*'s special telescopes. The crew follows a simple, single-shift schedule and works five days a week.

U.S. astronauts aboard *Mir* are in constant contact with support teams of science and engineering specialists from Houston's Johnson Space Center who have traveled to the Russian Mission Control Center in Moscow. These experts monitor the progress of experiments, solve technical and equipment problems, and are available to answer questions the astronauts might have. They conduct ten-minute communication sessions with *Mir* throughout the day, and are also in frequent contact with Mission Control back in Houston. Participants see this support system as a model of what will be needed to run the International Space Station.

Norman Thagard was the first U.S. astronaut to stay aboard *Mir,* arriving on a Russian launch vehicle (this ride was also an American first) on March 14, 1995. Subsequent astronaut residents have traveled to the space station by way of the U.S. *Atlantis* space shuttle. These residents include Lucid, Blaha, Foale, and Jerry Linenger—Wendy Lawrence and David Wolf are scheduled for future stays. The final *Mir*/Shuttle rendezvous will take place in May of 1998. By that time construction of the International Space Station will be underway.

Sources

Gordon, Michael R. "Russia Launches a Cargo Craft to Save Mir Space Station." *The New York Times.* July 6, 1997: 12.

ISS Phase I-Space Station Mir. [Online] Available http://www.osf.hq.nasa.gov/mirold/Welcome.html, December 5, 1996.

"Luck Sent Astronaut to Space Station." *The New York Times.* July 6, 1997: 12.

National Geographic Society

Founded January 27, 1888

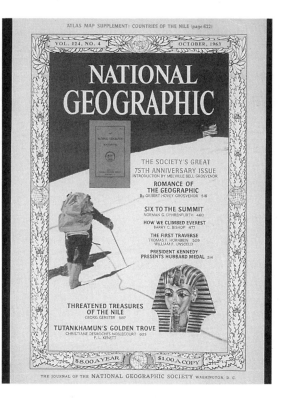

The National Geographic Society was established in 1888 "to increase and diffuse [spread] geographic knowledge." It has done this by sponsoring explorations and expeditions—beginning in 1890—that investigate the planet and its inhabitants. Awarding field scientists and other researchers grants that now total four million dollars a year, the society shares its findings with the rest of the world through the *National Geographic* magazine. Also founded in 1888, the magazine now has an international readership of many millions. Subscribers become society members, and a portion of their magazine fees supports the organization's scientific and educational projects.

The National Geographic Society is the largest nonprofit scientific and educational institution in the world.

The founding

The society was created by a diverse group of thirty-three men—geographers, explorers, teachers, lawyers, mapmakers, military officers, and businessmen—who had one thing in common: a passion for knowledge and a keen interest in discovery and human achievement. Over the course of two weeks in January 1888 they gathered in Washington, D.C., and talked about the purpose of the society, how it would be organized and run, and the qualifications of its members. On January 27 the National Geographic Society was officially founded, and headquartered in that city.

For its first president, the society chose Gardiner Greene Hubbard, a lawyer and businessman who had helped establish a school for the deaf (and promoted the experiments of his son-in-law, Alexander Graham Bell). Noting that he was neither "a scientific man, nor ... a geographer" in his first speech to the organization, Hubbard added, "By my election you notify the public that the membership of our Society will not be confined to professional geographers, but will include that large number who, like myself, desire to promote special researches by others, and to diffuse the knowledge so gained, among men, so that we may all know more of the world upon which we live."

The Committee for Research and Exploration

The National Geographic Society established a Committee for Research and Exploration to sponsor expeditions and field studies around the world. Geologist Israel C. Russell led the first society-sponsored expedition to Alaska in 1890. At that time, large parts of the globe were still unexplored. In 1909 the society backed the efforts of Robert Edwin Peary, as he led the first expedition to reach the North Pole. Other society-sponsored missions of exploration and human achievement included man's first flight over the South Pole by Richard Evelyn Byrd in 1929, and the first American expedition to reach the top of Mount Everest—the world's highest mountain, located in the Himalayas—in 1963.

As diving equipment and craft were developed in the twentieth century, the oceans became a new frontier for exploration. The National Geographic Society supported the pioneering work of oceanographer Jacques Cousteau as he explored the wonders of the sea and its unknown inhabitants. It also backed the deep-sea hunts of ocean scientist Robert Ballard, who found the sunken hull of the *Titanic* in 1985 on the ocean floor. The "unsinkable" luxury liner that went down in the North Atlantic in 1912 was remarkably preserved. The world got its first glimpse of the submerged *Titanic* from Ballard's deep-sea photographs, published in the *National Geographic* magazine.

The Committee for Research and Exploration has also sponsored scientific efforts to discover our prehistoric past and to better know the creatures with whom we share the planet. For decades the society supported the excavation work of scientists Louis and Mary Leakey in Tanzania's Olduvai Gorge, where they unearthed hundreds of prehistoric fossils, including the remains of early man. It has given long-term funding to primatologist Jane Goodall, who has studied the chimpanzees in Tanzania's Gombe National Park for more than thirty years. Hers has been the longest ongoing investigation of an animal species in the wild. The society also was behind the work of Dian Fossey, who studied and helped preserve the endangered mountain gorilla of Rwanda.

The National Geographic Society museum

The National Geographic Society museum—called Explorers Hall—is located near its headquarters in downtown Washington, D.C. Admission is free. There visitors can see Geographica, a permanent, hands-on exhibit about Earth and its geography. It allows participants to interact with a tornado, or to experience the dangers of Peary's trip to the North Pole. Visitors can also feel what it's like to fly 23,000 miles above Earth, through an interactive video program called Earth Station One presented in the museum's amphitheater. In addition, Explorers Hall offers temporary exhibits that investigate such subjects as dinosaurs, ancient civilizations, and wildlife, and lectures and live performances are given in its auditorium.

The society today

Today, the National Geographic Society has more ways than ever "to increase and diffuse geographic knowledge." Television specials allow viewers to observe scientific field work and discoveries firsthand. The organization offers books, maps, globes, and other geographic items for purchase. National Geographic members can participate in the society's educational travel tour programs. In fact, in 1984, the organization introduced the *National Geographic Traveler,* for readers who want to visit places profiled in the *National Geo-*

The National Geography Bee

The National Geographic Society sponsors a yearly Geography Bee. A school interested in participation registers with the society and receives materials to use in a school-level competition. The winner of that bee then takes a written test. Students with the top one hundred scores in their state (or territory) go on to the next level of competition.

State-level bees are held in the spring, and the winner from each state goes on to the national competition, held at National Geographic Society headquarters in Washington, D.C. The fifty-seven state and territory winners compete until ten finalists remain. Those students begin a new round of competition, this time for college scholarships. The third-place winner receives $10,000 scholarship, the second-place winner is granted a $15,000 scholarship, and the National Geography Bee victor wins a $25,000 scholarship.

In recent years the National Geographic Society has also sponsored a worldwide geography competition called the International Geography Olympiad. In 1995, for instance, teams of students who had won geography bees in their home countries of Australia, Canada, Russia, the United Kingdom, and the United States traveled to Epcot Center at Disney World in Florida to compete. The top three groups were awarded gold, silver, or bronze medals.

graphic magazine. Published six times a year, it contains practical trip-planning and travel advice.

When the magazine was first published in 1888, it was a scholarly scientific journal with no illustrations and a plain brown cover. It is now a colorful monthly filled with lively articles, stunning photographs, and supplemental maps. For the past twenty years the society has also offered a magazine of geographic discovery for young people called *National Geographic World.* The journal is part of the society's junior membership, which is open to youths ages eight to fourteen. Besides a subscription to *World,* junior members receive posters, trading cards, and activity booklets throughout the year, and can join the magazine's pen pal network. The magazine was recently honored with the publishing industry's Parents' Choice Gold Award, and has nearly one million readers.

Now in its second century, the National Geographic Society has expanded its focus to reflect today's world. It is active in conservation efforts to protect Earth's natural resources. The organization is also trying to improve young people's geographic knowledge.

Sources

NGS-The "Bee" Basics. [Online] Available http://www.nationalgeographic.com/society/ngo/geobee/basics.html, June 24, 1997.

NGS-Birth of the Society. [Online] Available http://www.nationalgeographic.com/ngs/hq/birth/, June 24, 1997.

NGS-Explorers Hall. [Online] Available http://www.nationalgeographic.com/ngs/hq/explorer/, June 24, 1997.

NGS-National Geographic Online. [Online] Available http://www.nationalgeographic.com/, April 1, 1997.

Nils Adolf Erik Nordenskjöld

Born November 18, 1832, Helsinki, Finland
Died August 12, 1901, Stockholm, Sweden

Swedish scientist Nils A. E. Nordenskjöld was the first person to travel between the Atlantic and Pacific Oceans by way of the Arctic Ocean north of Eurasia—a route known as the Northeast Passage.

Beginning in the sixteenth century, northern Europeans led expeditions to find new water routes to India and China, for existing routes to the Orient were controlled by the powerful maritime nations of Spain and Portugal. Most exploratory efforts were spent looking for a northwest passage, sailing between the Atlantic and Pacific Oceans over North America. However, English, Dutch, and Russian explorers did try to find a north*east* passage between the oceans, along the northern coast of Eurasia. While a number of them explored various parts of the passage (and some, like Dutchman Willem Barents, lost their lives in the process), no one traveled its full length until 1878–79, when Swedish scientist Nils A. E. Nordenskjöld made the year-long voyage in his converted whaling ship, the *Vega*. Russia would eventually develop the Northeast Passage into a busy commercial waterway known as the Northern Sea Route.

Nordenskjöld was born in Helsinki, Finland, on November 18, 1832, the son of Swedish parents. His father was a mineralogist with the mining administration there, and as a child Nils would accompany him on his field studies all over the country. He too became a mineralogist, graduating from the University of Helsingfors in Helsinki in 1853. Like his father, he joined Finland's mining administration, and the two of them traveled to the Ural Mountains in Russia, where they carried out scientific research. On his return Nils wrote a handbook about that country's minerals, which led to a teaching position at the Helsinki university.

During this time, Finland was a part of the Russian Empire. When Nordenskjöld spoke out against Russian rule he alarmed government authorities and lost both of his jobs. In 1858 he emigrated to Sweden, where he eventually became a citizen. He was offered a position at the Swedish National Museum of Natural History in Stockholm, heading its mineralogy department. He also became a professor at the University of Stockholm.

In 1858 Nordenskjöld joined an expedition led by Swedish geologist Otto Torell to the Spitsbergen island group (part of the Svalbard island group), which lies halfway between the north coast of Norway and the North Pole. There he collected many specimens that supplied information about the natural history of the area. In 1861 he and Torell made a second trip there, this time exploring the northern islands by dogsled, and drawing up the first scientific maps of the territory. In 1864 Nordenskjöld visited the islands again, his reputation as an Arctic explorer growing.

Polar expedition sets northern distance record

In 1868 Nordenskjöld led a polar expedition sponsored by the Swedish Academy of Science. Traveling on the naval iron steamer *Sofia,* the scientist's mission was to get as close to the North Pole as possible. The expedition headed north from Spitsbergen, and on September 18 reached the highest latitude ever by a ship in the eastern hemisphere: 81°42'.

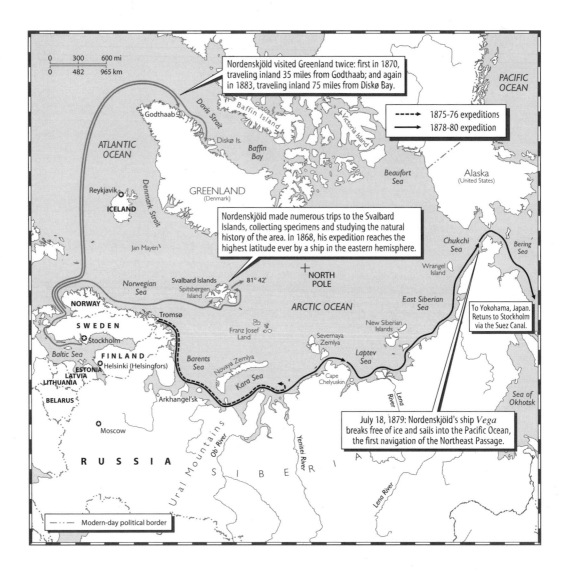

Nordenskjöld visited Greenland twice: first in 1870, traveling inland 35 miles from Godthaab; and again in 1883, traveling inland 75 miles from Diskø Bay.

Nordenskjöld made numerous trips to the Svalbard Islands, collecting specimens and studying the natural history of the area. In 1868, his expedition reaches the highest latitude ever by a ship in the eastern hemisphere.

To Yokohama, Japan. Retuns to Stockholm via the Suez Canal.

July 18, 1879: Nordenskjöld's ship *Vega* breaks free of ice and sails into the Pacific Ocean, the first navigation of the Northeast Passage.

- - - - → 1875-76 expeditions
———→ 1878-80 expedition

— · — · — Modern-day political border

First scientist to explore Greenland

In 1870 Nordenskjöld traveled to western Greenland, hoping to cross the ice cap that covers much of the island. No one had yet explored Greenland's interior, and information about the ice cap was important to understanding world weather and the history of glaciation (glaciers). Setting out by dogsled from the town of Godthaab with a fellow Swedish scientist and two Inuit (Eskimos), Nordenskjöld traveled thirty-five miles inland, to an altitude of twenty-two hundred feet, before being forced back. Yet the mineralogist would return for more explorations in the following decade.

Nordenskjöld returned to Spitsbergen in 1872, leading a second Swedish polar expedition. He planned to travel by sledge (heavy sled) over the frozen Arctic Ocean to the North Pole. But the ice proved too choppy to move over easily, and a storm that scattered the reindeer he used as pack animals further threatened his mission. When his ship became frozen in its port over the winter—leaving him short of supplies—he knew he had to abandon his attempt to reach the Pole. Waiting for the spring thaw, he spent his time exploring Nordaustlandet, Spitsbergen's northernmost island.

Prepares to sail Northeast Passage

After the ordeal of his second polar trip, Nordenskjöld decided to redirect his exploratory efforts to opening the Northeast Passage. He studied why other expeditions had .failed and came to the conclusion that earlier explorers had sailed too far from the mainland, mistakenly acting on the popular belief that there was an expanse of open, ice-free sea around the North Pole. Nordenskjöld thought it was better to sail close to the coast, for during the summer Russia's Ob, Yenisei, and Lena Rivers probably warmed the northern coastal waters just enough to clear a narrow passage. In 1875 and 1876 Nordenskjöld made two preparatory trips to test his theory, sailing as far as the mouth of the Yenisei River.

The success of these trips helped Nordenskjöld gain the backing of King Oscar II of Norway and Sweden for his final Northeast Passage expedition. Other supporters were wealthy Scandinavian and Russian businessmen, who looked forward to the opening of new markets for their goods. On July 21, 1878, Nordenskjöld set sail from the Norwegian Arctic port of Tromsö on a steam- and sail-driven ship, the three hundred-ton *Vega*. Aboard were four officers, four scientists, and twenty sailors. For the first part of the voyage, three Russian merchant ships that belonged to one of the expedition's backers sailed with Nordenskjöld, stopping to trade at ports along the way.

Weather conditions were good and the *Vega* reached Cape Chelyuskin without difficulty on August 19, 1878. It was the northernmost point of mainland Asia, and no ship had ever passed it before. The expedition continued on to the mouth of the great Lena River, where the last of the merchant ships landed. There Nordenskjöld tried to turn north to explore the New Siberian Islands, but heavy ice forced him back. As the summer passed and the ship moved eastward, the ice became thicker. On September 28 the *Vega* passed North Cape, the westernmost point that Captain James Cook had reached in his search for the Northeast Passage in 1779, approaching from the Pacific Ocean. There Nordenskjöld and his shipmates were stopped by frozen seas, only 120 miles from Bering Strait, which separates Siberia from Alaska.

An Arctic winter with the Chukchi

The *Vega* expedition spent the Arctic winter trapped in the ice. Nordenskjöld used the time to conduct plant, animal, and other scientific studies. He and his crew members also came to know the native people of northeastern Siberia, the Chukchi, very well. In his book about the expedition, Nordenskjöld told about a breakfast served in a Chukchi household: "first seals' flesh and fat, with a sort of sauerkraut of fermented willow-leaves, then seals' liver, and finally seals' blood—all frozen."

Expedition completes historic journey

The *Vega* was able to break free of ice on July 18, 1879, and within two short days was sailing into the Pacific Ocean. The expedition headed for Yokohama, Japan, where on September 2 Nordenskjöld telegraphed news of his epic achievement back to Sweden. After three centuries of failed attempts, the first navigation of the Northeast Passage had been made. No lives had been lost in the process.

Nordenskjöld and his crew celebrated with a victory cruise around the Eurasian landmass, adding this first-ever circumnavigation to their accomplishments. They sailed from

Japan through the Suez Canal in northeast Africa, arriving to a hero's welcome in Stockholm harbor on April 24, 1880. That date is now a national holiday in Sweden—Vega Day.

Made a baron for his achievement, Nordenskjöld spent the next three years writing about his historic journey. His *Voyage of the Vega Round Asia and Europe,* published in 1881, became a bestseller. He also wrote a five-volume work on the expedition's scientific findings.

Nordenskjöld returned to Greenland in 1883, in what would be his tenth—and last—Arctic expedition. He was convinced that far into the island's interior, beyond the ice cap, lay green pastureland. He and his party scaled the ice cover at Disko Bay, reaching an altitude of five thousand feet. Traveling about seventy-five miles inland, they saw nothing but ice. This led the scientist to rethink his ideas, concluding that all of Greenland was ice-covered. Nordenskjöld later shared this theory with a young Norwegian explorer, Fridtjof Nansen, who successfully crossed the world's largest island on skis in 1888.

With his years of exploring behind him, Nordenskjöld devoted himself to scholarship. He published important works on geology and mineralogy, and on the history of mapmaking and exploration. He died on August 12, 1901, in Stockholm, Sweden.

Sources

Baker, Daniel B., ed. *Explorers and Discoverers of the World.* Detroit: Gale Research, 1993.

Bohlander, Richard E., ed. *World Explorers and Discoverers.* New York: Macmillan, 1992.

Maxtone-Graham, John. *Safe Return Doubtful: The Heroic Age of Polar Exploration.* New York: Scribner, 1988.

Waldman, Carl, and Alan Wexler. *Who Was Who in World Exploration.* New York: Facts on File, 1992.

Ida Pfeiffer

Born October 14, 1797, Vienna, Austria
Died October 27 or 28, 1858, Vienna, Austria

Austrian Ida Pfeiffer was one of the first women to travel around the world alone, which she did twice during the mid-nineteenth century.

Ida Reyer was the only girl in a family of six children. Her father was a wealthy Viennese merchant who allowed his daughter to dress like a boy and to be taught alongside her brothers. Although Ida's father died when she was nine and her mother tried to correct her "unladylike" upbringing, it was already too late. The girl was strong-willed, fearless, and independent. These characteristics would serve her well on the extraordinary world travels she would undertake later in her life.

At seventeen Ida fell in love with her piano teacher (an instrument she hated to play) but the match was considered beneath her social station. So she consented to an arranged marriage with Dr. Mark Anton Pfeiffer, a distinguished lawyer from Lemberg who was much older than she. After her husband exposed dishonest government officials, he lost his practice and had difficulty finding other employment. The couple's luxurious lifestyle disappeared, and Ida was forced to give drawing and music lessons to help feed their two young sons. When her mother died in 1831 and left her a small in-

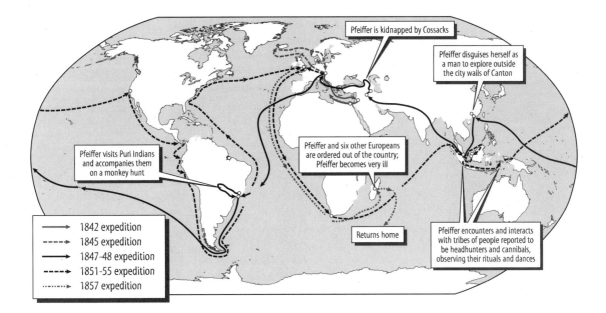

Pfeiffer is kidnapped by Cossacks

Pfeiffer disguises herself as a man to explore outside the city walls of Canton

Pfeiffer visits Puri Indians and accompanies them on a monkey hunt

Pfeiffer and six other Europeans are ordered out of the country; Pfeiffer becomes very ill

Returns home

Pfeiffer encounters and interacts with tribes of people reported to be headhunters and cannibals, observing their rituals and dances

1842 expedition
1845 expedition
1847-48 expedition
1851-55 expedition
1857 expedition

heritance, Ida separated from her husband and returned to Vienna, where she lived comfortably and raised their children.

Begins exotic travels

When Ida was forty-five and her sons were living on their own, her thoughts turned to travel. She decided to visit Jerusalem—alone. The journey stretched over the course of nine months, as she viewed Egypt and crossed the Arabian Desert from Cairo to the Isthmus of Suez. She kept a diary of her trip and published it on her return in 1843. It became quite popular and went through several printings. With the money it earned she financed a trip to Iceland and Scandinavia in 1845. A published account of her journey there, along with the sale of rock and plant samples she had gathered, allowed her to plan an even grander undertaking—a voyage around the world.

Pfeiffer sailed for South America. She landed in Brazil, traveling inland from Rio de Janeiro to Petropolis. While she found little to admire in the country's city life, she was very interested in visiting its unseen places and little-known peoples. She and a guide trekked into the lush forests, and Pfeiffer became enchanted by the ferns, flowers, vines, and tropical birds there. Searching for Indians, she came upon the Puri tribe, and stayed with them, sleeping on the ground in their open huts. She accompanied them on a monkey hunt and afterwards ate a special meal of roast monkey, roots, and corn.

From Brazil, Pfeiffer sailed around South America's Cape Horn to Tahiti. She then visited Hong Kong before boarding a Chinese junk (ship) on its way to Canton. Europeans were not welcome in China, but the curiosity-driven traveler insisted on walking about the city. She was fascinated by Chinese habits and customs: in her diary she wrote about the cruel punishments criminals faced, the foot binding of young girls, and the awful poverty of the boat dwellers.

Hunts tigers and crosses desert

During the next months, Pfeiffer traveled throughout India. She went on a tiger hunt there, and often wandered alone, collecting plants and insects. All the while she depended on the kindness of those she met for her food and shelter. She wrote: "What they can live on, I can, and if I do not like their food, it must be because I am not really hungry." From India she went to Persia, traveling up the Tigris River to Baghdad. There she joined a desert caravan to Mosul (in what is now Iraq); then she traveled to Tabriz, Kurdistan (now northern Iran). When she showed up on the doorstep of the Tabriz British consul, he was amazed that she had made the journey alone, with no knowledge of the country or the language of its people.

Pfeiffer crossed the Caucasus Mountains into Russia, a bit travel-worn and eager to be in an orderly Christian country ruled by a European king. To her dismay, as she walked near her caravan, armed cossacks (Russian soldiers on horseback) kidnapped her and held her overnight until she produced her passport. The traveler remarked that she had been more kindly treated by savages. She headed for home by way of Turkey, Greece, and Italy. She arrived in Vienna on November 4, 1848, after traveling twenty-eight hundred miles by land and thirty-five thousand miles by sea. The journey had taken nineteen months.

Upon her return, Pfeiffer published her diaries in *A Lady's Voyage Round the World*. The book made her quite famous and she was offered free passage on many ships and entertained by Europeans everywhere. In 1851 Pfeiffer went to England, hoping to catch a ship to Australia. Despite a grant from the Austrian government, she found she could not pay the fare, and so accepted the offer of free travel on a ship headed for the Dutch East Indies (now Indonesia). Sailing around southern Africa's Cape of Good Hope, she spent four weeks in Cape Town, hoping to visit the continent's interior. But lack of money stopped her again. So on she traveled to Singapore, and then to Sarawak, on the northern coast of the island of Borneo.

Visits with headhunters and cannibals

She remained in Borneo for six months. There she visited the Dyaks, a tribe known to be headhunters. She walked miles of difficult jungle paths to reach them and viewed the heads of their slain enemies, some three dozen hung in a row with their eye sockets filled with white shells. In her diary, Pfeiffer wrote that she did not find these people and their practices any more savage than Europeans, whose own history was filled with bloody and violent deeds—uncommon thinking for a Westerner at that time. In fact, she found the Dyaks "honest, good-natured, and modest."

Pfeiffer floated down the Kapuas River to the Dutch colonial port of Pontianak. Then she went to Sumatra, intent on visiting the Batak people, although she was strongly warned against it. They were cannibals, and as she started into their territory she left her diary behind on the awful chance that she would not come back. She traveled from one Batak district to another, observing tribal rituals and dances. Once she found herself surrounded by men who made it clear that they planned to kill and eat her. She recited a little speech in their language that she had prepared for just such an emergency, stating that she was too old and tough to make for good eating. The tribesmen laughed and let her go.

From Sumatra Pfeiffer traveled to remote eastern Indonesia where she visited the Alfora tribe on the island of

Ceram. Although they were reported to be wild headhunters, the Alforas turned out be very shy. On July 6, 1852, she left the East Indies on a sailing ship headed for San Francisco, California. There she hoped to visit with American Indians in the West, but was disappointed at how "civilized" they had become. Pfeiffer was then off to South America, with stops in Panama, Ecuador, and Peru. She visited the east coast of the United States before returning to London on June 14, 1855, her second world trip completed. It had spanned more than four years. She published her adventures in *A Lady's Second Journey Round the World*.

Two years later Pfeiffer started out on a third worldwide trip. She stopped at the island of Madagascar, off Africa's southeast coast, and traveled to its capital of Antanarivo. While there she was mistakenly accused of involvement in a plot to overthrow the island's cruel Queen Ranavola. She and six other Europeans were ordered out of the country, and were led to the harbor by armed guards. It took nearly fifty days of rough travel to reach the coast. The prisoners were treated very badly, and Pfeiffer came down with a fever for which she received no medical help. By the time they sailed away she was very sick. After a stop at the nearby British island of Mauritius to recover, Pfeiffer made her way home. She still planned to see more of the world, but the liver disease she contracted in Madagascar continued to weaken her. She died in Vienna during the night of October 27–28, 1858.

Sources

Baker, Daniel B., ed. *Explorers and Discoverers of the World.* Detroit: Gale Research, 1993.

Tinling, Marion. *Women Into the Unknown: A Sourcebook on Women Explorers and Travelers.* Westport, CT: Greenwood Press, 1989.

Vasily Danilovich Poyarkov

Died in 1668

Vasily Danilovich Poyarkov was born in the Russian town of Kashin, north of Moscow. His parents were serfs, members of Russia's servant class. Poyarkov become a cossack, a soldier who served the czar (Russian emperor) in territories on the Russian frontier. He traveled to eastern Siberia, and in 1638 was a member of a team that helped build a fort on the Lena River, a place that would later become the large city of Yakutsk, a center of Russian activity in the Far East.

Expedition searches for valley of riches

In 1643 the fort commander chose Poyarkov to lead an expedition to find the Shilka, or "Black Dragon," a river thought to extend south into China, through a valley rich with precious metals. Poyarkov and a military party of 133 men set out from Yakutsk, traveling south along the Lena River, which flows into the Arctic Ocean. They followed several tributaries (branches) of the great river—the Aldan, the Uchur, and the

Russian cossack Vasily Danilovich Poyarkov was the first European known to descend the Amur River, traveling across far eastern Russia to the Sea of Okhotsk and the Pacific Ocean.

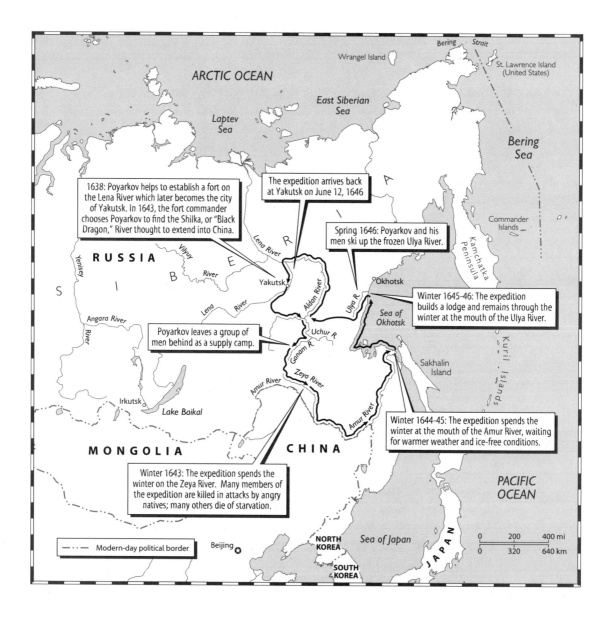

1638: Poyarkov helps to establish a fort on the Lena River which later becomes the city of Yakutsk. In 1643, the fort commander chooses Poyarkov to find the Shilka, or "Black Dragon," River thought to extend into China.

The expedition arrives back at Yakutsk on June 12, 1646

Spring 1646: Poyarkov and his men ski up the frozen Ulya River.

Winter 1645-46: The expedition builds a lodge and remains through the winter at the mouth of the Ulya River.

Poyarkov leaves a group of men behind as a supply camp.

Winter 1644-45: The expedition spends the winter at the mouth of the Amur River, waiting for warmer weather and ice-free conditions.

Winter 1643: The expedition spends the winter on the Zeya River. Many members of the expedition are killed in attacks by angry natives; many others die of starvation.

- - - Modern-day political border

Gonam—whose ice-cold waters and many rapids made progress difficult. At the Gonam River Poyarkov left a group of his men in a supply camp, continuing with the rest of the expedition southward over the mountains. Late in the year he came upon the Zeya River, an unknown tributary of the Amur River, which flows east to the Pacific Ocean (and which now marks the boundary between China and southern Siberia). They made camp on the Zeya, spending the winter there.

Warfare, starvation, and cannibalism

Running low on supplies, Poyarkov sent some of his men on a scouting mission. They came upon the Daurians, native people of the Amur River valley. The Daurians told the Russians that their land was not rich with precious metals and that the metal tools they did have were obtained in trade with the Chinese. Nevertheless, Poyarkov demanded a great deal of tribute money and supplies from the natives, who soon grew to hate the harsh foreign visitors. They attacked the Russians, killing many of them. The expedition's survivors barely lived through the winter in their Zeya camp, with forty men dying of starvation. It was said that the rest survived only because they turned to cannibalism.

Explorers reach Pacific Ocean

In the spring of 1644 the party of men Poyarkov had left on the Gonam River arrived with supplies, and the expedition was able to continue. The cossack commander and his group resumed their journey down the Zeya, eventually connecting with the Amur. They traveled eastward on the great river, frequently treating the peoples they met along the way cruelly. Understandably, the natives received them with hostility. Regardless, the expedition managed to reach the Amur's mouth on the Sea of Okhotsk, an inlet of the Pacific Ocean. There they spent the winter of 1644–45, waiting for warmer weather and ice-free waters in which to continue their travels.

Knowing that he and his men were too weak and undersupplied to fight their way back up the Amur on their return home, Poyarkov decided to sail north along the coast of the Asian mainland. The party set off again in the summer of 1645. Passing Sakhalin Island, the travelers followed the shore of the Sea of Okhotsk until they reached the mouth of the Ulya River, a waterway they knew about from an earlier expedition led by explorer Ivan Moskvitin. In 1639 Moskvitin had built a winter lodge there, the first Russian settlement on the Pacific coast. Poyarkov and his expedition decided to do the same, and set up camp at the mouth of the Ulya to wait out the winter of 1645–46. In the early spring the cossack and his men headed up the frozen Ulya on skis until they once again came upon the Aldan River. They followed it to the Lena River, which eventually led them home. The expedition arrived in Yakutsk on June 12, 1646. Poyarkov returned to Moscow two years later.

In a detailed report of his three-year expedition, Poyarkov described the territories he had visited, their inhabitants, and their geographical features. His journey had taken him across a large expanse of southeastern Siberia. He called for a major Russian effort to take over the Amur valley. This led to the launching of several Russian expeditions over the next several years. The information Poyarkov gathered was an early step in the expansion of Russian rule into the Pacific region, which took place on a large scale in the eighteenth and early nineteenth centuries.

Sources

Amur and Okhotsk Territories. [Online] Available http:// vladivostok. com/rus_mag/eng/N_1/AMUR.HTM, July 19, 1997.

Baker, Daniel B., ed. *Explorers and Discoverers of the World.* Detroit: Gale Research, 1993.

Waldman, Carl and Alan Wexler. *Who Was Who in World Exploration.* New York: Facts on File, 1992.

Heinrich Schliemann

Born January 6, 1822, Neubukow, Mecklenburg-
Schwerin, Germany
Died December 26, 1890, Naples, Italy

Since the Middle Ages, historians, mapmakers, and travelers have tried to find the actual sites where the events of Homer's epic poem the *Iliad* took place. Was the ancient Greek poet's account of the final years of the Trojan War based on fact, or merely a myth? Did the ancient city of Troy really exist? Listening spellbound to these stories as a boy, Heinrich Schliemann was certain that the tales were true, and determined that someday he would be the one to rediscover the city.

The son of a pastor, Schliemann had to leave school early to help with the family finances. He was apprenticed to a grocer when he was fourteen, and a short time later became an office boy for a firm located in Amsterdam, the Netherlands. All the while he studied about the ancient Greeks and even learned their language. He learned to read and write other languages as well, nearly a dozen in all. In 1844 he became a bookkeeper for a company in Amsterdam that sent him to St. Petersburg, Russia. There he started his own business, importing indigo (a

Heinrich Schliemann was a German businessman and amateur archaeologist who discovered the ruins of ancient Troy and Mycenae.

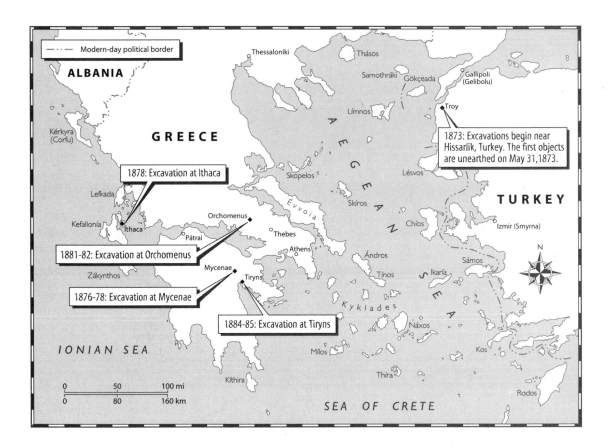

Modern-day political border

ALBANIA

GREECE

Kérkyra
(Corfu)

Lefkada

Kefallonía

Ithaca

1878: Excavation at Ithaca

Pátrai

Zákynthos

Orchomenus

Thebes

Athens

Mycenae

Tiryns

1881-82: Excavation at Orchomenus

1876-78: Excavation at Mycenae

1884-85: Excavation at Tiryns

IONIAN SEA

Thessaloníki

Thásos

Samothráki

Gökçeada

Límnos

Skópelos

Evvoia

Skíros

A E G E A N   S E A

Chíos

Ándros

Tínos

Ikaría

Sámos

Kyklades

Náxos

Mílos

Thíra

Kíthira

Gallipoli
(Gelibolu)

Troy

1873: Excavations begin near Hissarlik, Turkey. The first objects are unearthed on May 31, 1873.

Lésvos

TURKEY

Izmir (Smyrna)

N

Kos

Rodos

| 0 | 50 | 100 mi |
| 0 | 80 | 160 km |

SEA   OF   CRETE

plant used for dye) and tea. During the Crimean War—the conflict between Russia and France, England, and Turkey—he made his fortune as a military supplier. He made a second fortune as a banker while in California during the gold rush. Because he was living in the territory when it became a state in 1850, he was given American citizenship.

Unearths ancient treasures

Retiring from business at the age of forty-one, Schliemann studied and traveled for some time before taking up his childhood dream: that of finding Troy and other ancient Greek sites. At his own expense he began excavation of a desolate region near the village of Hissarlik, near Turkey's western coast, in 1873. At daybreak on May 31 the self-taught archaeologist unearthed the first object in an incredible collection of treasures, one of the richest archaeological finds ever made. It consisted of nearly nine thousand objects, including thousands of pieces of jewelry, such as diadems (royal headbands) of woven and hammered gold, rings, bracelets, earrings, necklaces, buttons, belts, and pins. Also among the collection were human figurines, bowls and vessels for perfumed oils, and copper weapons. Schliemann called his find "Priam's Treasure" after the *Iliad*'s Trojan king, certain he had uncovered the royal palace. The world was stunned by the magnificence of the objects the amateur archaeologist had found and grateful for the proof, at last, that Homer's epic poem was based on historical fact.

The science of archaeology was still in its early stages during Schliemann's time, with methods of digging, taking field notes, and dating finds not firmly established. Scholars later dated the objects he unearthed to a thousand years before the time of Homer's Troy. (There had actually been nine cities at various times on the site.) They also criticized Schliemann's crude methods of excavation, which actually destroyed layers representing the Homeric period as he dug beneath them. They questioned Schliemann's dramatic accounts of the discovery as well. For instance, he wrote that his wife Sophia had secretly whisked away the earliest treasures in her shawl to protect them from the untrustworthy hired help; later he admitted that she had not been there. Worse still, there were repeated rumors that the fame-seeking amateur archaeologist had added objects found elsewhere or purchased from the Turkish black market to the excavation site—all in an effort to prove his beliefs about Homer's writings and to further his own reputation.

Rules about ownership of archaeological finds were not well-defined during Schliemann's time—and later scholars agreed that he certainly took advantage of them. To start, the amateur archaeologist did not have the permission of the Ottoman (now Turkish) government when he began his original excavation. When he later agreed to split his findings with the Turks, he smuggled many of the objects out of the country. Turkey sued for the return of the treasures but received only a small amount of money representing its share. Schliemann tried to sell his finds in Europe, but with their ownership in

Homer and the Trojan War

Homer was an ancient Greek poet believed to have lived somewhere between 1200 and 850 B.C. He is thought to have written the epic works the *Iliad* and the *Odyssey,* which recount the Trojan War and the wanderings of Odysseus (Ulysses), a leader of Greek forces during that war.

The Trojan War was a conflict between the Greeks and the people of Troy. According to Greek mythology, the war began when Trojan prince Paris kidnapped Helen, the beautiful wife of Menelaus of the Greek city-state of Sparta. The Greeks gathered together and attacked Troy's surrounding cities and countryside. The city itself was well fortified, however, and the only way the Greeks were able to get inside was through trickery. They built a large hollow wooden horse in which to hide a small group of warriors. Despite warnings, the Trojans took the fascinating horse within their city walls, and at night the soldiers crept out and opened the city gates. Troy was destroyed. It is thought that the Trojan War might reflect a real war that took place around 1200 B.C. over the control of trade between the invading Greeks and the people of Troas (the territory surrounding the ancient city of Troy).

question, major museums turned him down. So in the early 1880s he donated Priam's Treasure to Germany, which gratefully accepted the dazzling collection. But questions of legal ownership continued to plague the archaeological treasures.

Other important discoveries

Despite Schliemann's personal flaws and careless science, there is no denying the importance of the objects he unearthed, which painted a picture of ancient Greek life that had only been imagined. The archaeologist made other important excavations over the next decade. From 1876 to 1878 he unearthed the ancient Greek trade and cultural center of Mycenae (legendary home of Agamemnon, leader of the Greeks in the Trojan War) and its royal tombs; in 1878 he found the remains of Ithaca, the reported home of Homer's Odysseus; from 1881 to 1882 he excavated Orchomenus, location of the ancient Boeotian city of Thebes; and from 1884 to 1885 he dug at the site of Tiryns, an ancient Mycenaen city of great splendor and palaces. Schliemann wrote several books colorfully describing his expeditions and finds, as well as an autobiography that was published in 1892. Between excavations he lived in a mansion in Athens with his second wife, Sophia Engastromenos, with whom he had two children. He died on December 26, 1890, in Naples, Italy.

Some fifty years later, at the start of World War II, the thousands of ancient objects that comprised Priam's Treasure were removed from the Berlin museum in which they had been exhibited. German chancellor and Führer (leader) Adolf Hitler had ordered that all museum collections be put into underground storage to protect them from bombs. When the Soviet Army entered Berlin in May of 1945 the treasure vanished altogether, and it was generally assumed that Russian soldiers had melted down the priceless artifacts and sold them.

Nations vie for priceless objects

But in the early 1990s the treasures of Priam were found. Officials at Moscow's Pushkin Museum, after years of denial, admitted with embarrassment that they had held the objects since the end of the war, when they were flown to Moscow. Researchers from England, Greece, Turkey, Germany, and the United States helped the Russians identify and catalog the artifacts. In 1996 an exhibition of 259 of the most stunning of the objects opened at the Pushkin, and the public was again able to journey into the remarkable ancient world that Schliemann's excavations had opened to them.

Still, not everyone was happy with the treasure's reappearance. The German government wanted it back, along with other artwork the Soviets had taken near the end of the war. And Turkey insisted, as it had all along, that Schliemann had illegally obtained the artifacts. The Turks claimed ownership of Priam's Treasure, hoping one day to retrieve it and place it in a museum at the site of Homer's Troy.

Sources

James, Jamie. "Treasures of Troy." *Opera News*. December 25, 1993: 17.

Lemonick, Michael D. "Troy's Lost Treasure." *Time*. April 22, 1996: 78.

Plagens, Peter. "The Golden Hoard; a Soviet Secret for Fifty Years, Ancient Trojan Treasure Goes Public in Moscow." *Newsweek*. April 8, 1996: 72.

Steiner, George. "Letter from Lyons." *Opera News*. August 1995: 38.

May French Sheldon

Born May 10, 1847, Beaver, Pennsylvania
Died February 10, 1936, London, England

An American who lived much of her life in England, May French Sheldon was one of the first women to explore East Africa, leading an expedition there in 1891.

During the mid-nineteenth century, Britain and Germany were laying plans to colonize the Mombasa region of East Africa (an area that is now Kenya and Tanzania). They hoped to set up plantations there, populated by white settlers. But in order to do so, they had to make native inhabitants give up their lands, a goal they achieved by harsh military expeditions and shows of force. May French Sheldon, a wealthy publisher interested in Africa, was convinced that such cruel methods by colonizers were not necessary. In 1891 she led an expedition into the area, hoping to prove that African tribes would accept white people who treated them with kindness and respect. She visited nearly three dozen different tribes, most of whom received her warmly. She, in turn, was one of the first Westerners to report on their lives and culture in a sympathetic and understanding way.

May (christened "Mary") French was born near Pittsburgh, Pennsylvania, on May 10, 1847. Her father was an engineer and her mother was a physician. While living much of

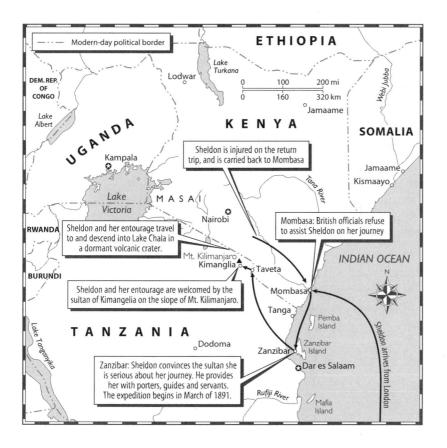

Map labels:
- Modern-day political border
- ETHIOPIA
- Lake Turkana
- Lodwar
- DEM. REP. OF CONGO
- Lake Albert
- UGANDA
- Kampala
- KENYA
- SOMALIA
- Jamaame
- Webi Jubba
- Lake Victoria
- MASAI
- Nairobi
- Tana River
- Jamaame
- Kismaayo
- RWANDA
- Sheldon is injured on the return trip, and is carried back to Mombasa
- Sheldon and her entourage travel to and descend into Lake Chala in a dormant volcanic crater.
- Mombasa: British officials refuse to assist Sheldon on her journey
- INDIAN OCEAN
- BURUNDI
- Mt. Kilimanjaro
- Kimanglia
- Taveta
- Sheldon and her entourage are welcomed by the sultan of Kimangelia on the slope of Mt. Kilimanjaro.
- Mombasa
- Tanga
- Lake Tanganyika
- TANZANIA
- Dodoma
- Zanzibar
- Pemba Island
- Zanzibar Island
- Sheldon arrives from London
- Zanzibar: Sheldon convinces the sultan she is serious about her journey. He provides her with porters, guides and servants. The expedition begins in March of 1891.
- Dar es Salaam
- Rufiji River
- Mafia Island

her young life in the United States, she was educated for a time in Europe and used family money to found a publishing house in London. In 1876 she married Eli Lemon Sheldon, an American banker and fellow publisher who was also based in that city. Among their friends was the explorer Henry Morton Stanley, whose adventures in Africa inspired May to plan an expedition there herself. Nearly everyone tried to discourage her, insisting that the African jungles were no place for a woman traveler.

Overcomes expedition's rocky start

When Sheldon arrived at the port of Mombasa, British authorities there refused to help her in any way, denying her porters to carry her provisions. So she went offshore to the island of Zanzibar, and convinced its sultan (ruler) that she was serious about her journey. He gathered more than one hundred Zanzibari porters, guides, and personal servants for her trip—for everything would have to be carried over narrow jungle trails—and she returned to the mainland. The sultan also gave her an official letter telling all she met to give her safe passage.

Sheldon brought an extraordinary amount of provisions on the journey. Besides the camping equipment, weapons, tools, and medical supplies they would need, the expedition required goods for bartering (trading) and gift-giving. Such presents would increase their welcome wherever they went. Sheldon brought toys for children—paints, tops, balls, kites, dolls, picture books, and fireworks. Among her supplies of gifts were several thousand finger rings, with her name engraved on each one. Also included in her provisions was a silk court dress studded with jewels, which she intended to wear when she met the chief of each new tribe. It was her way of showing respect to these African leaders, "as a woman of breeding should meet the highest officials in any land," she once said.

The expedition set off in March of 1891 and traveled inland to the town of Taveta (now on the Kenya-Tanzania border). While a litter (a covered and curtained couch carried on the shoulders of men by poles) was available for Sheldon to ride in, she usually walked with her caravan, leading the way. She was a good shot and, as a physician's daughter, a skillful healer. After a time, the men and women in her expedition became devoted to her, and gave her the Swahili name Bebe Bwana, which means "Lady Boss." During the trip she survived a thorn injury to her eye and the discovery of a fifteen-foot python in her bed. Yet true to her station as a well-bred lady of wealth, she enjoyed certain luxuries on the trail, including daily hot baths and massages.

Reaches Africa's highest mountain

Sheldon was thrilled when her caravan made it to majestic Mount Kilimanjaro, Africa's highest mountain. She visited the village of Kimangelia, 4,700 feet up the mountain slope. Kimangelia's sultan welcomed her graciously, and inhabitants from other mountain villages came to see the white lady and to invite her to their homes. Sheldon also traveled to Lake Chala, a nearly round body of water located in the crater of an old volcano. It had rarely been visited because of the difficulty of descent. Yet a determined Sheldon—along with a few reluctant members of her party—climbed down to the water by hanging onto branches and vines. Once there, she constructed a makeshift boat and explored the lake, jubilantly flying an American flag and putting up markers with her name on them along the shore.

Sheldon came upon thirty-five different tribes as she traveled inland, some of whom had never seen a white woman before. She found most of them happy and friendly. A few allowed her to witness their ceremonies, rituals never before seen by a Westerner. Interested in their food, clothing, customs, and religion, she collected artifacts along the way. Once, she cut points out of an orange skin and placed them in her mouth for a toothy grin. This so amused her hosts that the tribal chief pulled out one his own teeth and gave it to her, motioning in sign language that if she wore it around her neck she would never go hungry. She discovered that she had little trouble communicating with the natives, using gestures and the Swahili she had learned. Even tribes reported to be ferocious, like the Rombos, turned out to be quite pleasant. Next, Sheldon was intent on visiting the Masai tribe—Africa's most terrifying warriors.

Earlier in the journey, Sheldon had met up with a small group of Masai traders. One of the painted warriors had leapt before her, yelling and threatening her with his huge spear, which he eventually stuck in the ground at her feet. Sheldon had responded by yelling back and shooting her gun into the air, which drove the warrior away. She kept the spear as a souvenir. The frightening encounter made her question her desire to visit the Masai tribe, and the fearful reluctance of her guides and porters—of whom she had grown so fond—finally changed her mind.

Journey brings widespread fame

On her return trip to the coast, Sheldon was seriously injured when the porters carrying her palanquin—the special litter on which she occasionally rode—slipped and dropped it twenty feet off a rickety bridge. She was carried back to Mombasa and boarded a ship home, where she was able to recover. Her African journey had taken nearly ten months. She wrote about her experiences in *Sultan to Sultan,* which also included photographs she had taken. Published in 1892, the book made Sheldon famous. She was in demand as a speaker, lecturing at home and abroad. She was honored by Britain's Royal Geographical Society, which made her one of its first female fellows.

Sheldon traveled twice more to the African continent. In 1903 she toured the Belgian Congo (later Zaire and now the Democratic Republic of Congo), and in 1905 she visited the independent nation of Liberia. She worked as a fundraiser for the Red Cross during World War I. Afterward, she continued to travel and lecture until she was well into her seventies. She died at her home in London on February 10, 1936.

Sources

Baker, Daniel B., ed. *Explorers and Discoverers of the World.* Detroit: Gale Research, 1993.

Bohlander, Richard E., ed. *World Explorers and Discoverers.* New York: Macmillan, 1992.

Tinling, Marion. *Women Into the Unknown: A Sourcebook on Women Explorers and Travelers.* Westport, CT: Greenwood Press, 1989.

Vilhjalmur Stefansson

Born November 3, 1879, Arnes, Manitoba, Canada
Died August 26, 1962, Hanover, New Hampshire

C anadian anthropologist Vilhjalmur Stefansson was not the usual Arctic explorer. He loved the polar environment and studied Inuit (Eskimo) ways so that he could live harmoniously with the land. He advised that other explorers to the region do the same, instead of bringing in supplies in an attempt to make the Arctic more like the places from which they'd come. Stefansson felt sure that the polar region was not just a wasteland, but harbored great economic potential. His ideas would eventually prove true, with the discoveries of mineral wealth, natural gas, and oil there later in the twentieth century.

Stefansson was born in Arnes, Manitoba, on November 3, 1879, the son of Icelandic emigrants. When he was two they moved to the United States, settling in North Dakota. He attended the University of North Dakota for two years before being expelled for nonattendance and troublemaking. He completed his studies at the University of Iowa, graduating in 1903.

Vilhjalmur Stefansson was a Canadian anthropologist and explorer who spent many years in the Canadian Arctic, where he lived among the Inuit people and discovered the last unknown territories of the Canadian Arctic Islands.

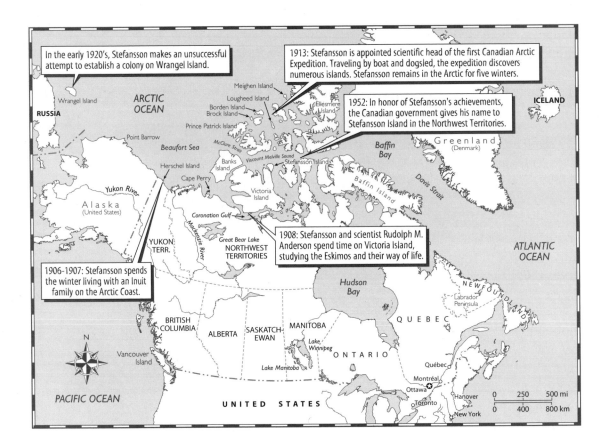

In the early 1920's, Stefansson makes an unsuccessful attempt to establish a colony on Wrangel Island.

1913: Stefansson is appointed scientific head of the first Canadian Arctic Expedition. Traveling by boat and dogsled, the expedition discovers numerous islands. Stefansson remains in the Arctic for five winters.

1952: In honor of Stefansson's achievements, the Canadian government gives his name to Stefansson Island in the Northwest Territories.

1908: Stefansson and scientist Rudolph M. Anderson spend time on Victoria Island, studying the Eskimos and their way of life.

1906-1907: Stefansson spends the winter living with an Inuit family on the Arctic Coast.

Joins Arctic expedition

He then attended Harvard Divinity School on a scholarship. Already an independent thinker, the young man insisted that he would study religion only as folklore. At the first opportunity, Stefansson changed his field to anthropology. In 1905 he did archaeological work in Iceland. The following year he was asked to serve as anthropologist on a polar expedition led by Danish explorer Ejnar Mikkelsen. Their mission was to study Victoria Island in the Canadian Arctic.

The expedition traveled down the Mackenzie River to Herschel Island in Mackenzie Bay, where its members boarded the ship that would take them to Victoria Island. Stefansson studied the Inuit they met along their river course. When the explorers reached Herschel Island they received bad news: their ship had become trapped in ice. Following a thaw, the damaged vessel sank and the expedition was abandoned. But Stefansson stayed on through the winter, living with an Inuit family on the Yukon Arctic coast. For nearly a year he learned their language, customs, and polar survival skills.

Returns to study Inuit people

Stefansson planned a second expedition to Victoria Island in 1908. He was accompanied by zoologist Rudolph M. Anderson, who was interested in Stefansson's theory that Arctic explorers could get all the food they needed simply by living off the land. Reaching the Arctic by sailing on Hudson Bay Company supply boats, the explorers studied the many Inuit groups that lived along Canada's northwest coast, from Point Barrow to Cape Parry. They did manage to reach Victoria Island this time, and along its southern shore—at Coronation Gulf—they encountered a band of Inuit that had never seen white men. Stefansson called the people Copper Eskimos, because they used copper tools. These were the "blond Eskimos" he had heard about in his earlier trip to the Arctic, for some of them had European features, blue eyes, and light hair. He stayed with the Copper Eskimos from 1910 to 1912, studying their way of life. When he returned to the United States, he proposed the sensational idea that these people were a mixture of native Inuit and Norsemen, Scandinavian Vikings who had settled in Greenland during the Middle Ages and then mysteriously disappeared. The theory caused quite a stir, but gained few believers.

Discovers unknown polar islands

Stefansson was appointed scientific head of the first Canadian Arctic Expedition of 1913, which was sponsored by the Canadian government. His mission was to explore the westernmost islands of the Canadian Arctic archipelago (a group of scattered islands). The expedition sailed in an old sealing ship, the *Karluk,* which was stopped by ice in August of 1913, just north of Alaska. Not wishing to be detained, Stefansson and a small party set out by dogsled over the frozen Arctic Ocean. Among the group was a young British adventurer named Hubert Wilkins, who had been hired by the London *Times* to photograph the expedition. They traveled more than five hundred miles and discovered unknown territories, including the islands of Borden, Meighen, Lougheed, and Brock, all located north of Prince Patrick Island. At times they traveled the Beaufort Sea by deliberately drifting on ice floes. The group never returned to the *Karluk,* which was pushed west by Arctic currents and crushed off the coast of Siberia. (Almost all crew members survived because of the brave efforts of Captain Bob Bartlett.) Stefansson remained in the Canadian Arctic until 1918, enduring five consecutive winters there. He was living proof that polar explorers could indeed survive by living off the hidden bounty of the land. In 1952 the Canadian government would give his name to the Stefansson Island, located in the Northwest Territories, in recognition of his exploratory efforts during those years.

Stefansson continued to pursue his interest in the Arctic region. From 1921 to 1925 he sponsored expeditions to northeastern Siberia's Wrangel Island and to Alaska. During that time he tried to set up an unauthorized colony on Wrangel Island, claiming it for Canada. It was a disaster, with the colonists dying tragically. It also caused serious problems between the Canadian government and the Soviet Union, which took possession of the island in 1924. Following that, Stefansson spent most of his time in New York City, lecturing and writing. He also served as a consultant to airlines that were developing transpolar routes, and during World War II advised the military on Arctic survival methods. In addition, he became involved in medical experiments to prove the healthfulness of an all-meat diet, the way of eating that had served him so well during his time in the Arctic.

Stefansson moved to Hanover, New Hampshire, in 1947, joining Dartmouth College's department of northern studies. There he established the Stefansson Collection, one of the world's largest libraries on polar exploration. His own books included *My Life with the Eskimo* (1913) and *The Friendly Arctic* (1921), which promoted the region as a livable place rich with hidden resources. In addition, he published the 1964 memoir *Discovery: The Autobiography of Vilhjalmur Stefansson*. He died in Hanover on August 26, 1962.

Sources

Baker, Daniel B., ed. *Explorers and Discoverers of the World*. Detroit: Gale Research, 1993.

Bohlander, Richard E., ed. *World Explorers and Discoverers*. New York: Macmillan, 1992.

Waldman, Carl and Alan Wexler. *Who Was Who in World Exploration*. New York: Facts on File, 1992.

Pedro de Teixeira

Born c. 1570–93, Castanheira, Portugal
Died June 4, 1640, São Luís do Maranhão, Brazil

Pedro de Teixeira was a Portuguese military officer who made the first full-length upstream exploration of the Amazon River. His trip established Portuguese control over the entire Amazon region.

The 1494 Treaty of Tordesillas was an agreement between Spain and Portugal that divided the non-Christian world into two separate areas that the powerful nations could explore, convert, and colonize. The division gave North America and most of South America to Spain, and the east end of South America, Africa, and India to Portugal. But in 1580 Spain's Philip II claimed the Portuguese throne, and for the next sixty years the two countries were ruled by the same king and were political allies, although they still had different governments. The nations also jealously guarded their colonial possessions. How is it, then, that army officer Pedro de Teixeira managed to claim an enormous region of South America—the whole Amazon River Basin—for Portugal?

Teixeira arrives in South America

During the late sixteenth and early seventeenth centuries, the English, Dutch, and French began to establish settlements

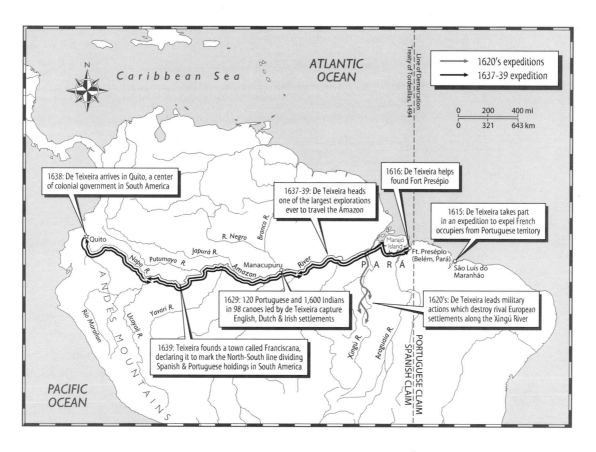

ATLANTIC OCEAN

Caribbean Sea

PACIFIC OCEAN

Line of Demarcation
Treaty of Tordesillas, 1494

0   200   400 mi
0   321   643 km

1638: De Teixeira arrives in Quito, a center of colonial government in South America

1637-39: De Teixeira heads one of the largest explorations ever to travel the Amazon

1616: De Teixeira helps found Fort Presépio

1615: De Teixeira takes part in an expedition to expel French occupiers from Portuguese territory

1629: 120 Portuguese and 1,600 Indians in 98 canoes led by de Teixeira capture English, Dutch & Irish settlements

1620's: De Teixeira leads military actions which destroy rival European settlements along the Xingú River

1639: Teixeira founds a town called Franciscana, declaring it to mark the North-South line dividing Spanish & Portuguese holdings in South America

Quito

R. Negro

Branco R.

Japurá R.

Napo R.

Putumayo R.

Amazon

Manacupuru

River

P A R Á

Marajó Island

Ft. Presépio (Belém, Pará)

São Luís do Maranhão

Yavari R.

Ucayali R.

Río Marañón

A N D E S   M O U N T A I N S

Xingu R.

Araguaia R.

PORTUGUESE CLAIM
SPANISH CLAIM

on the South American coast around the mouth of the Amazon. King Philip called upon his Portuguese subjects to defend that part of his realm. Teixeira, born into a noble family in the Portuguese town of Castanheira, traveled to Brazil in 1607 as a captain in the colonial forces. In 1615 he took part in an expedition that expelled French occupiers from the town of São Luís do Maranhão on the northern coast of Brazil. He then helped found Fort Presépio, located near the eastern mouth of the Amazon River, in 1616. This was to grow into the seaport of Belém, capital of the Brazilian state of Pará and the largest city in the Amazon Basin.

During the 1620s Teixeira led other military actions against European intruders, destroying settlements along the Xingu River, a southern tributary (branch) of the lower Amazon River. He also joined Luís Aranha de Vasconcelos on an expedition to map the area. In addition, he led a major expedition up the Amazon in 1629. His team of 120 Portuguese and 1,600 Indians traveled in 98 canoes. They captured English, Dutch, and Irish settlements in the area around Manacupuru. After more than two decades in Brazil, Teixeira had come to know the lower Amazon region and its tributaries very well, along with the Indian tribes who lived there.

With all foreign intruders gone, the Portuguese in Brazil looked to establish their own influence there, although much of it was officially Spanish territory. In 1637, when six Spanish soldiers and two Spanish priests arrived at Fort Presépio by traveling down the Amazon River from their mission in Spanish Quito (now Ecuador), the local Portuguese colonial governor was both surprised and alarmed. He was concerned that the Spanish, settled around the Amazon's western end in Quito and Peru, would be making their way east now that the way was clear. Teixeira was quickly appointed commander of an expedition that would escort the Spanish party safely home. In truth, the governor wanted Teixeira to explore and map the Amazon all the way to its source in the Andes Mountains, noting the best places to build forts and settlements. He also wanted Teixeira to establish good relations with the Indians he met along the way, and to mark a clear boundary between Spanish and Portuguese territories.

Leads first upstream exploration of Amazon

On October 28, 1637, Teixeira set off from Pará, heading one of the largest expeditions ever to travel the Amazon River. The party included 70 Portuguese soldiers and 2,000 Indian and Negro slaves, traveling in countless canoes. This was the first European expedition going *up* the length of the Amazon; earlier travelers—like Spanish explorer Francisco de Orellana—had floated down the river from its source. Rowing against the current made the trip much slower. The size of the group also slowed progress, for food had to be hunted and gathered constantly. Traveling upstream also required frequent scouting ahead, to see if a particular stretch of water was a tributary or part of the main river. One such branch was the unexplored Rio Negro, which Teixeira claimed for Portugal. He then proceeded up the Amazon to one of its eastern-most tributaries, the Napo River. There, after eight long months, he reached the first Spanish settlements on the eastern slopes of the Andes.

Traveling as far as they could by boat, Teixeira and his group made the last part of their journey on foot, through the mountains to the city of Quito, a center of Spanish colonial government. They arrived there in the late summer of 1638, after a journey of nearly a year. The people of Quito welcomed these travelers from the east warmly, celebrating their arrival with fireworks, bullfights, and banquets. But just as the visiting Spanish travelers in Pará had alarmed the Portuguese a year earlier, the appearance of Teixeira dismayed his Spanish hosts. They feared that the Portuguese planned to push their way into the upper Amazon from the east.

Marks Spanish-Portuguese border

The Spanish encouraged Teixeira to return home as soon as possible. He was joined by a group of Spanish observers led by Jesuit priest Cristóbal de Acuña, brother of Quito's colonial governor. The priest was to make a detailed report of the journey, noting the degree of Portuguese influence in the Amazon and mapping the region for future Spanish undertakings. Departing from Quito on February 16, 1639, Teixeira and his return expedition followed the Napo River until they reached the Amazon Basin. He rejoined a party of his men that he had left encamped there on his way upstream, and learned of their battles with a hostile tribe of Omagua Indians. Teixeira killed the Indians and founded a town called Franciscana on the site, claiming it for Portugal. He also put a carved log in the ground nearby, declaring that it marked the north-south line that divided Spanish and Portuguese holdings in South America. In the name of Portugal he took possession of all lands and rivers to the east. Surprisingly, his Spanish traveling companions did not protest the bold action. Although historians are not sure of the exact location of the marker, it is believed to be near the modern town of Tabatinga, close to the Brazil-Peru border.

Teixeira and his party finally returned to Pará on December 12, 1639, where they received a joyous welcome. The following year Spain and Portugal became separate kingdoms again, this time for good. Due in large part to Teixeira's continent-spanning expedition, the Amazon River—and with it a large part of South America—fell under Portuguese control. As a reward for his services, Teixeira received a military promotion to captain-major. He was also appointed governor of the province of Pará on February 28, 1640. Too ill to accept the offer, however, he died soon after, on June 4, 1640, in São Luís do Maranhão.

Sources

Baker, Daniel B., ed. *Explorers and Discoverers of the World*. Detroit: Gale Research, 1993.

Bohlander, Richard E., ed. *World Explorers and Discoverers*. New York: Macmillan, 1992.

Goodman, Edward J. *The Explorers of South America*. New York: Macmillan, 1972.

Waldman, Carl and Alan Wexler. *Who Was Who in World Exploration*. New York: Facts on File, 1992.

Alexine Tinné

Born October 17, 1835, The Hague, The Netherlands
Died August 1, 1969, near Ghat, Libya

Africa's Nile River was the site of many expeditions during the eighteenth and nineteenth centuries. The world's longest river, at more than four thousand miles, its waters had nourished ancient civilizations and its source had remained a mystery for centuries. Europeans visiting the vast unknown continent were drawn to the river and its far reaches. Alexine Tinné was one such explorer, eager to go farther and see more than those travelers who went before her.

She was born Alexandrina Petronella Francina Tinné on October 17, 1835, in the Netherlands. She was the only child of a wealthy Dutch businessman and his much younger second wife, who had family connections at the royal court. Once, when Tinné was ten years old, her uncle found her sprawled on the floor of the royal library with a large book on her favorite subject: geography. She also liked the natural sciences. While her life revolved around the set social activities of a well-born young lady, her family's extensive travels each summer fed her strong curiosity about the world outside her own.

Alexine Tinné was a wealthy Dutch woman who made several trips up the Nile River and was killed while attempting to be the first European woman to cross the Sahara Desert.

Alexine's father died when she was nine, and at twenty-one she took possession of the considerable fortune he had left her. She was the richest heiress in the Netherlands. A wedding engagement to a baron soon followed, but when the young woman discovered that he was marrying her largely for her money, she was heartbroken. Alexine's mother, Harriet, decided that a long trip would help her daughter forget her troubles. They planned to make a grand tour of Europe together in 1855.

Takes first trip up the Nile

The adventurous Alexine convinced her mother to extend their travels into the Middle East. For a while they stayed in Egypt's capital city of Cairo, enjoying the social life there. But Alexine had bigger plans in mind, and rented a *dahabeah* (a type of Egyptian boat) on which to cruise the Nile River. The travelers were able to take every luxury with them on the ninety-foot boat, including furniture, champagne, livestock, servants, and a full sailing crew. They went up the river as far as Aswan, visiting ancient Egyptian monuments along the way. Then they traveled by camel across the desert to Al-Quseir on the Red Sea. They returned down the river to Cairo, after a journey of ten weeks.

They were off to the Holy Land (Palestine) next, going as far as Beirut in Lebanon, where they stayed for some time in a monastery. They returned to Cairo to celebrate Christmas of 1856, having been gone most of the year. Nonetheless, Alexine was already planning another Nile trip, this time farther up the river, to Khartoum in the Sudan. She was told that the journey would be impossible without a steam-driven ship, but because one wasn't available, she rented an even larger *dahabeah,* outfitted with more supplies and an even bigger crew. The first part of the trip included stops at Asyut and Luxor, where Alexine, her mother, and other members of the traveling party tried without success to tour the surrounding desert by camel. Cataracts (steep rapids) at Aswan forced the group to change into a smaller boat. Still the travelers continued, viewing at Abu Simbel the enormous stone temple built

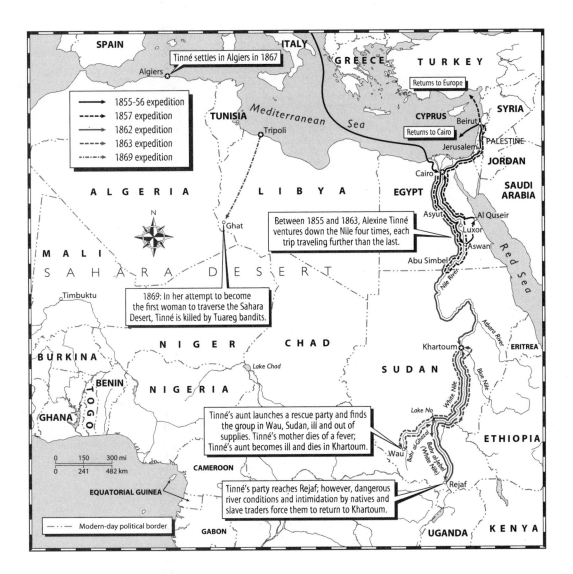

Tinné settles in Algiers in 1867

Returns to Europe

Returns to Cairo

→	1855-56 expedition
- - →	1857 expedition
→	1862 expedition
- - →	1863 expedition
-·-·→	1869 expedition

Between 1855 and 1863, Alexine Tinné ventures down the Nile four times, each trip traveling further than the last.

1869: In her attempt to become the first woman to traverse the Sahara Desert, Tinné is killed by Tuareg bandits.

Tinné's aunt launches a rescue party and finds the group in Wau, Sudan, ill and out of supplies. Tinné's mother dies of a fever; Tinné's aunt becomes ill and dies in Khartoum.

Tinné's party reaches Rejaf; however, dangerous river conditions and intimidation by natives and slave traders force them to return to Khartoum.

0	150	300 mi
0	241	482 km

-·-· Modern-day political border

for Egyptian pharaoh Ramses II. A second cataract finally forced them to turn back and they arrived in Cairo in March 1857. Mother and daughter later made stops in Beirut, Turkey, Italy, and Vienna before returning home.

Returns to Egypt for more river voyages

But Alexine was determined to travel farther south along the Nile. In the summer of 1861 she returned to Cairo, accompanied by her mother and an aunt. She rented a large house there, luxuriously equipped with china and silver from Europe and a grand piano. In January the huge household boarded three boats, packed with servants, pets, and provisions for a year. So large was the traveling party and its store of supplies that at the port of Korosko, where the boat finally landed, 102 camels were needed just to carry the luggage and animals.

On their way to Khartoum, Alexine and her party met other travelers sailing up the Nile. When they learned that she was going as far south as the Sudan, they called her the "Queen of the Equator." After twelve weeks, she and her group arrived at the capital city. It was here that the river branched into two great tributaries: the Blue Nile, reaching into northern Ethiopia; and the White Nile, coursing across east central Africa. While in Khartoum, Tinné met British explorer Samuel White Baker and his future wife, Florence. She also learned of John Hanning Speke and James Augustus Grant, two other British explorers whose return from an expedition up the White Nile—in an effort to locate its source—was long overdue. This information made Tinné change her mind about traveling up the Blue Nile as she made plans to meet Speke.

Tinné hired a steamer to tow her farther up the river. Thinking that she might want to build a house along the way, she added an assortment of building supplies to her already bulging store of provisions. She even paid a builder to come along. Tinné and her party left Khartoum on May 11, 1862, and traveled south to Jebel Dinka, a slave trading post. She became so distressed by the human suffering she witnessed there that she bought a family of six slaves and set them free. The travelers then headed up the Nile to Lake No, where they had to choose between two other river branches, the Bahr al-Ghazal and the Bahr al-Jebel. They selected the second, which seemed a bad decision as time wore on. For three weeks they fought their way through 150 miles of tangled swamps and streams. Then, near Gondokoro, a favorite crew member drowned. The trading settlement was considered the farthest navigable point on the Nile, but Tinné managed to push further, to Rejaf in southern Sudan. That was the end of the line, though, for the river became too dangerous, and the natives—frightened by slave traders—were hostile. When Tinné herself became sick, the party decided to return to Khartoum. The trip up the White Nile had taken five months.

Ventures into untraveled territory

After recovering, Tinné began planning a return trip up the White Nile for the following February. This time she would take the Bahr al-Ghazal branch that ran toward central Africa, perhaps even to the equator. She assembled an amazing array of companions and supplies for her journey: her steamer and several small boats held her mother, six servants, a Dutch traveler, a botanist (a scientist who studies plants), an ornithologist (a scientist who studies birds), and seventy-one soldiers, as well as ammunition, animals, and provisions for six months. While the expedition did go into territory never before visited by Westerners, it would ultimately prove a disaster. Tinné's aunt, who had stayed behind in Khartoum, led a rescue party to find the group after eight months had passed. She found the travelers in the south Sudanese town of Wau, ill and out of supplies. The group had been slowed by tropical storms and floods and hostile traders. Worse still, fever had killed Tinné's mother, two of the family's beloved maids, and one of the scientists. On their return trip, Tinné's aunt also became ill and died in Khartoum. (Alexine did manage to bring back an important botanical collection, which was given to the Imperial Herbarium of the court of Vienna.)

Stricken by grief, Tinné never returned to her home in the Netherlands, which reminded her of her dear mother. She lived in Cairo for a while, and then settled in Algiers, capital city of the French colony of Algeria, in 1867. She hoped to become the first European woman to cross the Sahara Desert on her way to the trade city of Timbuktu in the French Sudan. Setting out from the port of Tripoli in January of 1869, she and her traveling party were attacked by Tuareg bandits at the small oasis of Aberjoudj in early August. Tinné and most of her companions were killed. The few survivors brought the sad news back to Tripoli, and the Turkish governor organized a search to track down the murderers. Tinné's body was never found. Today her name appears on a monument honoring African explorers, located at Juba in the Sudan.

Sources

Baker, Daniel B., ed. *Explorers and Discoverers of the World*. Detroit: Gale Research, 1993.

Bohlander, Richard E., ed. *World Explorers and Discoverers*. New York: Macmillan, 1992.

Tinling, Marion. *Women Into the Unknown: A Sourcebook on Women Explorers and Travelers*. Westport, CT: Greenwood Press, 1989.

R.M.S. *Titanic*

First set sail April 10, 1912, Southampton,
Hampshire, England

Sank April 14–15, 1912, North Atlantic Ocean
Wreckage discovered September 1, 1985

During the late nineteenth and early twentieth centuries—long before the days of air travel—there was a great need for large ships to carry travelers between the United States and Europe. The trip could be made in about two weeks. Wealthy, first-class passengers stayed on the upper decks of the ships, in rooms that were quite luxurious—like those of the best hotels. Second-class passengers stayed in more modest staterooms, located in the middle section of the ship. And underpriviledged passengers stayed in crowded third-class quarters on the back and lower decks of the boat, called steerage. At that time thousands of European immigrants hoping to build better lives in America made the trip in this way.

World's largest ship is built

Bigger and faster ships were continually being built. Owned by the White Star Line, the R.M.S. *Titanic* was the largest ocean vessel of its time. It had taken nearly fifty thou-

The Titanic *struck an iceberg on its maiden voyage, sinking within a matter of hours in the North Atlantic Ocean. The most famous shipwreck of modern times was discovered on the ocean floor by a French–American expedition on September 1, 1985.*

sand men two years to build it. The ship was 900 feet long, 92 feet wide, and had eight decks. It weighed 46,328 tons. The *Titanic* was described as "practically unsinkable" because its 29 boilers—which powered three massive engines—were located in 16 watertight compartments. Even with two sections flooded, the ship could remain functioning and afloat. With a top speed of 24 knots, the trip from Great Britain to New York City would be accomplished in just seven days.

The *Titanic* was also the most luxurious ocean liner of its time. Its great oak and iron central staircase was 60 feet high and topped by a decorative glass dome. An orchestra played in the grand salon every night. The ship had a library, a squash court, a gym, and even an operating room. First-class passengers also enjoyed their own swimming pool and private promenade (strolling) decks.

Titanic begins its maiden voyage

Commanded by Captain Edward J. Smith, the great vessel set sail from Southampton, England, on April 10, 1912. It would stop in France and Ireland to pick up more travelers before heading out into the North Atlantic Ocean. Aboard were about 900 crew members and 1,320 passengers (since the records went down with the ship, no one knows the exact number for sure). Among the travelers were many rich and famous people, including multimillionaires John Jacob Astor, Isidor Straus, and Benjamin Guggenheim.

Hits deadly iceberg

On Sunday, April 14, the *Titanic* received several telegraph messages from other ships in the Atlantic, warning that the vessel was headed for icy waters. Still, the *Titanic* did not slow its pace, and at 11:40 that night it hit an iceberg. While the 80-foot mountain of ice was spotted by lookouts before the collision, the vessel was moving too fast to avoid it. The iceberg scraped across *Titanic*'s starboard (right) side, causing a gash that flooded three hull compartments within minutes.

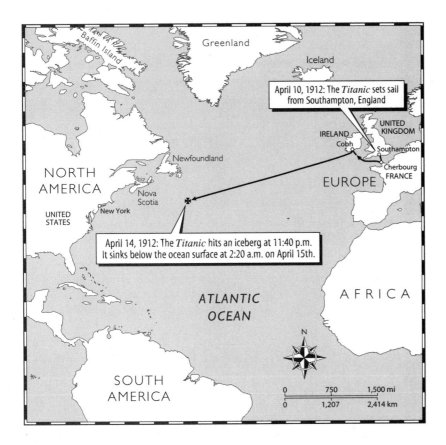

April 10, 1912: The *Titanic* sets sail from Southampton, England

April 14, 1912: The *Titanic* hits an iceberg at 11:40 p.m. It sinks below the ocean surface at 2:20 a.m. on April 15th.

Greenland

Iceland

UNITED KINGDOM

IRELAND

Cobh

Southampton

Cherbourg FRANCE

Newfoundland

NORTH AMERICA

EUROPE

Nova Scotia

New York

UNITED STATES

ATLANTIC OCEAN

AFRICA

N

SOUTH AMERICA

Baffin Island

| 0 | 750 | 1,500 mi |
| 0 | 1,207 | 2,414 km |

The captain and his crew knew almost immediately that the situation was hopeless, and began to telegraph distress signals. Forty-eight miles away, the ocean liner *Carpathia* received the message and began to speed to the site. Most of *Titanic*'s passengers were sleeping at the time of the collision, and when they were awakened and told the awful news, they found it hard to believe. The weather was fair and the sea was calm. And, afterall, the boat was "unsinkable."

Passengers prepare to abandon ship

But within an hour Captain Smith had the passengers gathered on deck and ready to abandon ship. Women and children were loaded into lifeboats first, and it was a confused operation for both crew and passengers, because the ship was new and no lifeboat practice drills had been run. Many of the lifeboats were lowered to the sea only partially full. Had they been filled to capacity, however, more than 1,000 people would still have been stranded, for the *Titanic* did not have enough lifeboats on board.

Families made their sad goodbyes as distress rockets were fired into the air to alert any passing ships. The *Titanic* was sinking rapidly. The ship's bow (front) pitched into the ocean and its stern (back) shot high into the air. Most of *Titanic*'s remaining passengers either leapt or were washed into the water. Some were picked up by lifeboats, but most were killed quickly by the frigid sea, its temperature only 28 degrees Fahrenheit. Some survivors reported that the ship broke in two before it sank below the ocean surface at 2:20 A.M., April 15.

Rescue vessel arrives too late

The *Carpathia* reached the scene at dawn. It took aboard the passengers who had escaped the *Titanic* in lifeboats and searched many more hours for survivors in the ice-filled sea. Only bodies were retrieved. The ship set sail for New York City, which it reached on the night of April 18. Other ships would come upon more bodies in the weeks following the disaster.

Both Great Britain and the United States quickly conducted investigations into the tragedy. The purpose was not so much to place blame as to make changes so that such a disaster would never happen again. New regulations mandated that all ships carry enough lifeboats for every one of their passengers and crew members. The universal distress signal "SOS" was adopted. And all ships were required to staff their telegraph rooms around the clock. (Another ship, the *Californian*, had been much closer to the *Titanic* than the *Carpathia* was that fateful night, but did not receive the distress calls because its equipment had been turned off.)

The gripping story of the *Titanic*'s first and last voyage has never faded from public interest. Many books have been written about it, and movies have retold the tale. Some people have even dreamed of raising the vessel from its watery grave. But before the huge problems involved with raising the *Titanic* can be solved, it would first have to be found.

Wreck discovered after seven decades

This would prove a difficult job, for the *Titanic* was thought to lie nearly three miles below the ocean surface—far deeper than any diver could go—perhaps even buried beneath the sea bed. More than seventy years passed before a deep-water tracking system allowed scientists to pinpoint where the vessel went down. On September 1, 1985, a French–American expedition aboard the research vessel the *Knorr* spotted what looked like one of the *Titanic*'s huge boilers on its special video screen. Later the team would find most of the shipwreck—remarkably intact—deeply embedded in the ocean floor.

Deep-sea photos captivate world

United States marine geologist Robert Ballard—from the Woods Hole Oceanographic Institution in Massachusetts—and French scientist Jean-Louis Michel were leading the project, testing underwater tracking equipment. The French team was from the Research Institute for the Exploration of the Sea (IFREMER) and sailed on the sonar search vessel *Le Suroit*. Attached to the *Knorr* was an underwater sled that Ballard had helped create, called the *Argo,* which was pulled along just above the ocean floor. Equipped with powerful lights and cameras, it transmitted moving pictures to the ship's video screen. For several weeks the scientists received pictures of nothing but mud. But after they spotted the *Titanic*'s boiler, they soon discovered the rest of the ship. It was upright but in two pieces: the stern lay some 2,600 feet from the much larger bow section, which was partially buried in mud. On the ocean floor around the site were well-preserved artifacts from the ship: wine bottles, metal serving trays, bedsprings, and chamberpots. Over the next several

Robert Ballard.

days the *Argo* and a similar vehicle took color photographs of the wreckage that appeared in newspapers and magazines around the world.

Scientists return to site with submarine and robot

Because the scientists could not see where they were pulling the *Argo,* they worried that they might damage things in the wreck site by crashing into them (the *Argo* was the size of a car). They needed to explore the *Titanic* and its artifacts with a vehicle that they could better control. Ballard and his team returned to the site in July 1986 on the *Atlantis II,* bringing with them a small deep-sea submarine. For nearly two weeks they planned to photograph the *Titanic* more closely than ever. Called the *Alvin,* the three-man submarine had been heavily reinforced to withstand the water pressure near the ocean floor, about 6,000 pounds per square inch. The water was so deep (12,460 feet) that it took the vessel two-and-a-half hours for each trip to and from the wreck site.

Attached to *Alvin* by a 250-foot line was a remote-controlled robot equipped with cameras, called Jason Junior, or JJ. As small as a lawn mower, it could travel into the interior of the *Titanic* and send video images and photos back to the crew on *Alvin.* Over the next several days, Ballard and his team learned much more about the wreck. They discovered that all things made out of organic materials, like wood, cloth, flesh, and bones, had long ago been eaten by deep-sea organisms. Therefore, no human remains were found. The ship's deck and beautiful woodwork were gone, but the elegant crystal chandeliers were still hanging and the vessel's brass trimmings shone like new. (Much of the iron hull was covered with hanging rust formations, though, or "rustsicles.") JJ traveled everywhere on the *Titanic:* to the gymnasium, the officers' quarters, the lookout tower, and to the bridge, where the ship was piloted. Many more artifacts were found, including a ship's safe, which JJ tried to open with its mechanical arm.

The expedition was a great success. Ballard and his team and their remarkable equipment had gathered more than sixty thousand camera shots of the *Titanic* site to examine. They took nothing from the wreck, but left two metal plaques behind. One—donated by the Titanic Historical Society of Springfield, Massachusetts—was a memorial placed on the stern, where the largest number of people had died. The second was set on the bow, and asked that anyone who visited the site leave it undisturbed.

Storm erupts over fate of ship

Because the *Titanic* was located in international waters, Ballard worried that treasure hunters would strip the wreckage site of the artifacts that he had revealed in his photographs. Not long after his discovery, he went before the U.S. Congress

The submerged hull of the sunken Titanic *is illuminated by* Alvin.

and asked that the site be protected as an international memorial. But in 1987 a French salvage expedition brought up hundreds of objects from the wreck, including a leather bag full of jewelry and money (the tannin in leather items aboard the *Titanic* kept them from disintegrating). A storm of controversy about the fate of the great ship began.

Some people felt that the *Titanic* should be left undisturbed out of respect for the many people who lost their lives there. To them, any attempt to take objects from the site would be like grave robbing. Others felt that the ship's artifacts should be retrieved and restored for the sake of history, so that more could be learned about that time, and about the lessons that the tragedy might still teach. And some people, of course, saw the remains of the *Titanic* as an opportunity for profit.

Company granted salvage rights

In 1993 George Tulloch's company, RMS Titanic, Inc., was granted the legal right in a U.S. district court to salvage the wreckage. This was under the condition that none of the recovered objects be sold for profit. In a number of expeditions, Tulloch and his team—with the help of IFREMER—have retrieved several thousand items from the *Titanic*; these have been restored and preserved in a French conservation laboratory. Many of the objects have gone on display in exhibits in Great Britain and the United States.

While RMS Titanic, Inc., has always argued that its top priority is to protect and preserve the historical and archaeological value of the great ship and its artifacts, some of its activities appear to be driven more by profit. The company sells *Titanic* merchandise and souvenirs, for instance, like T-shirts and authentic pieces of the ship's coal, the only items from the wreck legally available for purchase. In 1997 RMS Titanic also chartered cruises to the wreck site, where it attempted to raise a fifteen-ton piece of the ship's hull to the surface. Eight huge diesel-driven, air-filled balloons were used to float the section to the top, but the rigging used to lift it to the recovery ship snapped, and the piece sank back to the ocean floor ten miles from the rest of the *Titanic*. Tulloch plans to make another attempt next year. In the meantime, organizations continue to work to protect the site from further excavation.

Sources

Ballard, Robert. *Finding the Titanic.* New York: Scholastic, 1993.

Ballard, Robert. "How We Found Titanic." *National Geographic.* December 1985: 696–719.

Dudman, John. *The Sinking of the Titanic.* New York: Bookwright Press, 1988.

News 2. [Online] Available http://www.irishnews.com/110496/news2.html, May 26, 1997.

On the dock: Titanic buoyed by cash. [Online] Available http://library.msnbc.com/scitech/titanic/25020.asp, May 24, 1997.

RMS Titanic, Inc. Online. [Online] Available http://www.titanic-online.com/, June 3, 1997.

Sloan, Frank. *Titanic.* New York: Franklin Watts, 1987.

Titanic: The Discovery. [Online] Available http://www.fireflyproductions.com/titanic/ffdisc.htm, May 5, 1997.

The Titanic cyber cruise. [Online] Available http://library.msnbc.com/scitech/titanic/25023.asp, May 30, 1997.

Titanic Live Online. [Online] Available http://www.discovery.com/DCO/doc/1012/world/specials/titanic/titanic1.1.html, June 2, 1997.

Chronology of Exploration

As an aid to the reader who wishes to trace the history of exploration or the explorers active in a particular location, the major expeditions within a geographical area are listed below in chronological order.

Explorers with entries in Explorers and Discoverers, Volume 5 *are in* **boldface** *and have page numbers following their names; explorers whose names are not in boldface appear in Volumes 1–4.*

Africa: central

1802–14	Pedro João Baptista and Amaro José
1854–56	David Livingstone
1858–64	David Livingstone
1872–73	David Livingstone
1873–77	Henry Morton Stanley
1877–80	Hermenegildo de Brito Capelo and Roberto Ivens
1884–85	Hermenegildo de Brito Capelo and Roberto Ivens
1888–90	Henry Morton Stanley
1896–98	Jean-Baptiste Marchand
1903	**May French Sheldon 140**
1924–25	Delia Akeley

Africa: coast

1416–60	Henry the Navigator
1487–88	Bartolomeu Dias

Africa: east

1490–1526	Pero da Covilhã
1848	Johannes Rebmann
1848–49	Johann Ludwig Krapf
1848–49	Johannes Rebmann
1849	Johannes Rebmann
1851	Johann Ludwig Krapf
1855–57	**Alexine Tinné 155**
1857–59	Richard Burton and John Hanning Speke (with Sidi Mubarak Bombay)

1860–63	John Hanning Speke and James Augustus Grant (with Sidi Mubarak Bombay)
1862–63	Alexine Tinné
1862–64	Samuel White Baker and Florence Baker
1865–71	David Livingstone
1869	Alexine Tinné
1870–73	Samuel White Baker and Florence Baker
1871–73	Henry Morton Stanley (with Sidi Mubarak Bombay)
1883–84	Joseph Thomson
1891	**May French Sheldon 140**
1905–06	Delia Akeley
1909–11	Delia Akeley
1930s–60s	**Louis and Mary Leakey 91**
1968–	**Richard Leakey 91**

Africa: south

1849	David Livingstone
1850	David Livingstone
1851–52	David Livingstone
1851–55	**Ida Pfeiffer 126**

Africa: west

1352–53	Abu Abdallah Ibn Battutah
1795–99	Mungo Park
1805	Mungo Park
1827–28	René Caillié
1850–55	Heinrich Barth
1856–60	Paul Du Chaillu
1861–76	Friedrich Gerhard Rohlfs
1863	Paul Du Chaillu
1867	Paul Du Chaillu
1875–78	Pierre Savorgnan de Brazza

1879	Henry Morton Stanley
1879–81	Pierre Savorgnan de Brazza
1883–85	Pierre Savorgnan de Brazza
1891–92	Pierre Savorgnan de Brazza
1893	Mary Kingsley
1894	Mary Kingsley
1903	**May French Sheldon 140**

Antarctica

1819–21	Fabian Gottlieb von Bellingshausen
1837–40	Jules-Sébastien-Cé sar Dumont d'Urville
1839–40	Charles Wilkes
1903–05	**Jean-Baptiste Charcot 28**
1907–09	Ernest Shackleton
1908–10	Jean-Baptiste Charcot
1910–12	Roald Amundsen
1914–16	Ernest Shackleton
1921–22	Ernest Shackleton
1928	Hubert Wilkins
1928–29	Richard Evelyn Byrd
1929	Hubert Wilkins
1933–34	Lincoln Ellsworth
1933–35	Richard Evelyn Byrd
1935–36	Lincoln Ellsworth
1937	Lincoln Ellsworth
1939–40	Richard Evelyn Byrd
1946–47	Richard Evelyn Byrd
1956	Richard Evelyn Byrd
1956–58	Vivian Fuchs
1989–90	Will Steger

Arabia

| 25 B.C. | Aelius Gallus |
| 1812–13 | Hester Stanhhope |

1854–55	Richard Burton
1877–78	Anne Blunt and Wilfrid Scawen Blunt
1879–80	Anne Blunt and Wilfrid Scawen Blunt
1913	Gertrude Bell
1990	**Nicholas Clapp 40**
1991–92	Nicholas Clapp

Arctic *(see also* Northwest Passage)

1827	Edward Parry
1858	**Nils Adolf Erik Nordenskjöld 120**
1860	**Charles Francis Hall 68**
1861	Nils Adolf Erik Nordenskjöld
1864	Nils Adolf Erik Nordenskjöld
1864–69	Charles Francis Hall
1868	Nils Adolf Erik Nordenskjöld
1871	Charles Francis Hall
1872	Nils Adolf Erik Nordenskjöld
1893–96	Fridtjof Nansen
1902	**Jean-Baptiste Charcot 28**
1902	Robert Edwin Peary
1905–06	Robert Edwin Peary (with Matthew A. Henson)
1906–07	**Vilhjalmur Stefansson 145**
1908–09	Robert Edwin Peary (with Matthew A. Henson)
1908–12	Vilhjalmur Stefansson
1913–18	Vilhjalmur Stefansson
1921–25	Vilhjalmur Stefansson
1925	Roald Amundsen
1925	Richard Evelyn Byrd
1926	Roald Amundsen and Umberto Nobile
1926	Louise Arner Boyd
1926	Richard Evelyn Byrd
1926–27	Hubert Wilkins
1928	Louise Arner Boyd
1928	Hubert Wilkins
1931	Hubert Wilkins
1940	Louise Arner Boyd
1955	Louise Arner Boyd
1958	U.S.S. *Nautilus*
1986	Will Steger

Asia: interior

1643–46	**Vasily Danilovich Poyarkov 131**
1866–68	Francis Garnier
1870–72	Nikolay Przhevalsky
1876	Nikolay Przhevalsky
1883–85	Nikolay Przhevalsky
1893–95	Sven Hedin
1895–97	Isabella Bird
1899	Fanny Bullock Workman
1899–1901	Sven Hedin
1900	Aurel Stein
1903–05	Sven Hedin
1906	Fanny Bullock Workman
1906–08	Aurel Stein
1913–15	Aurel Stein
1927–33	Sven Hedin
1932	**Ella Maillart 98**
1934	Ella Maillart
1934–36	Sven Hedin
1953	Edmund Hillary
1977	Edmund Hillary

Asia/Europe (see Eurasia)

Asia, south/China

629–45 B.C.	Hs Ÿan-tsang
138–26 B.C.	Chang Ch'ien
399–414	**Fa-Hsien 54**
1405–07	Cheng Ho
1407–09	Cheng Ho
1409–11	Cheng Ho
1413–15	Cheng Ho
1417–19	Cheng Ho
1421–22	Cheng Ho
1433–35	Cheng Ho
1847–48	**Ida Pfeiffer 126**
1851–55	Ida Pfeiffer
1935	**Ella Maillart 98**
1939	Ella Maillart
1949	Ella Maillart
1994	Ella Maillart

Australia

1605–06	Willem Janszoon
1642	Abel Tasman
1644	Abel Tasman
1770	James Cook
1798–99	Matthew Flinders
1801–02	Matthew Flinders
1801–02	Joseph Banks
1802–03	Matthew Flinders
1813	**Gregory Blaxland 24**
1839	Edward John Eyre
1840–41	Edward John Eyre
1860–61	Robert O'Hara Burke and William John Wills
1869–70	**John Forrest 58**

1874	John Forrest
1876	John Forrest
1880	John Forrest

Aviation

1927	Charles Lindbergh
1928	Amelia Earhart
1930	Beryl Markham
1930	Amy Johnson
1931	Amy Johnson
1931	Wiley Post
1932	Amelia Earhart
1932	Amy Johnson
1933	Wiley Post
1935	Amelia Earhart
1936	Amelia Earhart
1936	Beryl Markham
1947	Chuck Yeager
1986	Dick Rutan and Jeana Yeager
1995	**Steve Fossett 62**
1996	Steve Fossett
1997	Steve Fossett

Central America

1523–26	**Pedro de Alvarado 1**

Europe

1845	**Ida Pfeiffer 126**
1848	Ida Pfeiffer
1851	Ida Pfeiffer
1855	**Alexine Tinné 155**
1857	Alexine Tinné
1873	**Heinrich Schliemann 135**
1876–78	Heinrich Schliemann
1884–85	Heinrich Schliemann
1993	**Barry Clifford 47**

Eurasia

454–43 B.C. Herodotus
401–399 B.C. Xenophon
334–23 B.C. Alexander the Great
310–06 B.C. Pytheas
921–22 **Ahmad Ibn Fadlan 75**
1159–73 Benjamin of Tudela
1245–47 Giovanni da Pian del Carpini
1271–95 Marco Polo
1280–90 Rabban Bar Sauma
1487–90 Pero da Covilhã
1492–93 Christopher Columbus
1497–99 Vasco da Gama
1502–03 Vasco da Gama
1537–58 Fernã o Mendes Pinto
1549–51 Saint Francis Xavier
1595–97 Cornelis de Houtman
1598–99 Cornelis de Houtman
1697–99 Vladimir Atlasov
1725–30 **Vitus Bering 19**
1733–41 Vitus Bering
1787 Jean François de Galaup, Comte de La Pérouse
1879–80 **Nils Adolf Erik Nordenskjöld 120**
1930s **Ella Maillart 98**

Greenland

982 Erik the Red
1870 **Nils Adolf Erik Nordenskjöld 120**
1871 **Charles Francis Hall 68**
1883 Nils Adolf Erik Nordenskjöld
1886 Robert Edwin Peary
1888 Fridtjof Nansen

1891–92 Robert Edwin Peary (with Matthew A. Henson)
1893–95 Robert Edwin Peary (with Matthew A. Henson)
1926–36 **Jean-Baptiste Charcot 28**
1931 Louise Arner Boyd
1933 Louise Arner Boyd
1937 Louise Arner Boyd
1938 Louise Arner Boyd

Middle East

1842–43 **Ida Pfeiffer 126**
1847–48 Ida Pfeiffer
1856 **Alexine Tinné 155**
1857 Alexine Tinné

Muslim World

915–17 Abu al-Hasan 'Ali al-Mas'udi
918–28 Abu al-Hasan 'Ali al-Mas'udi
921–22 **Ahmad Ibn Fadlan 75**
943–73 Abu al-Kasim Ibn Ali al-Nasibi Ibn Hawkal
1325–49 Abu Abdallah Ibn Battutah

North America: coast

1001–02 Leif Eriksson
1493–96 Christopher Columbus
1497 John Cabot
1498 John Cabot
1502–04 Christopher Columbus
1508 Sebastian Cabot
1513 Juan Ponce de León
1513–14 Vasco Núñez de Balboa
1518–22 Hernán Cortés
1519–22 Pedro de Alvarado
1524 Giovanni da Verrazano

1534	Jacques Cartier
1534–36	Hernán Cortés
1535–36	Jacques Cartier
1539	Hernán Cortés
1540–41	**Pedro de Alvarado 1**
1541–42	Jacques Cartier
1542–43	João Rodrigues Cabrilho
1584	Walter Raleigh
1585–86	Walter Raleigh
1587–89	Walter Raleigh
1603	Samuel de Champlain
1604–07	Samuel de Champlain
1606–09	John Smith
1608–10	Samuel de Champlain
1609	Henry Hudson
1610	Samuel de Champlain
1614	John Smith
1792–94	George Vancouver

North America: interior

1666–71	**Jacques Marquette 104**
1673	Jacques Marquette
1674–75	Jacques Marquette
1822	**William Henry Ashley 6**

North America: sub-Arctic

1654–56	Médard Chouart des Groselliers
1668	Médard Chouart des Groselliers
1668	Pierre Esprit Radisson
1670	Pierre Esprit Radisson
1679	Louis Jolliet
1682–83	Médard Chouart des Groselliers
1684	Pierre Esprit Radisson

1685–87	Pierre Esprit Radisson
1689	Louis Jolliet
1694	Louis Jolliet
1725–30	**Vitus Bering 19**
1733–41	Vitus Bering
1789	Alexander Mackenzie
1795	Aleksandr Baranov
1799	Aleksandr Baranov
1819–22	John Franklin
1825–27	John Franklin

North America: west

1527–36	Álvar Núñez Cabeza de Vaca (with Estevanico)
1538–43	Hernando de Soto
1539	Estevanico
1540–42	Francisco Vásquez de Coronado
1611–12	Samuel de Champlain
1613–15	Samuel de Champlain
1615–16	Samuel de Champlain
1615–16	Ètienne Brulé
1621–23	Ètienne Brulé
1657	Pierre Esprit Radisson
1659–60	Mé dard Chouart des Groselliers
1659–60	Pierre Esprit Radisson
1669–70	René-Robert Cavelier de La Salle
1672–74	Louis Jolliet
1678–83	René-Robert Cavelier de La Salle
1684–87	René-Robert Cavelier de La Salle
1769–71	Daniel Boone
1775	Daniel Boone
1792–94	Alexander Mackenzie

1792–97	David Thompson
1797–99	David Thompson
1800–02	David Thompson
1804–06	Meriwether Lewis and William Clark
1805–06	Zebulon Pike
1806–07	Zebulon Pike
1807–11	David Thompson
1811–13	Wilson Price Hunt and Robert Stuart
1823	**William Henry Ashley** (with Jedediah Smith) **6**
1823–25	Jedediah Smith
1824–25	William Henry Ashley
1824–25	Peter Skene Ogden
1825–26	Peter Skene Ogden
1826	William Henry Ashley
1826–27	Peter Skene Ogden
1826–28	Jedediah Smith
1828–29	Peter Skene Ogden
1829–30	Peter Skene Ogden
1842	John Charles Frémont
1843–44	John Charles Frémont
1845–48	John Charles Frémont
1848–49	John Charles Frémont
1850–51	Jim Beckwourth
1851–55	**Ida Pfeiffer 126**
1853–55	John Charles Frémont

North Pole *(see* Arctic)

Northeast Passage

1607	Henry Hudson
1878–79	**Nils A. E. Nordenskjöld 129**
1918–20	Roald Amundsen
1931	Lincoln Ellsworth

Northwest Passage

1610–13	Henry Hudson
1776–79	James Cook
1819–20	Edward Parry
1821–23	Edward Parry
1824–25	Edward Parry
1845–47	John Franklin
1850–54	Robert McClure
1903–06	Roald Amundsen

Oceans

1872–76	H.M.S. *Challenger*
1901	Jean-Baptiste Charcot
1912	**R.M.S** *Titanic* **161**
1921	Jean-Baptiste Charcot
1942–42	Jacques Cousteau
1948	August Piccard
1954	August Piccard
1960	Jacques Piccard
1968–80	*Glomar Challenger*
1969	Jacques Piccard
1984	**Barry Clifford 47**
1985	R.M.S. *Titanic*

South America: coast

1498–1500	Christopher Columbus
1499–1500	Alonso de Ojeda
1499–1500	Amerigo Vespucci
1501–1502	Amerigo Vespucci
1502	Alonso de Ojeda
1505	Alonso de Ojeda
1509–10	Alonso de Ojeda
1519–20	Ferdinand Magellan
1526–30	Sebastian Cabot
1527	Giovanni da Verrazano

1528	Giovanni da Verrazano
1534	**Pedro de Alvarado 1**
1594	Walter Raleigh
1595	Walter Raleigh
1615	**Pedro de Teixeira 150**
1617–18	Walter Raleigh
1735–43	**Charles-Marie de La Condomine 85**
1743–44	Charles-Marie de La Condomine
1831–34	Charles Darwin
1847–48	**Ida Pfeiffer 126**
1851–55	Ida Pfeiffer

South America: interior

1524–25	Francisco Pizarro
1526–27	Francisco Pizarro
1531–41	Francisco Pizarro
1540–44	Álvar Núñez Cabeza de Vaca
1541–42	Francisco de Orellana
1620s	**Pedro de Teixeira 150**
1629	Pedro de Teixeira
1637–38	Pedro de Teixeira
1639	Pedro de Teixeira
1743	**Charles-Marie de La Condomine 85**
1769–70	Isabel Godin des Odonais
1799–1803	Alexander von Humboldt
1903	Annie Smith Peck
1904	Annie Smith Peck
1908	Annie Smith Peck
1911	Hiram Bingham
1912	Hiram Bingham
1915	Hiram Bingham

South Pacific

1519–22	Ferdinand Magellan
1577–80	Francis Drake
1642–43	Abel Tasman
1721–22	Jacob Roggeveen
1766–68	Samuel Wallis
1766–69	Philip Carteret
1767–69	Louis-Antoine de Bougainville
1768–71	James Cook (with Joseph Banks)
1772–75	James Cook
1776–79	James Cook
1785–88	Jean François de Galaup, Comte de La Pérouse
1791	George Vancouver
1826–29	Jules-Sébastien-César Dumont d'Urville
1834–36	Charles Darwin
1838–39	Jules-Sébastien-César Dumont d'Urville
1838–42	Charles Wilkes
1847–48	**Ida Pfeiffer 126**
1851–55	Ida Pfeiffer
1923	**Evelyn Cheesman 35**
1928–30	Evelyn Cheesman
1930	Michael J. Leahy
1931	Michael J. Leahy
1932–33	Michael J. Leahy
1933–42	Evelyn Cheesman

Space

1957	*Sputnik*
1958–70	*Explorer 1*
1959–72	*Luna*
1961	Yury Gagarin

1962	John Glenn
1962–75	*Mariner*
1963	Valentina Tereshkova
1967–72	*Apollo*
1969	Neil Armstrong
1975–83	*Viking*
1977–90	*Voyager 1* and *2*
1983	Sally Ride
1987	**Mae Jemison 80**
1990–	Hubble Space Telescope
1992	Mae Jemison
1986–	***Mir* space station 109**

Tibet

1624–30	Antonio de Andrade
1811–12	Thomas Manning
1865–66	Nain Singh
1867–68	Nain Singh
1879–80	Nikolay Przhevalsky
1892–93	Annie Royle Taylor
1898	Susie Carson Rijnhart
1901	Sven Hedin
1915–16	Alexandra David-Neel
1923–24	Alexandra David-Neel

Explorers by Country of Birth

If an expedition was sponsored by a country other than the explorer's place of birth, the sponsoring country is listed in parentheses after the explorer's name.

Explorers with entries in Explorers and Discoverers, Volume 5 *are in **boldface** and have page numbers following their names; explorers whose names are not in boldface appear in Volumes 1–4.*

Angola

Pedro João Baptista (Portugal)
Amaro José

Australia

John Forrest 58
Michael J. Leahy
Hubert Wilkins
William John Wills

Austria

Ida Pfeiffer 126

Canada

Louis Jolliet

Peter Skene Ogden
Susie Carson Rijnhart
Vilhjalmur Stefansson 145

China

Rabban Bar Sauma
Chang Ch'ien
Cheng Ho
Fa-Hsien 54
HsŸan-tsang

Denmark

Vitus Bering (Russia) **19**

Ecuador

Isabel Godin des Odonais

England

Samuel White Baker
Joseph Banks
Gertrude Bell
Isabella Bird
Gregory Blaxland 24
Anne Blunt
Wilfrid Scawen Blunt
Richard Burton
Philip Carteret
H.M.S. *Challenger*
Evelyn Cheesman 35
James Cook
Charles Darwin
Francis Drake
Edward John Eyre
Matthew Flinders
John Franklin
Vivian Fuchs
Henry Hudson (Netherlands)
Amy Johnson
Mary Kingsley
Mary Leakey 91
Thomas Manning
Beryl Markham (Kenya)
Edward Parry
Walter Raleigh
John Smith
John Hanning Speke
Hester Stanhope
Annie Royle Taylor
David Thompson
R.M.S. *Titanic* (built in Belfast, Ireland)
161
George Vancouver
Samuel Wallis

Estonia

Fabian Gottlieb von Bellingshausen
(Russia)

Finland

Nils Adolf Erik Nordenskjöld (Sweden)
120

France

Louis-Antoine de Bougainville
Étienne Brulé
René Caillié
Jacques Cartier
Samuel de Champlain
Jean-Baptiste Charcot 28
Médard Chouart des Groselliers
Paul Du Chaillu (United States)
Jacques Cousteau
Alexandra David-Neel
Jules-Sébastien-César Dumont d'Urville
Francis Garnier
Charles-Marie de La Condomine 85
Jean François de Galaup, Comte de La
Pérouse
René-Robert Cavelier de La Salle
Jean-Baptiste Marchand
Jacques Marquette 104
Pierre Esprit Radisson

Germany

Heinrich Barth (Great Britain)
Alexander von Humboldt
Johann Ludwig Krapf
Johannes Rebmann
Friedrich Gerhard Rohlfs
Heinrich Schliemann 135

Greece

Alexander the Great
Herodotus
Pytheas
Xenophon

Hungary

Aurel Stein (Great Britain)

Iceland

Leif Eriksson

India

Nain Singh

Iraq

Abu al-Kasim Ibn Ali al-Nasibi Ibn Hawkal
Ahmad Ibn Fadlan 75
Abu al-Hasan 'Ali al-Mas'udi

Ireland

Robert O'Hara Burke (Australia)
Robert McClure
Ernest Shackleton

Italy

Pierre Savorgnan de Brazza (France)
John Cabot (Great Britain)
Sebastian Cabot (England, Spain)
Giovanni da Pian del Carpini
Christopher Columbus (Spain)
Marco Polo
Giovanni da Verrazano (France)
Amerigo Vespucci (Spain, Portugal)

Kenya

Louis S. B. Leakey 91
Richard Leakey 91

Malawi

Sidi Mubarak Bombay (Great Britain)
James Chuma (Great Britain)

Morocco

Abu Abdallah Ibn Battutah
Estevanico

Netherlands

Willem Barents 13
Cornelis de Houtman
Willem Janszoon
Jacob Roggeveen
Abel Tasman
Alexine Tinné 155

New Zealand

Edmund Hillary

Norway

Roald Amundsen
Erik the Red (Iceland)
Fridtjof Nansen

Portugal

Antonio de Andrade
Hermenegildo de Brito Capelo
João Rodrigues Cabrilho (Spain)
Pedro da Covilhã
Bartolomeu Dias

Vasco da Gama
Henry the Navigator
Roberto Ivens
Ferdinand Magellan (Spain)
Fernão Mendes Pinto
Pedro de Teixeira 150

Romania

Florence Baker

Rome

Aelius Gallus
Russia *(see also* **Union of Soviet Socialist Republics**
Vladimir Atlasov
Aleksandr Baranov
Vasily Danilovich Poyarkov 131
Nikolay Przhevalsky

Scotland

David Livingstone
Alexander Mackenzie
Mungo Park
Robert Stuart (United States)
Joseph Thomson

Spain

Pedro de Alvarado 1
Benjamin of Tudela
Álvar Núñez Cabeza de Vaca
Francisco Vásquez de Coronado
Hernán Cortés
Vasco Núñez de Balboa
Alonso de Ojeda
Francisco de Orellana

Francisco Pizarro
Juan Ponce de León
Hernando de Soto
Saint Francis Xavier
Sweden
Sven Hedin
Switzerland
Ella Maillairt 98
Auguste Piccard
Jacques Piccard

Union of Soviet Socialist Republics

Yury Gagarin
Luna
Mir space station 109
Sputnik
Valentina Tereshkova

United States of America

Delia Akeley
Apollo
Neil Armstrong
William Henry Ashley 6
Jim Beckwourth
Hiram Bingham
Daniel Boone
Louise Arner Boyd
Richard Evelyn Byrd
Nicholas Clapp 40
William Clark
Barry Clifford 47
Amelia Earhart
Lincoln Ellsworth
Explorer 1
Steve Fossett 62

John Charles Frémont
John Glenn
Glomar Challenger
Charles Francis Hall 68
Matthew A. Henson
Hubble Space Telescope
Wilson Price Hunt
Mae Jemison 80
Meriwether Lewis
Charles Lindbergh
Mariner
National Geographic Society 115
U.S.S. *Nautilus*
Robert Edwin Peary
Annie Smith Peck
Zebulon Pike

Wiley Post
Sally Ride
Dick Rutan
May French Sheldon 140
Jedediah Smith
Will Steger
Viking
Voyager 1 and *2*
Charles Wilkes
Fanny Bullock Workman
Chuck Yeager
Jeana Yeager

Wales
Henry Morton Stanley (United States)

Cumulative Index to Volumes 1–5

Boldface indicates main entries in Volume 5 and their page numbers; *1–4:* refers to entries in the four-volume base set; *5:* refers to entries in Volume 5; (ill.) following a page number refers to illustrations.

A

A-erh-chin Shan-mo mountains *1–4:* 421, 706

Abd al-Hamid II *1–4:* 105

Abominable Snowman *1–4:* 453

Aborigines *1–4:* 147–148, 260, 302, 356–357, 367, 487, 857; *5:* 58–60

Abu Simbel, Egypt *5:* 156

Abyssinia *1–4:* 287, 289, 503, 789

Académie Française *1–4:* 286; *5:* 90

Acadia *1–4:* 212, 214–215

Acapulco, Mexico *1–4:* 481

Accra, Ghana *1–4:* 416

Acoma, New Mexico *1–4:* 271

Acre, Israel *1–4:* 786

Acropolis *1–4:* 656

Across the Tian Shan to Lop-Nor 1–4: 706

Adam's Peak *1–4:* 79

Adelaide, Australia *1–4:* 144, 355, 357, 362; *5:* 59, 60

Adelaide Island *1–4:* 853; *5:* 31, 32

Adélie Coast *1–4:* 328–329

Adelie Land *5:* 33

Aden, Yemen *1–4:* 289, 290, 503–504, 772–773, 775

Admiralty Islands *1–4:* 127, 190

Adriatic Sea *1–4:* 157, 184, 186

Adventure 1–4: 261–264, 298, 300

Adwa *1–4:* 503

Aegean Islands *1–4:* 433

Aegean Sea *1–4:* 6, 96, 325

"Aeroplane Girl" *1–4:* 492

Afghanistan *1–4:* 78, 462, 808; *5:* 103

Amu Darya River *1–4:* 8, 808; *5:* 101

Amundsen, Roald *1–4:* 14–22, 56, 130, 158, 160, 337, 429, 641, 747, 859

Amundsen Gulf *1–4:* 17

Amundsen-Scott Base *1–4:* 377, 804

Amur *1–4:* 705

Amur River *5:* 22, 131–133

"Amy, Wonderful Amy" *1–4:* 492

Anabasis 1–4: 868, 870

Anadyr River *1–4:* 41

Añasco Bay *1–4:* 248

Ancient Greeks *5:* 135

Andalusia, Spain *1–4:* 287

Andaman Islands *1–4:* 693

Anders, William *1–4:* 28

Anderson, Rudolph M. *5:* 147

Anderson, William R. *1–4:* 611, 613

Andes Mountains *1–4:* 99, 101, 157, 174, 299–301, 409, 479, 654, 768; *5:* 4, 88, 152

Andrade, Antonio de *1–4:* 23–25

Andronicus II *1–4:* 67

Andronicus III *1–4:* 77

Andros Island *1–4:* 697

Aneityum *5:* 37, 38

Angareb River *1–4:* 45

Angediva Island *1–4:* 390

Angkor, Cambodia *1–4:* 395

Angmagssalik, Greenland *1–4:* 342

Angola *1–4:* 57, 137–138, 313, 500

Angostura *1–4:* 479

Annam, Vietnam *1–4:* 394

Annapolis Royal, Nova Scotia *1–4:* 214

Antanarivo, Madagascar *5:* 130

Antarctic Circle *1–4:* 91, 262; *5:* 32

Antarctic Peninsula *1–4:* 92–93, 803, 853

Antarctic Treaty *1–4:* 340

Antarctica *1–4:* 90–93, 158, 160–163, 325–329, 336, 375, 452–453, 744–747, 801, 804, 853, 856; *5:* 28–30, 32–34

Anticosti Island *1–4:* 194–195, 498

Antigua *1–4:* 635

Antioch, Syria *1–4:* 97, 220, 598

Antivari, Yugoslavia *1–4:* 186

Apalachen *1–4:* 769

Aparia *1–4:* 629, 630

Apollo 1–4: 26–33, 37, 402, 558

Appalachian Mountains *1–4:* 118, 529, 770

Appenine Mountains *1–4:* 31

Apuré River *1–4:* 478

Aqualung *1–4:* 282–284

Arab Bureauscuba *1–4:* 89

Arabian Desert *5:* 127

Arabian Peninsula *1–4:* 108, 223, 772; *5:* 40, 42

Arabian Sea *1–4:* 435

Aral Sea *1–4:* 78, 597

Arawak (tribe) *1–4:* 248–249

Archimedes Crater *1–4:* 556

Arctic *1–4:* 129–132, 159, 255, 336, 646, 856

Arctic Circle *1–4:* 328, 612, 640

Arctic Ocean *1–4:* 14, 21, 469, 509, 801, 821, 857; *5:* 13, 120, 123, 131, 147

Arctic Researches and Life Among the Esquimaux 5: 71

Arequipa, Peru *1–4:* 99

Areta (tribe) *1–4:* 384

Arghūn *1–4:* 67

Argo 5: 166

Arguin Island *1–4:* 426

Arias, Pedro *1–4:* 767

Arikara (tribe) *1–4:* 483, 532

Aristotle *1–4:* 5, 9

Arkansas *5:* 106

Arkansas (tribe) *1–4:* 516

Arkansas River *1–4:* 83, 372, 497, 662, 663, 761

Armenia *1–4:* 67, 597, 689, 868

Armstrong, Neil *1–4:* 29, 34–39, 523, 558

Arnhem Land *1–4:* 812

Around the World in Eight Days 1–4: 700

Arrillaga, José de *1–4:* 834

Bahia dos Vaqueiros *1–4:* 312

Bahía San Miguel *1–4:* 616

Bahr al-Ghazal River *1–4:* 582; *5:* 158, 159

Bahr al-Jebel River *5:* 158

Bahr-el-Salam River *1–4:* 45

Baikonur Space Center *1–4:* 380, 778, 818

Baja, California *1–4:* 28, 177, 281, 834

Baker, Florence *1–4:* 43–51, 114, 156, 776

Baker, Samuel White *1–4:* 43–51, 114, 156, 580, 776; *5:* 158

Bakongo (tribe) *1–4:* 581

Baku, Azerbaijan *1–4:* 418

Balboa, Vasco Núñez de. *See* Núñez de Balboa, Vasco

Balchen, Bernt *1–4:* 338

Bali *1–4:* 304, 457

Baliem River *1–4:* 522

Balkan Peninsula *1–4:* 5–6, 44

Balkan Wars *1–4:* 856

Balkh *1–4:* 462

Ballard, Robert *5:* 117, 165–167, 169

Balloon aviation *5:* 66

Balloons *5:* 62, 64–67

Baluchistan *1–4:* 808

Bamako, Mali *1–4:* 634, 636

Bamian *1–4:* 462

Bancroft, Ann *1–4:* 802

Banda Sea *1–4:* 487

Bangala (tribe) *1–4:* 796

Bangkok, Thailand *1–4:* 491, 666

Bangladesh *1–4:* 575

Bangui *1–4:* 581

Banks, Joseph *1–4:* 52–56, 91, 257, 262, 360, 575, 601, 632–633, 635, 638; *5:* 25

Banks Island *1–4:* 601–602

Bantam *1–4:* 456–457, 486–487

Baptista, Pedro Joâo *1–4:* 57–60, 139

Bar Sauma, Rabban *1–4:* 65–68

Baranof Island *1–4:* 63

Baranov, Aleksandr *1–4:* 61–64

Baranov, Peter *1–4:* 62

Barbosa, Duarte *1–4:* 571

Barcelona, Spain *1–4:* 95, 247

Barents, Willem 5: 13–18, 14 (ill.), 15 (ill.), 120

Barents Sea *5:* 13, 14

Bari *1–4:* 50

Barka Khan *1–4:* 688

Barker, Frederick *1–4:* 794

Barotse *1–4:* 548

Barrow, John *1–4:* 638–639

Barrow Strait *1–4:* 639

Barrow Submarine Canyon *1–4:* 612

Barth, Heinrich *1–4:* 69–74, 737

Bartlett, Bob *1–4:* 430–431, 648, 652; *5:* 148

Basel, Switzerland *1–4:* 503–504

Bashkirs *5:* 77

Basra, Iraq *1–4:* 77, 89, 416–417

Bass, George *1–4:* 360

Bass Strait *1–4:* 360

Basundi (tribe) *1–4:* 581

Batak (tribe) *5:* 129

Batavia, Dutch East Indies (Djakarta, Indonesia) *1–4:* 64, 261, 733, 810

Bates, Henry Walter *1–4:* 304

Bathori, Sigismund *1–4:* 763

Bathurst, Australia *1–4:* 302

Bathurst Plains, Australia *5:* 26

"Battle" of Cahuenga *1–4:* 83

Battle of Coruña *1–4:* 784

Battle of Las Salinas *1–4:* 673

Battle of New Orleans *1–4:* 365

Battle of Okeechobee *1–4:* 83

Battle of Omdurman *1–4:* 583

Battle of Trafalgar *1–4:* 365

Battle of Wounded Knee *1–4:* 532

Batu *1–4:* 184–186

Baudin, Nicolas *1–4:* 362

Bauer, Ferdinand *1–4:* 361

Baxter, John *1–4:* 356, 357

Bay of Arguin *1–4:* 426

Bay of Bengal *1–4:* 693

Bay of Fundy *1–4:* 213–215; *5:* 64

Bay of Guayaquil *1–4:* 671

Bay of San Julián *1–4:* 568

Boldface indicates main entries in Volume 5 and their page numbers; *1–4:* refers to entries in the four-volume base set; *5:* refers to entries in Volume 5; (ill.) following a page number refers to illustrations.

191 | Index

Boldface indicates main entries in Volume 5 and their page numbers; *1–4:* refers to entries in the four-
volume base set; *5:* refers to entries in Volume 5; (ill.) following a page number refers to illustrations.

193 | Index

Caloris 588

Calypso *1–4:* 285

Cambridge, England *1–4:* 499

Cambridge Bay *1–4:* 17

Cambridge University *5:* 92

Camden, Arkansas *1–4:* 770

Camelford, Baron *1–4:* 835

Cameron, Verney Lovett *1–4:* 116, 234

Camp VIII *1–4:* 451

Canadian Arctic *1–4:* 361, 364–365, 525, 560; *5:* 68, 145–148

Canadian Arctic Expedition *1–4:* 856; *5:* 147

Canadian Arctic islands *1–4:* 858

Canadian Rockies *1–4:* 701

Cañar *1–4:* 481

Canary Islands *1–4:* 174, 244, 248, 288, 426, 455, 500, 568, 631

Cannanore, India *1–4:* 289

Canton, China *1–4:* 79, 105, 577, 667, 866; *5:* 57, 128

Cao, Diogo *1–4:* 311

Cap Haitien, Haiti *1–4:* 246

Capara *1–4:* 696

Cape Blanco *1–4:* 426

Cape Bojador *1–4:* 425

Cape Breton Island *1–4:* 170

Cape Canaveral, Florida *1–4:* 26, 28–29, 37, 353, 725; *5:* 82

Cape Chelyuskin *5:* 124

Cape Cod, Massachusetts *1–4:* 213–215; *5:* 47

Cape Columbia *1–4:* 430, 431, 650, 652

Cape Cross *1–4:* 311

Cape Dan *1–4:* 605

Cape Delgado *1–4:* 505

Cape Disappointment *1–4:* 832

Cape Fear, North Carolina *1–4:* 837–838

Cape Hatteras *1–4:* 837

Cape Hecla *1–4:* 648, 650

Cape Hood *1–4:* 832

Cape Horn *1–4:* 258, 297, 510, 732, 834, 853; *5:* 128

Cape Leeuwin *1–4:* 361

Cape Maria van Diemen *1–4:* 811

Cape Mendocino *1–4:* 178

Cape of Good Hope *1–4:* 116, 127, 190, 192, 241, 258, 260–262, 265, 288, 311, 313–314, 319, 386, 388, 390, 455, 566, 666, 832, 865; *5:* 129

Cape of Masts *1–4:* 426

Cape of the Virgins *1–4:* 569

Cape Parry *5:* 147

Cape Race, Newfoundland *1–4:* 170, 540

Cape Royds *1–4:* 746, 747

Cape Sheridan *1–4:* 650

Cape Town, South Africa *1–4:* 92, 302, 493, 501, 544, 548, 578, 829; *5:* 129

Cape Verde Islands *1–4:* 174, 294, 319, 387, 426, 455, 572, 631

Cape Wolstenholme *1–4:* 472

Cape York *1–4:* 647

Cape York Peninsula *1–4:* 487

Capelo, Hermenegildo de Brito. *See* Brito Capelo, Hermenegildo de

Caracas, Venezuela *1–4:* 99, 476, 477

Carantouan, New York *1–4:* 142

Cárdenas, Garcia Lopez de *1–4:* 271

Carib (tribe) *1–4:* 248, 838

Caribbean *5:* 48, 87

Caribbean Sea *1–4:* 192, 247, 600, 616, 713, 831, 855

Carlos IV *1–4:* 476

Carlyle, Thomas *1–4:* 358

Carmathians *1–4:* 597

Caroline Islands *1–4:* 326, 328

Caroni River *1–4:* 715, 716

Carpathia *5:* 163, 164

Carpathian Mountains *1–4:* 475

Carpentaria *1–4:* 147

Carpenter, William B. *1–4:* 209

Carpini, Giovanni da Pian del *1–4:* 183–186

Carranca, Andrés Dorantes de *1–4:* 346

Boldface indicates main entries in Volume 5 and their page numbers; *1–4:* refers to entries in the four-volume base set; *5:* refers to entries in Volume 5; (ill.) following a page number refers to illustrations.

195 | Index

Chibcha *1–4:* 479

Chicago River *5:* 107

Chickahominy River *1–4:* 764

Chickasaw (tribe) *1–4:* 770

Chihuahua, Mexico *1–4:* 348, 663

Childersburg, Alabama *1–4:* 770

Children's Crusade *1–4:* 96

Chile *1–4:* 510, 732, 834

Chillicothe, Ohio *1–4:* 120

Chiloe Island *1–4:* 300

Chimbu Valley *1–4:* 521

Chin-liu, China *1–4:* 460

China *1–4:* 461, 463, 469, 484, 509–510, 513, 687, 691–692, 814; *5:* 13, 40, 44, 54–57, 64, 98, 100, 101, 120, 128, 131, 132, 158

China Inland Mission *1–4:* 814

Chinese Nationalists *5:* 98

Chinese Turkistan *1–4:* 461

Chira River *1–4:* 672

Chirikov, Alexei Ilyich *5:* 22, 23

Chitambo *1–4:* 554

Cho Oyu *1–4:* 450

Chobe River *1–4:* 547–548

Choctaw Bluff, Alabama *1–4:* 770

Cholon (Saigon, Vietnam) *1–4:* 394

Cholula, Mexico *1–4:* 278

Choqquequirau, Peru *1–4:* 99

Chouart des Groseilliers, Médard *1–4:* 225–230

Christian, Fletcher *1–4:* 189

Christmas Island *1–4:* 265

Chryse Planitia *1–4:* 845

Chu Chan-chi *1–4:* 223

Chu Ti, Prince *1–4:* 222

Ch'üan-chou, China *1–4:* 79

Chukchi Peninsula *1–4:* 62

Chukchi Sea *1–4:* 611

Chuma, James *1–4:* 116, 231–237, 552, 554, 826

Churchill, Winston *1–4:* 748

Churchill River *1–4:* 561

Church Missionary Society *1–4:* 503, 505

Church of England *1–4:* 316

Church of Vidigueira *1–4:* 392

Cíbola. *See* Seven Cities of Cíbola)

Cilicia, Turkey *1–4:* 88

Cimarron River *1–4:* 761

Ciudad Bolivar *1–4:* 479

Clapp, Nicholas *5:* **40–46,** 40 (ill.), 41 (ill.)

Clapperton, Hugh *1–4:* 72, 637

Clark, George Rogers *1–4:* 119, 529

Clark, William *1–4:* 485, 528–537; *5:* 6

Clearwater River *1–4:* 534

Cleopatris, Egypt *1–4:* 384

Cleveland, Ohio *1–4:* 702

Clifford, Barry *5:* **47–53,** 47 (ill.), 48 (ill.), 49 (ill.), 50 (ill.)

Clinch River *1–4:* 118

Clinch River valley *1–4:* 119

Clitus *1–4:* 9

The Coast of Northeast Greenland 1–4: 132

Coats Land *1–4:* 748

Cochin, China *1–4:* 394, 397

Cocos Islands *1–4:* 302

Coelho, Nicolau *1–4:* 387

Cofitachequi *1–4:* 769

Coiba *1–4:* 615

Collins, Michael *1–4:* 29, 37

Collinson, Richard *1–4:* 17, 368, 600, 602

Colombia *1–4:* 479, 615, 625

Colorado River *1–4:* 166, 270–271, 530, 621, 759–760

Columbia 1–4: 37, 38, 725, 832

Columbia River *1–4:* 372, 483–484, 530, 534–535, 621–622, 821, 824, 832

Columbia River valley *1–4:* 824

Columbus, Bartholomew *1–4:* 239, 241, 249, 251–252

Columbus, Christopher *1–4:* 169–170, 238–254, 275, 288, 313, 386, 487, 614, 623, 695, 796, 839

Columbus, Diego *1–4:* 238, 240, 251, 254, 696

Columbus, Ferdinand *1–4:* 239, 241, 252

Comanche *1–4:* 761

Boldface indicates main entries in Volume 5 and their page numbers; *1–4:* refers to entries in the four-volume base set; *5:* refers to entries in Volume 5; (ill.) following a page number refers to illustrations.

197 | Index

Boldface indicates main entries in Volume 5 and their page numbers; *1–4:* refers to entries in the four-volume base set; *5:* refers to entries in Volume 5; (ill.) following a page number refers to illustrations.

199 | Index

Boldface indicates main entries in Volume 5 and their page numbers; *1–4:* refers to entries in the four-
volume base set; *5:* refers to entries in Volume 5; (ill.) following a page number refers to illustrations.

201 | Index

Fort Mandan *1–4:* 532

Fort New Archangel, Alaska *1–4:* 63

Fort Presépio *5:* 151, 152

Fort Prud'homme *1–4:* 516

Fort Ross, California *1–4:* 64

Fort St. Louis *1–4:* 518

Fort Vancouver, Washington *1–4:* 761

Fossett, Steve *5:* **62–67,** 62 (ill.), 63 (ill.)

Fossey, Dian *5:* 117

Foweira, Africa *1–4:* 49

Fox, Jack *1–4:* 522

Fox, Luke *1–4:* 640

Fox, Tom *1–4:* 522

Fox River *1–4:* 496; *5:* 106

Foxe Basin *1–4:* 640

Fra Mauro Highlands *1–4:* 31

Fraehn, C. M. *5:* 78

Fram *1–4:* 18, 19, 21, 607–608

Français *5:* 29–31

France *5:* 28, 31, 33, 85–88, 104, 107, 136, 162

Francia, José *1–4:* 482

Francis of Assisi *1–4:* 183

Franciscana *5:* 153

Franco-Prussian War *1–4:* 134, 397

François I (of France) *1–4:* 193–196, 837–838

Frankincense *5:* 40, 42, 44–46

Frankincense trade route *5:* 40, 45

Franklin, Jane Griffin *1–4:* 367–368

Franklin, John *1–4:* 14, 361, 364–369, 599, 639; *5:* 68

Franklin Strait *1–4:* 16, 368

Franz Josef Land *1–4:* 130, 607

Fraser, Simon *1–4:* 563

Fraser River *1–4:* 563

Frederick the Great (of Prussia) *1–4:* 474

Free Svanetia *5:* 99

Freetown, Sierra Leone *1–4:* 180, 500

Freiburg, Germany *1–4:* 475

Frémont, Jessie Benton *1–4:* 371, 374

Frémont, John Charles *1–4:* 370–374

Fremont Peak *1–4:* 372

French and Indian War *1–4:* 117, 122, 508

French Antarctic Expedition *5:* 32, 33

French Canada *5:* 104, 107

French Congo *1–4:* 136

French Equatorial Expedition *5:* 87

French Foreign Legion *1–4:* 736

French Geographical Society *1–4:* 182, 329

French Guiana *1–4:* 717

French Legion of Honor *1–4:* 326

French Polynesia *1–4:* 733; *5:* 36

French Revolution *1–4:* 511

French River *1–4:* 142, 216

The Friendly Arctic *5:* 148

Friendship *1–4:* 332, 402–404

Frobisher, Martin *1–4:* 344, 472; *5:* 70

Frobisher Bay *5:* 70

Frontenac, Count de *1–4:* 496, 513

Frozen Strait *1–4:* 640

Fuchs, Vivian *1–4:* 375–377, 452–453, 801

Funatsu, Keizo *1–4:* 803–804

Fur trade *5:* 6, 8

Furneaux Islands *1–4:* 360

Fury *1–4:* 641–642

Fury Strait *1–4:* 641

G

Gabet, Joseph *1–4:* 814

Gabon *1–4:* 135, 321–322, 500

Gades, Phoenicia *1–4:* 710

Gagarin, Yuri *1–4:* 378–382, 402, 559, 782, 818

Galapagos Islands *1–4:* 301, 303; *5:* 36

Galfridus of Langele *1–4:* 68

Galileo *1–4:* 32, 464

Boldface indicates main entries in Volume 5 and their page numbers; *1–4:* refers to entries in the four-volume base set; *5:* refers to entries in Volume 5; (ill.) following a page number refers to illustrations.

203 | Index

Boldface indicates main entries in Volume 5 and their page numbers; *1–4:* refers to entries in the four-volume base set; *5:* refers to entries in Volume 5; (ill.) following a page number refers to illustrations.

205 | Index

Boldface indicates main entries in Volume 5 and their page numbers; *1–4:* refers to entries in the four-volume base set; *5:* refers to entries in Volume 5; (ill.) following a page number refers to illustrations.

207 | Index

J

Jackson, Frederick *1–4:* 608

Jackson, Thomas "Stonewall" *1–4:* 374

Jackson Hole, Wyoming *1–4:* 484

Jaén *1–4:* 481

Jaette Glacier *1–4:* 131

Jahangir, Emperor *1–4:* 23

Jalapa, Mexico *1–4:* 277

Jamaica *1–4:* 249, 253–254, 357–358, 626

Jamaica Channel *1–4:* 253

James I (of England) *1–4:* 712, 716

James II (of England) *1–4:* 229

James Bay *1–4:* 472

James River *1–4:* 764

Jameson, Robert *1–4:* 293

Jamestown, Virginia *1–4:* 763

Jan Mayen Island *1–4:* 469

Janszoon, Willem *1–4:* 486–488

Japan *1–4:* 492, 809; *5:* 21, 22, 63, 64, 82, 98, 101, 109, 124, 125

Jarra *1–4:* 633

Jason 1–4: 490, 492

Jason Junior (JJ) *5:* 166

Jauf, Saudi Arabia *1–4:* 110

Java *1–4:* 222–223, 457, 486, 488, 667, 862

Java Man *5:* 91

Jeannette 1–4: 606

Jebel Dinka *5:* 158

Jefferson, Thomas *1–4:* 482, 528–530, 533, 536

Jefferson River *1–4:* 533

Jemison, Mae *5:* **80–84,** 80 (ill.), 82 (ill.)

Jemison Group *5:* 84

Jersey Island, English Channel *1–4:* 716

Jerusalem, Israel *1–4:* 65, 76, 87, 96–97, 597, 786; *5:* 127

Jessup, Morris K. *1–4:* 647

Jesuit missionaries *1–4:* 23–25, 494, 498, 512, 668, 866

Jet Propulsion Laboratory *1–4:* 847; *5:* 42

Jhansi *1–4:* 491

Jhelum River *1–4:* 9, 11

Jidda, Saudi Arabia *1–4:* 76, 152, 290

Jih-k'a-tse, Tibet *1–4:* 308, 753

Jinja, Uganda *1–4:* 3

Johansen, Hjalmar *1–4:* 607

John Bishop Memorial Hospital *1–4:* 105

John F. Kennedy Space Center *1–4:* 402, 587

John I (of Portugal) *1–4:* 240, 247, 288, 424, 425

John II (of Portugal) *1–4:* 288, 290, 291, 311, 313, 386

John III (of Portugal) *1–4:* 864

John of Monte Corvino *1–4:* 68

Johns Hopkins University *1–4:* 337

Johnson, Amy *1–4:* 333, 489–493

Johnson, Lyndon B. *1–4:* 404

Johnston, Keith *1–4:* 235, 236, 826

Johnson Space Center *5:* 114

Johore *1–4:* 458

Joinville Land *1–4:* 328

Joliba 1–4: 636, 637

Jolliet, Louis *1–4:* 494–498, 513, 516; *5:* 104, 106–108

Jordan Valley *1–4:* 597

José, Amaro *1–4:* 57–60 139

Josephine Ford 1–4: 160

Journal of a Voyage by Order of the King to the Equator 5: 89

A Journey in Ashango Land 1–4: 324

"*J.T.*" : *The Biography of an African Monkey 1–4:* 2

Juan Fernández Islands *1–4:* 124, 188, 569, 732

Juba, Somalia *1–4:* 223

Juba, Sudan *1–4:* 591; *5:* 160

Jumano (tribe) *1–4:* 347

Jungle Portraits 1–4: 4

Junkers, Hugo *1–4:* 422

Jupiter *1–4:* 464, 468, 847–850

Jupiter Inlet *1–4:* 697

Jur River *1–4:* 582

Boldface indicates main entries in Volume 5 and their page numbers; *1–4:* refers to entries in the four-volume base set; *5:* refers to entries in Volume 5; (ill.) following a page number refers to illustrations.

209 | Index

K

Ka-erh *1–4:* 754–755
Ka'abah *1–4:* 152
Kabalega Falls *1–4:* 43
Kabara *1–4:* 636
Kabul, Afghanistan *1–4:* 8, 434, 808
Kabul River *1–4:* 434, 462; *5:* 56
Kabylia campaigns *1–4:* 736
Kadiköy *1–4:* 869
Kafu River *1–4:* 47
Kagoshima *1–4:* 667
K'ai-feng *1–4:* 687
Kai Island *1–4:* 487
Kailas Mountains *1–4:* 421
Kalahari Desert *1–4:* 544, 546
Kalami River *1–4:* 10
Kalgan, China *1–4:* 705
Kalomo River *1–4:* 549
Kalongosi River *1–4:* 553
Kamalia *1–4:* 634
Kamchadals *1–4:* 42
Kamchatka *1–4:* 511
Kamchatka Mountains *1–4:* 41
Kamchatka Peninsula *1–4:* 40–42, 267, 510; *5:* 20
Kamchatka River *1–4:* 41, 42
Kamehameha (of Hawaii) *1–4:* 64, 832, 834
Kan-chou River *1–4:* 808
Kanawha valley *1–4:* 121
Kanbaya, port *1–4:* 596
Kane, Elisha Kent *1–4:* 644; *5:* 71, 72
Kangaroo Island *1–4:* 362
Kannauj *1–4:* 462
Kano, Nigeria *1–4:* 71
Kanpur *1–4:* 462
Kansas (tribe) *1–4:* 662
Kansu *5:* 102
Kapuas River *5:* 129
Kara Sea *5:* 16
Karachi, Pakistan *1–4:* 10, 434, 491
Karagwe *1–4:* 776
Karakorum, Mongolia *1–4:* 184–185

Karakorum Range *1–4:* 862–863
Karankawa (tribe) *1–4:* 518
Karbala, Iraq *1–4:* 88
Karlsefni, Thorfinn *1–4:* 527
Karuma Falls *1–4:* 48
Kasai River *1–4:* 548–549
Kasanje, Africa *1–4:* 58–59
Kashgar, China *1–4:* 419–421, 463, 690, 808; *5:* 56, 102
Kashmir, India *1–4:* 24, 105, 462, 755, 807, 862; *5:* 98, 102
Kasonia, Gascony, France *1–4:* 67
Kassange *1–4:* 549
Katanga *1–4:* 58
Katmandu, Nepal *1–4:* 452, 753
Katsina, Nigeria *1–4:* 72
Kauai, Hawaii *1–4:* 64
Kayak Island *5:* 23
Kazakhstan *1–4:* 778
Kazeh *1–4:* 553, 774, 790
Kazembe, Zambia *1–4:* 58–59, 233
Kealakekua Bay *1–4:* 266
Kearny, Stephen W. *1–4:* 373
Keeling Atoll *1–4:* 302
Kellett, Henry, Captain *1–4:* 602–603
Kemys, Lawrence *1–4:* 716–717
Kenai Peninsula *5:* 23
Kennedy, John F. *1–4:* 26, 34, 402, 404
Kennedy Space Center *5:* 82, 83
Kentucky River *1–4:* 118–119
Kenya *1–4:* 504, 589–591, 594, 719, 773, 828; *5:* 81, 91, 92, 96, 97, 140, 142
Kerguelen Island *1–4:* 265
Kerman *1–4:* 12
Keyzer, Pieter de *1–4:* 455–456
Khabarovsk *1–4:* 701–703
Khadija (of Maldive Islands) *1–4:* 78
Khanbalik *1–4:* 688, 691–693
Kharashahr *1–4:* 461
Khartoum, Sudan *1–4:* 4, 45, 49–50, 591, 776; *5:* 156, 158, 159
Khawak Pass *1–4:* 8
Khazars *1–4:* 597; *5:* 77

Boldface indicates main entries in Volume 5 and their page numbers; *1–4:* refers to entries in the four-volume base set; *5:* refers to entries in Volume 5; (ill.) following a page number refers to illustrations.

211   Index

L

La Boussole *1–4:* 509, 511

La Concepción de Urbana *1–4:* 478

La Condamine, Charles-Marie de *1–4:* 409–410, 476–477, 481; *5:* **85–90,** 85 (ill.), 86 (ill.)

La Dauphine *1–4:* 837–838

La Guajira *1–4:* 624–625

La Hogue *1–4:* 638

La Motte, Dominique *1–4:* 513

La Navidad (Limonade-Bord-de-Mer, Haiti) *1–4:* 246, 248

La Paz, Bolivia *1–4:* 654

La Paz Bay *1–4:* 280–281

La Pérouse, Jean-François de Galaup, comte de *1–4:* 326, 508–511

La Pérouse Strait *1–4:* 510

La Relación y Comentarios *1–4:* 168

La Rochelle, France *1–4:* 766; *5:* 87

La Salle, René-Robert Cavelier de *1–4:* 512–518

La Salle, Illinois *1–4:* 516

Labrador *1–4:* 173, 338, 432, 498, 526, 652

Lacerda, Francisco José de *1–4:* 57–58

Lachine Rapids *1–4:* 142, 195, 497

Ladakh, India *1–4:* 105, 755

Lady Alice *1–4:* 794–795

A Lady's Life in the Rocky Mountains *1–4:* 104

A Lady's Second Journey Round the World *5:* 130

A Lady's Voyage Round the World *5:* 129

Lae, New Guinea *1–4:* 520

Laetoli, Tanzania *5:* 95

Lagos, Portugal *1–4:* 239, 737

Lagrée, Ernest Doudart de *1–4:* 395

Laing, Alexander Gordon *1–4:* 181

Lake Alakol *1–4:* 185

Lake Albert *1–4:* 3, 43, 47–48, 50, 794, 798

Lake Athabaska *1–4:* 822

Lake Baikal *5:* 22

Lake Bangweulu *1–4:* 232–234, 551–552, 554

Lake Chad *1–4:* 69–72, 136, 737

Lake Chala *5:* 143

Lake Champlain *1–4:* 215

Lake Chilwa *1–4:* 550

Lake Courte Oreille *1–4:* 226

Lake Dilolo *1–4:* 548

Lake Edward *1–4:* 798

Lake Erie *1–4:* 142, 513–514

Lake Eyre *1–4:* 356; *5:* 60

Lake Huron *1–4:* 142, 216, 496, 514

Lake Illiwarra *1–4:* 360

Lake Issyk-Kul *1–4:* 419

Lake Itasca *1–4:* 662

Lake Kazembe *1–4:* 233

Lake Leopold *1–4:* 796

Lake Malawi *1–4:* 550–552, 826

Lake Manitoba *1–4:* 823

Lake Maracaibo *1–4:* 624

Lake Michigan *1–4:* 216, 496–497, 514; *5:* 106, 107

Lake Mweru *1–4:* 552

Lake Naivasha *1–4:* 827

Lake Ngami *1–4:* 544, 546

Lake Nipissing *1–4:* 142, 216

Lake No *5:* 158

Lake Nyasa, Malawi *1–4:* 112, 231–232, 236, 505, 773, 789, 826

Lake of the Woods *1–4:* 823

Lake Ontario *1–4:* 513

Lake Parima *1–4:* 479

Lake Raeside *5:* 59

Lake Rukwa *1–4:* 826

Lake Simcoe *1–4:* 142

Lake Superior *1–4:* 142, 225–227, 823; *5:* 106

Lake Tahoe, Nevada *1–4:* 104

Lake Tanganyika *1–4:* 113, 115–116, 155–156, 233–234, 236, 551–553, 774, 790, 792, 794, 826

Lake Terrens *1–4:* 356

Lake Texcoco *5:* 2

Boldface indicates main entries in Volume 5 and their page numbers; *1–4:* refers to entries in the four-volume base set; *5:* refers to entries in Volume 5; (ill.) following a page number refers to illustrations.

213 | Index

M

Macao *1–4:* 510
Macedonia *1–4:* 5, 433
Mach, Ernst *1–4:* 872
Machiparo *1–4:* 630
Machu Picchu *1–4:* 98, 100, 102
Mackenzie, Alexander *1–4:* 367, 560–565, 834
Mackenzie, Charles Frederick *1–4:* 231
Mackenzie Bay *5:* 146
Mackenzie Delta *1–4:* 601
Mackenzie Pass *1–4:* 563
Mackenzie River *1–4:* 18, 367, 560, 562, 601, 801; *5:* 146
Mackinac *1–4:* 496, 514
Macquarie Island *1–4:* 92
Mactan Island *1–4:* 570
Madagascar *1–4:* 456, 458; *5:* 130
Madeira *5:* 36
Madeira Islands *1–4:* 19, 239, 425
Madeira River *1–4:* 630
Madison, James *1–4:* 533
Madison River *1–4:* 533
Madura *1–4:* 457
Magadha *1–4:* 462; *5:* 56
Magdalen Islands *1–4:* 194
Magdalena River *1–4:* 479, 615
Magellan, Ferdinand *1–4:* 174, 566–573
Magomero, Africa *1–4:* 231
Maharashtra *1–4:* 463
Mahdia, Tunisia *1–4:* 415
Maigaard, Christian *1–4:* 645
Maillart, Ella *5:* **98–103,** 98 (ill.), 100 (ill.)
Makatéa Island *1–4:* 733
Makololo *1–4:* 546–550
Makran Coast, Pakistan *1–4:* 10–11
Malacca, Malaya *1–4:* 223, 667, 865
Malaga, Spain *1–4:* 79
Malagarasi River *1–4:* 790
Malakal *1–4:* 591
Malange, Angola *1–4:* 138
Malawi *1–4:* 828
Malay Archipelago *1–4:* 327, 459, 666, 742, 865

Malay Peninsula *1–4:* 105, 666, 692
Maldive Islands *1–4:* 78, 223
Maldonado, Pedro Vicente *5:* 87, 88
Malheur River *1–4:* 620
Mali *1–4:* 578–580
Malindi, Kenya *1–4:* 223, 290, 389–390
Malta Island *1–4:* 785
Malthus, Thomas
Mambirima Falls *1–4:* 140
Mana, India *1–4:* 24
Mana Pass *1–4:* 24, 754
Manacupuru *5:* 152
Manchukuo *5:* 101
Manchuria *5:* 101
Manco *1–4:* 672
Manco II *1–4:* 99
Mandan (tribe) *1–4:* 532, 823
Mandarin *1–4:* 460
Manhattan *1–4:* 470
S.S. *Manhattan 1–4:* 17
Mankinga (of the Chagga) 719–721
Manning, Thomas *1–4:* 574–577
Manoa, South America *1–4:* 715
Manta *5:* 87
Manuel Comnenus *1–4:* 95, 96
Manuel I (of Portugal) *1–4:* 313, 386, 390–391
Manuel II *1–4:* 566
Maori (tribe) *1–4:* 259, 260, 302, 810
A Map of Virginia, 1–4: 764
Maragheh, Azerbaijan *1–4:* 66
Marañón River *1–4:* 411, 413; *5:* 88, 89
Marchand, Jean Baptiste *1–4:* 136, 578–584
Marcos, Fray *1–4:* 176
Mare Crisium *1–4:* 559
Mare Imbrium *1–4:* 556
Margarita, Venezuela *1–4:* 630
Margarita Island *1–4:* 251, 624
Mariame (tribe) *1–4:* 347
Mariana Islands *1–4:* 569, 573
Mariana Trench *1–4:* 211, 659
Marias River *1–4:* 533
Mar'ib, Yemen *1–4:* 384

Merchant Adventurers *1–4:* 175

Mercury *1–4:* 481, 587–588, 850

Mercury 1–4: 31, 401

Mercury 5 1–4: 28

"Mercury Seven" *1–4:* 401, 404

Mercy Bay *1–4:* 602–603

Méré *1–4:* 582

Meru *1–4:* 3

Meryon, Charles *1–4:* 784–785, 787

Mesawa *1–4:* 503

Mesopotamia *1–4:* 8, 87, 97, 219–220, 808

Messina, Sicily *1–4:* 97

Mestiza 1–4: 479

Metternich, Clemens von *1–4:* 475

Metzenbaum, Howard *1–4:* 405

Mexico *5:* 1–3, 5, 11, 104, 106

Mexico City, Mexico *1–4:* 167, 270, 272, 273, 541; *5:* 2

Michel, Jean-Louis *5:* 165

Michilimackinac *1–4:* 216, 496, 516

Micronesia *1–4:* 327

Middle East *5:* 42–44, 156

Midjökull *1–4:* 342

Mikkelsen, Ejnar *5:* 146

Miletus *1–4:* 6

Mill, John Stuart *1–4:* 358

Minab River *1–4:* 10

Mindanao Island *1–4:* 571

Minnetaree (tribe) *1–4:* 532, 534

***Mir* space station *5:* 109–114,** 109 (ill.), 110 (ill.), 112 (ill.)

Mir/Shuttle rendezvous program *5:* 109

Mirambo *1–4:* 790

Miranda *1–4:* 850

Mirnyi 1–4: 91–92

Miss Boyd Land *1–4:* 131

Mission San Gabriel *1–4:* 760

Mississippi River *1–4:* 165, 494, 496–497, 513–518, 529–530, 661–662, 767, 770, 823; *5:* 6, 104

Mississippi Valley *1–4:* 517

Missoula, Montana *1–4:* 620

Missouri *1–4:* 483, 533, 662; *5:* 6–9, 11, 43, 64, 65, 106

Missouri (tribe) *1–4:* 531

Missouri River *1–4:* 483, 496, 516, 530–533, 535–536, 759, 823; *5:* 6–9, 106

Mitchell, Edgar *1–4:* 31

Mocha, Yemen *1–4:* 666

Moffat, Robert *1–4:* 544

Mogadishu, Somalia *1–4:* 223

Mohawk (tribe) *1–4:* 215, 225

Mohi, Hungary *1–4:* 184

Mojave (tribe) *1–4:* 621, 760

Mojave Desert *1–4:* 760

Mojave River *1–4:* 760

Môle St. Nicolas, Haiti *1–4:* 245

Mollison, Jim *1–4:* 492, 493, 592

Moluccas (Spice Islands) *1–4:* 127, 174, 318, 457, 567, 570–571, 573, 733, 865

Mombasa, Kenya *1–4:* 3, 113, 223, 289, 389, 504, 718, 828; *5:* 140, 141, 144

Möngkhe *1–4:* 184

Mongol Empire *1–4:* 688

Mongolia *1–4:* 704–705

Mongolia and the Tangut Country 1–4: 706

Mongols *1–4:* 65–67, 77, 97, 183, 185, 576, 687, 691–693

Moniz, Felipa Perestrello de *1–4:* 238

Montana *1–4:* 484, 533

Monterey, California *1–4:* 83, 510, 761, 834

Montevideo, Uruguay *1–4:* 296, 299

Montezuma *1–4:* 274–276, 278, 279

Montgomerie, Thomas George *1–4:* 751

Monticello *1–4:* 482

Montpelier, France *1–4:* 95

Montreal, Quebec *1–4:* 195, 226, 483–484, 497, 512–513, 516, 518

Monts, Pierre de *1–4:* 214

Moore, John *1–4:* 784

Moors *1–4:* 241–242, 424

Boldface indicates main entries in Volume 5 and their page numbers; *1–4:* refers to entries in the four-volume base set; *5:* refers to entries in Volume 5; (ill.) following a page number refers to illustrations.

217 | Index

N

Nairobi *5:* 91, 92, 95, 96

Najaf, Iraq *1–4:* 77

Najran, Saudi Arabia *1–4:* 384

Nalanda *1–4:* 462, 463

Namibe, Angola *1–4:* 139

Nan Shan mountains *1–4:* 707; *5:* 55

Nanking, China *1–4:* 222–223; *5:* 57

Nansemond River *1–4:* 765

Nansen, Fridtjof *1–4:* 15, 18–19, 604–609, 645; *5:* 125

Naples, Italy *1–4:* 95

Napo River *1–4:* 627–629; *5:* 153

Napoléon Bonaparte *1–4:* 474, 528, 784–785

Napoleonic Wars *1–4:* 56, 365, 476, 482, 638, 831

Nares, George *1–4:* 209, 210; *5:* 74

Narragansett Bay *1–4:* 838

Narrative of the United States Exploring Expedition 1–4: 854

Narváez, Pánfilo de *1–4:* 165, 176, 278, 346

NASA. *See* National Aeronautics and Space Administration (NASA)

NASA Space Flight Center *1–4:* 466

Nass River *1–4:* 622

Natchez (tribe) *1–4:* 516

Natchitoches, Louisiana *1–4:* 664

National Aeronautics and Space Administration (NASA) *1–4:* 26, 29, 31, 36, 39, 465–467, 660, 723–724, 726, 780, 847; *5:* 42, 46, 81, 82, 84, 109, 112–114

National African Company *1–4:* 828

National Air and Space Museum *1–4:* 743, 845

National Geographic Society *1–4:* 159, 377, 652; *5:* 66, 95, **115–119,** 115 (ill.)

National Geographic magazine *5:* 115, 117

National Space Development Agency of Japan (NASDA) *5:* 82

Native American *1–4:* 470, 478, 495–496, 514, 516, 518, 527–528, 530, 532, 534–536; *5:* 11, 104, 106

U.S.S. *Nautilus 1–4:* 610–613, 859

Navasota, Texas *1–4:* 518

Navidad, Mexico *1–4:* 177

Nduye, Zaire *1–4:* 4

Nearchus *1–4:* 10–13

Nearest the Pole: A Narrative of the Polar Expedition of the Peary Arctic Club 1–4: 652

Necho, King *1–4:* 435

Needles, California *1–4:* 621

A Negro at the North Pole 1–4: 432

Negros Island *1–4:* 571

Nelson, Horatio *1–4:* 359

Nelson River *1–4:* 229

Nepal *1–4:* 450–453, 751; *5:* 56, 103

Neptune *1–4:* 847, 849–850

Nestorians *1–4:* 65, 66

Nestorius *1–4:* 66

The Netherlands *5:* 13, 89, 135, 155, 156, 159

Netsilik *1–4:* 16

Neva 1–4: 63

Nevado Coropuna *1–4:* 99, 101

New Archangel, Alaska *1–4:* 64

New Brunswick *1–4:* 194–195, 214

New Caledonia *1–4:* 264; *5:* 38

New France (Canada) *1–4:* 141, 212, 216–217, 225, 494, 496, 497, 512–513, 516

New Guinea *1–4:* 3, 127, 190, 328, 487–488, 519–520, 523, 811–812

New Hebrides *5:* 36, 37

New Holland *1–4:* 488, 812

New Ireland *1–4:* 127, 190

New London *5:* 70, 71

New London Company *1–4:* 763

Boldface indicates main entries in Volume 5 and their page numbers; *1–4:* refers to entries in the four-volume base set; *5:* refers to entries in Volume 5; (ill.) following a page number refers to illustrations.

219 | Index

Boldface indicates main entries in Volume 5 and their page numbers; *1–4:* refers to entries in the four-volume base set; *5:* refers to entries in Volume 5; (ill.) following a page number refers to illustrations.

221 | Index

Boldface indicates main entries in Volume 5 and their page numbers; *1–4:* refers to entries in the four-volume base set; *5:* refers to entries in Volume 5; (ill.) following a page number refers to illustrations.

223 | Index

Boldface indicates main entries in Volume 5 and their page numbers; *1–4:* refers to entries in the four-volume base set; *5:* refers to entries in Volume 5; (ill.) following a page number refers to illustrations.

225 | Index

S

Sakhalin *1–4:* 510
Sakhalin Island *5:* 133
Salapunco, Peru *1–4:* 99
Samaná Bay *1–4:* 246
Samana Cay, Bahama Islands *1–4:* 245
Samar Island *1–4:* 570
Samaritans *1–4:* 97
Samarkand, Uzbekistan *1–4:* 78, 461; *5:* 101
Samudra, Sumatra *1–4:* 79
San Antonio *1–4:* 567, 569
San Antonio, Texas *1–4:* 166, 539
San Antonio Bay *1–4:* 347
San Bernardino, California *1–4:* 621
San Diego, California *1–4:* 539, 760
San Diego Bay *1–4:* 177
San Diego Harbor *1–4:* 178
San Domingo, Cuba *1–4:* 319
San Fernando de Apuré *1–4:* 478
San Francisco, California *1–4:* 104; *5:* 63, 130
San Francisco Bay *1–4:* 832, 834
San Germain, Puerto Rico *1–4:* 696
San Gerónimo, Mexico *1–4:* 270
San Joaquin Valley *1–4:* 372, 621, 760
San Jose, Trinidad *1–4:* 715
San Juan, Puerto Rico *1–4:* 671, 696, 698
San Kuri *1–4:* 3
San Luis Rey *1–4:* 537
San Miguel, California *1–4:* 83, 672
San Miguel Island *1–4:* 177
San Salvador, Bahama Islands *1–4:* 176, 245, 696
San Sebastián *1–4:* 615
San Tomás *1–4:* 717
San'a, Yemen *1–4:* 597
Sancti Spiritus, Argentina *1–4:* 174
Sandwich Islands *1–4:* 510
Sandy Hook *1–4:* 470

Sangha (monks) *5:* 56
Sangre de Cristo Mountains *1–4:* 373, 663
Sanlúcar de Barrameda *1–4:* 568, 573
Sansanding *1–4:* 634, 636
Sanskrit *1–4:* 462–463
Santa Barbara Channel *1–4:* 177
Santa Catalina Island *1–4:* 177
Santa Cruz *1–4:* 511, 697
Santa Cruz Islands *1–4:* 189
Santa Fe, Argentina *1–4:* 299
Santa Fe, New Mexico *1–4:* 662–664, 761
Santa Fe Trail *1–4:* 83
Santa Maria *1–4:* 243, 245–246, 248
Santa Maria de la Antigua del Darién *1–4:* 615
Santa Maria Island *1–4:* 246
Santangel, Luis de *1–4:* 242
Santiago *1–4:* 567, 569
Santiago, Cuba *1–4:* 275
Santiago Island *1–4:* 572
Santo Domingo, Dominican Republic *1–4:* 165, 249, 251–254, 274, 615, 625, 696, 840
Santos, Brazil *1–4:* 157
Sao Gabriel *1–4:* 387, 390
Sâo Jorge da Mina, Benin *1–4:* 239
São Luís do Maranhão, Brazil *5:* 150, 151, 154
Sao Rafael *1–4:* 387, 390
Sao Tiago *1–4:* 294
Sarawak, Borneo *5:* 129
Sargasso Sea *1–4:* 244
Saskatchewan, Canada *1–4:* 561, 822–823; *5:* 63
Sasquatch *1–4:* 453
Saturn *1–4:* 464, 467, 847, 849–850
Saturn *1–4:* 37
Saturn V *1–4:* 27
Sault Ste. Marie, Michigan *5:* 105
Savannah River *1–4:* 769
Savitskaya, Svetlana *1–4:* 723
Sawyer, Herbert *1–4:* 105

Boldface indicates main entries in Volume 5 and their page numbers; *1–4:* refers to entries in the four-volume base set; *5:* refers to entries in Volume 5; (ill.) following a page number refers to illustrations.

227 | Index

Shuttle Imaging Radar (SIR) *5:* 25, 42, 68–70, 74, 85

Siam *1–4:* 812

Sian *1–4:* 461, 463, 692

Siberia *1–4:* 267, 469, 482, 492, 509–510; *5:* 19–23, 124, 131, 132, 134, 148

Sicily, Italy *1–4:* 67, 95, 434, 710

Sidayu *1–4:* 457

Siddhartha Gautama *1–4:* 307; *5:* 56

Sierra de Quareca *1–4:* 616

Sierra Leone *1–4:* 387, 426; *5:* 58, 81

Sierra Nevada *1–4:* 83, 372–373, 621, 760

Sijilmasa, Morocco *1–4:* 416

Sikkim *1–4:* 308, 751, 814, 816

The Silent World 1–4: 285

Silk Road *1–4:* 218, 220

Silla *1–4:* 634

Silverstein, Abe *1–4:* 26

Simbing *1–4:* 633

Simla, India *1–4:* 105

Simonstown *1–4:* 501

Simpson, George *1–4:* 619

Simpson Strait *1–4:* 17

Sinai, Egypt *1–4:* 290

Sinai Desert *1–4:* 97

Sinai Peninsula *1–4:* 76

Sinaloa, Mexico *1–4:* 281

Sind, Pakistan *1–4:* 151, 434

Singapore *1–4:* 105, 491; *5:* 129

Singh, Duleep *1–4:* 44

Singh, Kalian *1–4:* 754

Singh, Kishen *1–4:* 752

Singh, Mani *1–4:* 751, 753–754

Singh, Nain *1–4:* 750–756

Sinkiang Uighur, China *1–4:* 66, 704–706; *5:* 56, 101, 102

Sino-Japanese War *1–4:* 106

Sino-Swedish Scientific Expedition *1–4:* 422

Sinta, Pedro de *1–4:* 426

Sioux (tribe) *1–4:* 227, 532

Sioux City, Iowa *1–4:* 531

Siple, Paul A. *1–4:* 163

Sitka Island *1–4:* 63

Six Months in the Sandwich Islands 1–4: 104

Skate 1–4: 860

Sketches Awheel 1–4: 862

Skraelings *1–4:* 527

Sky Roads of the World 1–4: 493

Slave River *1–4:* 561

Slidell, John *1–4:* 854

Smith, Edward J. *5:* 162

Smith, Jedediah *1–4:* 620–621, 757–761; *5:* 8

Smith, John *1–4:* 470, 762–766

Smith Sound *5:* 71

Smithsonian Institution *1–4:* 743

Smoky River *1–4:* 563

Snaefellsnes *1–4:* 342

Snake River *1–4:* 372, 484, 534, 619–620

Snook, Neta *1–4:* 331

Society Islands *1–4:* 733

Society of Geography *1–4:* 138

Socrates *1–4:* 867, 870

Sofala, Mozambique *1–4:* 289, 392

Soko (tribe) *1–4:* 796

Sokoto, Nigeria *1–4:* 72

Solis, Juan Diaz de *1–4:* 173, 568

"Solo Challenger" *5:* 64

Solomon Islands *1–4:* 126, 189–190, 326, 328, 511

Somali Desert *1–4:* 3

Somaliland *1–4:* 773

Somers, Geoff *1–4:* 803

Somerset Island *1–4:* 16

Son-tay, Vietnam *1–4:* 398

Songkhla, Thailand *1–4:* 491

Sonora, Mexico *1–4:* 167

SOS *5:* 164

Soto, Hernando de *1–4:* 164, 167, 767–771

South 1–4: 749

South America *5:* 30, 32, 33, 85, 87, 90, 127, 128, 130, 150, 153, 154

South Australia *5:* 59, 60

South China Sea *1–4:* 222

South Georgia Island *1–4:* 91, 749

Boldface indicates main entries in Volume 5 and their page numbers; *1–4:* refers to entries in the four-volume base set; *5:* refers to entries in Volume 5; (ill.) following a page number refers to illustrations.

229 | Index

T

Boldface indicates main entries in Volume 5 and their page numbers; *1–4:* refers to entries in the four-volume base set; *5:* refers to entries in Volume 5; (ill.) following a page number refers to illustrations.

231 | Index

Tierra del Fuego *1–4:* 53, 258, 264, 296–297, 299–300

Tigeux, New Mexico *1–4:* 271

Tigeux War *1–4:* 272

Tigre *1–4:* 503

Tigris River *1–4:* 108, 110, 868; *5:* 128

Tikrat, Iraq *1–4:* 596

Timbuktu, Mali *1–4:* 69, 73, 80, 179–181, 634, 636, 737

Timor, Malay Archipelago *1–4:* 189, 491

Tinian Island *1–4:* 192

Tinné, Alexine *5:* **155–160,** 155 (ill.), 157 (ill.)

Tintellust *1–4:* 71

Tinto River *1–4:* 243

Tiribazus *1–4:* 868

Tiryns, Greece *5:* 138

Tissaphernes *1–4:* 868

Titan *1–4:* 849

Titania *1–4:* 850

R.M.S. *Titanic* *5:* 117, **161–168,** 161 (ill.), 163 (ill.), 165 (ill.), 167 (ill.)

Titanic Historical Society *5:* 167

Titov, Gherman *1–4:* 380

Tlaxcala, Mexico *1–4:* 277–279

Tlingit-Haida *1–4:* 63

Tockwough (tribe) *1–4:* 765

Tokugawa *1–4:* 866

Tom Thumb *1–4:* 360

Tonga Island *1–4:* 265, 328, 809, 811

Tongariro National Park *1–4:* 449

Tonquin *1–4:* 484

Tonty, Henri de *1–4:* 513, 514, 516

Tookolito *5:* 70, 71, 73

Toowoomba *1–4:* 520

Töregene *1–4:* 185

Torell, Otto *5:* 121

Torres, Luis Vaez de *1–4:* 126, 261, 488

Torres Strait *1–4:* 126, 261, 362, 487

Toulon, France *1–4:* 182, 282, 326, 659

Tovar, Pedro de *1–4:* 271

Tower of London *1–4:* 714, 716

Trabzon *1–4:* 694, 869

Traits of American-Indian Life and Character *1–4:* 618

Trans-Siberian Railroad *1–4:* 701

Transantarctic Mountains *1–4:* 20

Transcontinental Air Transport *1–4:* 541

Transylvania Company *1–4:* 119

Trapezus *1–4:* 869

Travancore, India *1–4:* 865

Travels in West Africa *1–4:* 501

Treaty of Tordesillas *1–4:* 386, 567; *5:* 150

Trebizond, Greece *1–4:* 67

Trent Affair *1–4:* 854

Triana, Rodrigo de *1–4:* 244

Trieste *1–4:* 659

Trieste, Italy *1–4:* 157, 659

Trinidad *1–4:* 567, 571, 573

Trinidad *1–4:* 251, 276, 624, 715; *5:* 36

Tripoli, Libya *1–4:* 55, 70, 71, 737; *5:* 159

Triton *1–4:* 850

Trois-Rivières, Canada *1–4:* 226–227; *5:* 105

Trojan War *5:* 135, 138

Tromsö *5:* 123

Trondheim, Norway *1–4:* 711

Troy, Greece *1–4:* 6; *5:* 135–139

True Relation of Virginia *1–4:* 764

Trujillo, Peru *1–4:* 627, 481

Truman, Harry S *1–4:* 428

Tsaidam, China *1–4:* 219, 705

Tsangpo River *1–4:* 752, 753

Tsaparang, Tibet *1–4:* 24–25

Tswana *1–4:* 544

Tuakau, New Zealand *1–4:* 449

Tuamotu Archipelago *1–4:* 92, 124, 189, 191, 733

Tuat, Algeria *1–4:* 737

Tübingen *1–4:* 502

Tucker, HL *1–4:* 101

Tudela, Spain *1–4:* 94, 97

Tukulors *1–4:* 579

Boldface indicates main entries in Volume 5 and their page numbers; *1–4:* refers to entries in the four-volume base set; *5:* refers to entries in Volume 5; (ill.) following a page number refers to illustrations.

233 | Index

Venezuela *1–4:* 476, 842

Venus, 256, 259, 585, 587–588, 781–782

Venus de Milo 1–4: 325–326

Ver-sur-Mer, France *1–4:* 160

Veracruz, Mexico *1–4:* 277

Veranzano, Girolamo da *1–4:* 837

Verkhne-Kamchatsk *1–4:* 42

Verne, Jules *1–4:* 610, 658

Verón, Pierre Antoine *1–4:* 123, 126

Verrazano, Giovanni da *1–4:* 193, 470, 836–838

Verrazano-Narrows Bridge *1–4:* 836

Veslekari 1–4: 131

Vespucci, Amerigo *1–4:* 623–624, 839–842

Vestfold Hills *1–4:* 860

Victoria 1–4: 567, 571, 573

Victoria Falls *1–4:* 549

Victoria Island *1–4:* 17; *5:* 146, 147

Victoria Land *1–4:* 163, 377

Victoria Nile *1–4:* 48, 50, 794

Vidin, Bulgaria *1–4:* 44

Vienna, Austria *1–4:* 184; *5:* 126–128, 130, 157, 159

Vientiane, Laos *1–4:* 395

Viking 1–4: 843–846

Viking (ship) *1–4:* 604

Viking Lander Atlas of Mars 1–4: 846

Vikings *5:* 17, 77, 147

Vilcabamba mountains *1–4:* 99

Vilcabamba River *1–4:* 99–100

Ville de Bruges 1–4: 581

Ville de Paris 1–4: 638

Vincennes 1–4: 853

Vinland *1–4:* 524, 526–527

Virgin River *1–4:* 759

Virginia *1–4:* 529, 713, 763

Visconti, Teobaldo *1–4:* 689

Viscount Melville Sound *1–4:* 639

Visscher, Frans Jacobszoon *1–4:* 810–811

Vitcos *1–4:* 98–102

Vogel, Edward *1–4:* 73

Volga Bulgars *5:* 75

Volga River *1–4:* 77, 184, 688, 818; *5:* 75–77

Vostok 1–4: 91–92, 380, 402, 559, 781, 818–819

Vostok Island *1–4:* 92

A Voyage of Discovery to the North Pacific Ocean and Round the World 1–4: 835

Voyage of the Vega Round Asia and Europe 5: 125

Voyage to Terra Australis 1–4: 363

Voyager (airplane) *1–4:* 740–743

Voyager 1 and *2 1–4:* 847–851

Voyages 1–4: 227

The Voyages and Adventures of Fernao Mendes Pinto 1–4: 668

Voyages to the Frozen and Pacific Oceans 1–4: 564

W

Wabag Valley *1–4:* 521

Wagner, Johannes *1–4:* 721

Wahgi Valley *1–4:* 521

Wainwright, Jacob *1–4:* 234

Wakamba *1–4:* 505–506

Walker, Alan *5:* 96

Walker Lake *1–4:* 760

Walla Walla, Washington *1–4:* 620–622

Wallace, Alfred Russell *1–4:* 304–305

Wallace Line *1–4:* 304

Waller, Horace *1–4:* 235

Wallis, Samuel *1–4:* 124, 187–192 257

Wallis Islands *1–4:* 192

Walsh, Donald *1–4:* 659

Walvis Bay *1–4:* 312

Wamba, Zaire *1–4:* 4

War of 1812 *1–4:* 64, 365

War of the Austrian Succession *1–4:* 187

Boldface indicates main entries in Volume 5 and their page numbers; *1–4:* refers to entries in the four-volume base set; *5:* refers to entries in Volume 5; (ill.) following a page number refers to illustrations.

235 | Index

X

Y

Boldface indicates main entries in Volume 5 and their page numbers; *1–4:* refers to entries in the four-volume base set; *5:* refers to entries in Volume 5; (ill.) following a page number refers to illustrations.

237   Index